HANNIBAL—

The colossus of Carthage whose sixty-four-year lifespan left its imprint on the maps of time and history!

"This book is considerably more than a readable account of a great person. It paints a warm and sympathetic picture of Carthage's history and civilization. The author has considerable historical insight . . . a refreshing way of dealing with minor characters—"
—The New York Times

"Harold Lamb has added another to his list of splendid historical works."
—The Springfield Republican

"Hannibal emerges from Harold Lamb's pages with a most satisfying solidity."
—Christian Science Monitor

HANNIBAL

by Harold Lamb

PINNACLE BOOKS   NEW YORK CITY

A Pinnacle Books edition, published by special arrangement with Doubleday and Company, Inc.

ISBN: 0-523-00901-1

First printing, August 1976

Cover illustration by Ken Kelly

Printed in the United States of America

PINNACLE BOOKS, INC.
275 Madison Avenue
New York, N.Y. 10016

Foreword

Hannibal, son of Hamilcar Barca, a Carthaginian, lived twenty-two centuries ago. Yet his name is as familiar as something of yesterday.

Today school children read Julius Caesar's *Commentaries* on the Gallic wars without illusion. To their minds Caesar's victories over the Gauls took place a long time ago and very far away from them. On the other hand they read how Hannibal took his elephants over the Alps with an odd sense of sharing in the adventure themselves, a childish peculiarity that the satirist Juvenal noticed at an early date. In fact, in Juvenal's time, mothers had a habit of frightening children with the cry, *"Hannibal's at the gates!"*

He lived for sixty-four years, approximately one century before Caesar and one century after Alexander, king of Macedonia. That was the time of the great change in the Mediterranean world. Until then people dwelt in tribal societies and the ancient city-states scattered about the shores under the rule of elders or councils. The change began with the Greeks and their advancement of individuality, with an awareness of belonging to a whole—the single cosmos that became in the end the Roman Empire. Hannibal had as much to do with this transition as had the better-known Alexander or Caesar but in a quite different way.

"Of all that befell . . ." Polybius tells us, "the cause was one man." And this despite the fact that Hannibal was defeated in his last battle, and soon after that, perhaps in some measure because of it, his city of Carthage was utterly destroyed.

Destroyed, however, Carthage has lingered on in our memories, not merely as a city or a mistress of the sea, or a place of silent people with strange gods. So has the memory of Hannibal endured in spite of the deep obscurity that covers everything about him except his name and dates. What was his actual rank—king or merely general; what purpose drove him on like a thunderbolt upon Italy; what species of army did he lead, toward what destination, until the earliest chroniclers spoke of the catastrophe as the "Hannibalic War"? Above all, why, after he was hunted down in his last years to end his own life on a distant shore, did he appear to have won an odd personal victory over the strong militant people who defeated him? He did not claim as much. A dependable tradition has preserved his words: "It is time now to end the great anxiety of the Romans who have grown weary of waiting for the death of a hated old man."

The irony of these few words gives us his only self-portrait. No likeness of this man of Carthage survives; coins yield the images of the Carthaginian elephants but not a head of Hannibal; nor was his portrait statue, apparently, ever erected. He had one bronze memorial tablet made; it was merely a list of his victories in battle, to be left behind in a temple when he departed from Italy. He liked to write; yet the only writing by his hand preserved for a time is an account of some ancient history for the people of the island of Rhodes. Admitted to be a master of warfare more understanding than Alexander and more effective than Napoleon Bonaparte, he left to modern strategists the triumph of Cannae, which they have tried often enough to duplicate; he left no maxims—unlike the others—or comments to be followed. It is as if he answered the questioning of history with, "No comment."

Plutarch, the indefatigable biographer of great men of the Graeco-Roman epoch, wrote the lives of several who gained fame by opposing Hannibal, with no more than relevant anecdotes about the Carthaginian himself. The remarkable Scipio Africanus, worthy as G. Julius Caesar of our study, is known best for his defeat of this silent antagonist; his "carrying the war into Africa" has become a proverb, as have the Fabian tactics of Fabius Maximus, the Delayer. Cato the Censor, a major figure in events, is remembered chiefly for his iterated *Delenda est Carthago* (Carthage must be destroyed). In truth these three Romans are known to us solely because in three different ways they opposed themselves to Hannibal.

In the same way his memory lies over all the Middle Sea that became the Mare Nostrum of the Romans after his death. For he watched the swell of Ocean break against the Sacred Promontory where the sun goes down, and where the sun rises in the east, near the ruins of Troy, he said his farewell to his enemies. On a road under the snow of the Alps you will be told that Hannibal came that way, but you will not be told who accompanied him, or why. It is as if his passing had a significance that cannot be easily explained. You have the feeling that his coming made a change in the people of that time—that something very unusual happened to them, so that things were not quite the same afterward—and the secret of the unusual happening is buried in the stony hills which cannot speak.

Now it is exceptional for the memory of a single man to endure for so long a time; it is most unusual in those circumstances for the significance of his life to be shrouded in secrecy. Mystery seemed to follow close upon his footsteps. The riddle of his route through the Alps, leading an army with elephants, has fascinated scholars for several centuries; their attempted solutions of the riddle fill more than a hundred volumes on library shelves. On their part military historians have studied him in the role of a master of warfare to lay bare his secret of success with armies—more elusive than Napoleon's—and their volumes are almost as numerous as those of the searchers after the way through the Alps. On the other hand, a published life of Hannibal son of Hamilcar hardly exists, unless it is threaded through the account of his campaigns.

Historians give us reasons for this silence as to the man himself, and they are valid reasons. The Carthaginians, they explain, were a secretive folk who kept few records, and Hannibal was no exception. Then, too, after the final destruction of their great city, its surviving libraries were given away to neighboring African princes who could read Punic, but who, it seems, did not care very much for books. The art treasures of Carthage were carried off to Rome or bestowed on deserving allies of the victors. The remnant of people who survived, scattered along the African coast, never managed to build another city, and their ancient traditions were lost to memory in time.

After the last conflagration died out on the temple height of Carthage, the Roman general commanding— the younger Scipio, the Aemilian—uttered the obituary of the doomed metropolis and its inhabitants: "God of Death and War, bring infernal terrors into this cursed city of Carthage, and against its armies and its people. We curse, with the utmost strength of our being, this people and army. We curse whoever occupied these palaces, whoever worked in these fields, whoever lived upon this soil. We implore that they may never again behold light from above. Let eternal silence and desolation remain here. Accursed be they who return. Let a two-fold curse be upon those who try to resurrect these ruins."

Not that Scipio Aemilianus voiced his anger in this way against all life that had been Carthaginian; his curse was a ritual matter, the ending of his military duty, like the sealing of a tablet before putting it away. In fact Polybius, who accompanied him at the moment, noticed that the soldier's face was drawn, and heard him murmur a verse from Homer: "The day will come when sacred Ilium will perish with its people." Polybius asked why he said anything so pessimistic. The Roman victor answered that he was thinking that this same fate might some day befall his own city.

In this way the memory of Hannibal's time eclipsed with the culture and life of the city. What remained to be dug up by modern archaeologists was the necropolis, the foundations of some temples with the graveyards around them, and the prayers inscribed on the tombs told nothing of Hannibal.

Furthermore, historians made certain that the writings of the two secretaries, both Greeks, who accompanied Hannibal, were destroyed or lost, except for some fragments quoted by later writers. Since these were all Romans or Roman-employed, the history of Carthage during the great war for mastery of the Mediterranean became that of the enemy. When Rome gained supremacy as the Empire under Augustus, her very talented historians naturally rewrote much of the record of her rise to glorify the Empire and pay tribute to the Divine Augustus. By their recording, the memory of Hannibal changed into that of the most terrible antagonist of the Senate and the Roman People. His human attributes and the reality of the vanished Carthage tended to disappear from the record of history.

What remains is like a palimpsest, on which the earliest writing has been erased and covered with quite different inscriptions. Still, on a palimpsest the imprint of the earliest writing can be made out faintly, and perhaps some of it may be restored as the oldest hand traced it.

The purpose of this book is to try to restore to sight the traces of the life of Hannibal son of Hamilcar before he ended it in 183 B.C. We will search for only what related to his individuality, whether it be the shape of a Celtic sword blade, or a stone that he took in his hand, or some wigs he carried with him, or the view from the Collina height outside a gate of Rome. Historians have made clear the events of his time; we can try to journey back in imagination to the man who was the cause of those events.

We will begin with a mountain on the coast of the island of Sicily in the year 241 B.C., the year of the peace that was no peace.

Contents

Of all that befell both the Romans and the Carthaginians, the cause was one man, and one mind—Hannibal's.

POLYBIUS

HANNIBAL

I. Retreat from the Sea

"Thy Rowers Have Brought Thee into Great Waters."

Like many others Hannibal emerged from childhood within sight of the sea. He did not leave the mountain until he was five years old. This Mount Eryx (Erkte) thrust like a giant's watchtower out into deep water beside the shallow half-moon bay. It overlooked the small walled town on the bay. Hannibal could not have visited the town because there was a state of war between it and the inhabitants of the mountain.

Thus, unlike most other first-born sons, his earliest remembered environment had been an armed camp. Not that the men around him usually carried arms; they repaired the reed-roofed huts when it rained or watched their women string silver coins into necklaces as a provision against hard times. Their prisoners raised barley on the level shelves of the mountain, while their elder boys kept the herds of sheep and goats grazing as a source of meat for the pot. It was a somewhat unusual circumstance that Hannibal should know, first of all, this manner of subsistence within a sheltered spot in enemy territory. The steep bastions of Mount Eryx safeguarded the community ruled by Hamilcar Barca.

When food began to fail toward the end, Hannibal

heard more often the heavier tramp of helmeted men with shields slung, moving down the trails in detachments. They went off toward sunset, down the guarded trails of the slopes, to return under cover of darkness, driving donkeys and prisoners loaded with wine and grain jars, and perhaps driving cattle taken from the broad valley below. Because he went out to watch their comings and goings, the five-year-old boy did not think it strange that these active men spoke in a variety of languages—being mercenaries from a dozen shores or islands. After the custom of men in camp they managed to get along with rude native African talk or trade Greek. And the boy picked up this talk readily when he wanted to find out anything. The merecenaries would always drop their work to sit down and explain things to the first-born of the Lord Hamilcar, who was prone to roaring anger as well as solicitude for their needs. Perhaps Hannibal was most impressed by the giant Libyan of the clashing earrings who could carry a trussed colt on his mighty shoulders. In any case this camp became the child's nursery, attended by the mercenaries who served his father for silver shekels or loyalty or hope of loot. Hamilcar Barca had a canny way of winning over the most dissimilar men, including Roman deserters. He allowed enslaved captives the right of marriage and a pittance of pay—an egg for their nests. Yet the women of his house on Mount Eryx were young and skilled prostitutes.

The mountain impressed itself on Hannibal. Its summit, wind-whipped, shrouded at times by moving cloud masses, stood apart from the dark summits of the island's interior. Black storms gathered inland, veined by lightning flashes. The human watchers on Eryx became a part of the sky's anger or benevolence. In later life Hannibal remained sensitive to these apparitions in the sky, which might presage the will of the earth gods. He kept seers about him rather as interpreters than as augurs, to read as it were the horoscope of the skies. This may or may not have had anything to do with the circumstance that the family name of Barca meant "Thunderbolt."

Then, too, at dawn on Eryx you looked past the shadows of the shore to the apparition of the sun over the sea in the east. The priests faced the sunrise when they

2

poured sacrificial wine from the vials before the terraphim of the tabernacle tent. Hamilcar, moving his abode constantly, kept the household images in this small pavilion. All Carthaginians looked to the east from a necessity which they felt rather than understood. There lay the birth land of their ancestors the Phoenician Semites, the Red Land of most ancient days—which may have been the shore of the Persian Gulf—from which the ancestors had migrated to Canaan and the fertile shore of the Middle Sea. Out of the sea the folk of the Red Lands had made their living, not only from its fishery—Sidon, the Fishery had been their first port—or from the purple dye they gleaned from its murex, but from carrying trade across it daringly in vessels of their making. "A merchant of the people into many isles," the prophet Ezekiel had named them. Seafarers, they built strong cities on the stony isles adjacent to the coast yet protected in a measure from the armed hosts that swarmed there. The strongest of the Phoenician cities was crowded upon such an isle, Tyre, the Rock. From the depths of the continent, by the caravans of Damascus, Judah, Sheba, and Edom, the merchants of Tyre had drawn the raw materials that formed in turn the handiwork of artisans, the linen of Egypt, or the glass of Byblos.

The rocky shelf of Tyre, of course, held no resources for its people, who depended on farming the adjacent mainland for food. The people, crowded into lofty apartment buildings, probably numbered no more than 25,000. "The riches of Tyre," Strabo relates, "came from the skill of its inhabitants." That peculiar skill of the Semitic Phoenicians lay in the carrying of trade, the bartering of raw materials against finished goods, and vice versa. In the day of Hiram the King they built a fleet in the Red Sea for Solomon, King of Israel, from timber out of the stright-growing cedars of Lebanon, with spikes of the iron of the Taurus, and sails of Egyptian linen. In return for this they drew gold from the mines of Ophir, and precious incense of myrrh and frankincense from the coast of Sheba. Hiram also furnished the timber for the temple built by Solomon.

The Phoenicians were the first people, and perhaps the last, to base their culture on their commerce. Inevitably,

3

then, they prospered in tranquil times, the intervals between strife and invasion. Sennacherib's host was only one of many to besiege the offshore citadel of Tyre. When this mother city yielded to Persian rule in 538—nearly three centuries before Hamilcar held his mountain citadel against the Romans—the Phoenicians maintained themselves by furnishing sea transport to the Persian Great Kings of the land. The structure of Tyre with its artifical harbors remained unchanged, and its wealth may have increased under the Persian empire; but its people had become subjects, no longer able to follow their destiny upon the sea.

"Thy rowers have brought thee into great waters," Ezekiel had said of them. The great waters were the Ocean itself, and the Phoenicians had mastered it by constructing ships powered by sail as well as oars, to venture on the deep sea routes to far lands instead of hugging the coasts or steering by sight from island to island. In their black vessels the Phoenician captains laid their courses by the changing pattern of the stars, in so doing drawing upon their early knowledge of Chaldean astronomical science. ("Thy wise men, O Tyre, were they pilots.") They ventured where light rowing galleys could not survive, riding the seasonal winds of the Mediterranean, aware of unseen currents, marking in their minds how unnamed capes stood as sentinels along western shores, and drawing the entrances to safe harbors and river mouths on the charts they concealed jealousy from other seafarers. For they had learned how to ride out storms, or shelter from them. They faced a greater hazard in the far-ranging vessels of the Cretan sea kings, which were followed in time by the oared fleets of the barbaric Greek city-states. The open sea lay under no rule of empire; no code of law had been written for it, and a cargo vessel lay at the mercy of a strongly armed ship that caught up with it. Phoenician guard ships, beaked with bronze rams, shepherded weaker craft to distant trading posts. Those posts, like Tyre itself, sheltered on rock-bound islets off a fertile coast, or at the end of a peninsula open to approach by water but difficult to reach from the land, as was the case with Carthage—*Kart hadasht*, the New City.

So Hannibal's ancestors had the sea in their blood.

4

Those who go down to the sea in ships grow accustomed to danger, and caution becomes a part of their natures. Paradoxically a thirst for freedom never leaves those who pilot a vessel beyond the horizon of the land. Sea-borne, the Phoenicians sought by every expedient to avoid the havoc of war. They had made the great discovery that the paths over the deep sea were the safest to all the isolated, strife-torn peoples of its shores; the Middle Sea became their thoroughfare to the continents, and they tried to deceive their rivals by tales of mythical terrors upon it—of the isle where Aeolus kept the winds imprisoned, and the far-off coast where night always equaled day and giant Laestrygonians ate the flesh of shipwrecked crews. Such tales found their way into the legends of Homer. Yet these deceptive, peace-seeking Tyrians fought to the last of their despairing strength to defend the freedom of Tyre. When that was lost, Tyre itself "was brought to silence in the midst of the sea."

Until then Carthage, the New City, had sent each year a gift of money to the temples of the ancestral gods in Tyre. They did that although the temples of those same gods, of Tanit and Eshmoun the Healer and Melcart, stood on the height of Carthage. The tradition of a thousand years made Hamilcar's priests pray to the east, with a sense of foreboding. Hamilcar's name signified the son of Melcart, ancient Lord of the City.

Now Hamilcar himself had a lion's restless courage. Because of that mercenaries came from afar to serve him, and he never stinted reward to them. But more than that, he had set his face in a new direction. The magnates of Carthage, the oldest families that traced their descent from the Tyrians—and the Barcas who came from Cyrene were not among them—went through life with divided minds, tradition-bound in worship of the ancient gods of Canaan, submissive to sacrifice, withdrawn from other peoples, conscious of impending doom that would demand the sacrifice even of themselves. They prayed to the east of their forefathers. The other and very different aspect of the Carthaginian mind sought the aid of inventions, manipulating circumstances to its advantage, even breaking down the age-old symbols of speech into the separate letters beginning with *alaph-beth,* as did the Syrians and cer-

5

tain Greeks. This Carthaginian imagination of better ways led them to fertilize ordinary soils, to devise new methods of labor, to seek out the wealth of hidden metals, and in so doing to explore the unknown west with its barbaric inhabitants. Hamilcar Barca had set his face that way, breaking with tradition to seek a new destiny. For one thing, after the island of Sicily had been occupied by victorious Roman armies, he found a way to carry on the war without cost to the exhausted treasury of Carthage by holding to Mount Eryx with a few thousand men paid by himself. His impregnable mountain could not be stormed. Even with food failing, Hamilcar would not surrender his bridgehead.

Fishermen brought their catches of heavy tuna to the foot of the mountain; sometimes a fast trireme would slip into the guarded cove, to be hauled up on the beach with its stores from Carthage before daybreak. All these needed to run the blockade of Roman warships and the oared fleet of mighty Syracuse that could be seen patrolling the outer sea and the adjacent harbor of the port of Panormus. This was the reason of the despair of Carthage. During the intermittent struggle of twenty-three years these northern fleets had prevailed over the ships of the African coast and the supremacy of Carthage at sea had come to an end. That seemed to the traditionalists of Carthage to be the will of the gods, not to be altered by human efforts. Hamilcar's effort at Eryx was a makeshift, a defiance of fate that could not bring a victory.

It was a clever move on the part of the Carthaginian Council to name the one man who would not hear of surrender as its spokesman for terms of peace with the equally exhausted Latin enemy. The Council, being made up of the eldest heads of wealthy families, had many traditionalists and also antagonists of the Barca family, and a majority resolved upon peace. If Hamilcar Barca could gain favorable terms from the distant power that called itself the Republic of the Roman People, so much to the good. If he failed, why so much the worse for the prestige of the Barca family. Habitually the elders of the Council distrusted a successful general, although the resourceful Hamilcar was exceptional in many ways.

The boy Hannibal was aware of the end only when a myriad of sails moved in from the western horizon, and the Roman guard ships let them pass. The fleet of transports had come from Carthage to take off the garrison of Mount Eryx and it anchored in the half-moon bay. Hamilcar himself appeared with bearers waving branches, carrying jars of date wine and olive oil at the head of carts of grain. By so doing he dramatized the end of hunger as well as of the war.

Then befell an incident slight in itself yet one that must have lingered in Hannibal's memory. By the gate pillars of his house waited two throngs drawn up on either side. Part were mercenaries with weapons carefully furbished, standing in company formation. They were Italians, deserters from Roman command. Across from them waited escaped slaves, still wearing the iron neck ring, with ragged women gathered behind them.

One of the soldiers stepped out, and Hamilcar gave him permission to speak. The man explained in curt Latin that he and his companions were to be surrendered, after long service to Hamilcar; on surrender they would be killed by crucifixion. The slaves, having no right to speak, merely prostrated themselves. Over their bodies the giant Libyan broke into a deep-throated chant, throwing back his head until his earrings clashed. A natural leader of the Africans, he enjoyed general favor and often presumed upon it.

Hamilcar nodded and stretched out his arm toward the Libyan. In the diadem that ringed his headcloth a rare emerald shone and it flashed in the sun when he spoke. He had listened to enough, he said, and he would answer them all on the third morning.

As he had promised he appeared at the gateposts after the sacrifice of the third morning. He struck his powerful hands together and spread them apart, and he told the listeners this: the peace was fair and the peace would be kept. No deserters would be surrendered, and no fugitive slaves given up; they would all be transported to the city of Carthage, their master. For his own command ended with the peace. Before the throngs shouted in amazed exultation, Hamilcar went back to his house.

So after three years the garrison of Mount Eryx

marched down entire from the mountain to the waiting transports. They showed no joy in leaving the huts; they were thinned by hunger and they carried little spoil. On the ships they passed their time calculating how much back pay was due them from the magnates of Carthage who had surrendered their mountain with a word. Thus it befell that the grievance of the mercenaries led them to mutiny, which caused a revolt of the slaves and grew into the merciless civil war that changed the plans of their Lord Hamilcar and the masters of Carthage.

All this could have left only a faint memory in the boy Hannibal, who hardly understood what was happening. Besides, he went from the ships to the luxury of a palace home in the great city, where dwelt his sisters and younger brothers, where tutors awaited him with servants to answer his call. Yet he did not entirely forget the encampment where armed men contrived a living.

Queen of the Seas

The New City was five centuries old by then. Originally a staging port of the Phoenicians on the route to Spain, she still showed the marks of her origin. At the tip of a narrow peninsula projecting into the bay of Tunis—across from the horned peaks of the Sacred Mountain—a harbor had been improvised behind a 400-foot stone mole. At its broad quays vessels were sheltered from the dangerous northwest winds. Hills on the neck of the peninsula protected the approach by land to the harbor of Carthage.

A second, inner harbor had been excavated for warcraft. In shape this was round as a wheel, within a great portico that covered the berths of some 200 galleys. Each berth had ceremonial marble pillars for mooring posts. An island formed the hub of the wheel, housing the administrative building of the admiralty. Here a lofty tower, like a miniature Pharos, gave observation of the outer waters. It served also as a signal tower. Behind the circular portico locked warehouses stored timber, cordage, weapons, and gear of war. Although Carthage no longer maintained the navy of the century when she had been queen of the western sea, the materials for such a fleet were stored up. A guarding wall kept unauthorized persons from spying out this inner emergency harbor.

A broad thoroughfare led up to the ancient citadel, the Byrsa. This height of some 200 feet, with barely half the area of the Acropolis at Athens, had been given over entirely now to the great temples, of Tanit the Earth Mother, Eshmoun the Healer—the Aesculapius of the Greeks—and Melcart. Since space was so restricted in the heart of Carthage the manufacturies rose seven stories about the Byrsa, stepped back in terraces to catch the sunlight, crowned with cisterns to catch the rain water. Here labored the artisans and traders who supplied the markets of the Mediterranean. They had their trade associations that met at common tables and made their voices heard in the affairs of the city.

Winding past the Byrsa height, the great boulevard ran nearly seven miles along the peninsula through gardens that were cemeteries sprinkled with the unique handiwork of Punic (Phoenician) art, the tomb towers. Toward the sea, other walled gardens sheltered the great families who had gained their treasures from commerce. Some of them, like the aristocratic Magos and adroit Hannos, had held supremacy in the city for generations. The Hanno clan were the open antagonists of the upstart, successful Hamilcar.

Along the crest boulevard passed a multitude who were no citizens of the New City. Cloaked Numidians bestrode nimble horses, to the whistling cry of their pipes; Soudanese paced the dusty road, shoulders erect under their burdens; Massylian warriors strode before their clustered families toward the city of unimagined wealth; Libyan peasants—the original inhabitants of the fertile coast—guided their carts through the traffic stream. Swarthy Greek overseers cracked their whips to make way for their old-fashioned but imposing chariots. Outland horse teams shied at elephants impassive under loads of timber. Caravans emerged from the southern roads out of the Land of Slaves in the depths of Africa.

In fact the highways of the Carthaginians had become arteries of the continent. Through them the products of

Africa passed into the city to be transformed into the cargoes of vessels outbound to the other ports of the Mediterranean.

Carthage had become a nerve center of peoples, a cosmopolis at the edge of the sea. In its shops the Punic (Phoenician) speech mingled with native dialects, and trade Greek with the Aramaic of the east. And in reality Carthage was a city of the east. The red heights of the African shore resembled the Red Lands beyond Canaan.

Carthage had another peculiarity. The city had always been free. Tyre had submitted to Chaldean and then to Persian rule, only to be demolished by Alexander and his Macedonian host. Refugees from that destruction in the year 332—old men and women with infants—escaped to safety in the New City. The proudest of the northern cities, Athens and Capua, had seen enemies invade their walls.

Strangely, Carthage had no city wall for defense. Until then none had been needed, because the enveloping sea protected the city.

Unlike Tyre, the New City drew its sustenance from the hinterland. The ridge of the peninsula looked down on a plain green with irrigated plantations. These extended to the fertile valley of the Bagradas River, beyond which stretched the dark sheathing of ancient forests, where skilled hands replanted tree growth, oak and pine, as fast as it was cut away.

At first Hannibal must have accompanied his restless father out to the limits of civilization, where the Libyans tended animals at the will of a chieftain dwelling in a palace of mud bricks. Perhaps they visited Cirta (Constantine) of the desert folk, on the river in the west. But the great revolt of 241—238, spreading like a conflagration through the hinterland, must have confined the boy to the villa in Carthage and to the workroom that he shared with a Greek mathematician and a reader who recited hero poems to his infant brothers.

The revolt very quickly became a civil strife in which the subjected hinterland sought to throw off the control of the city on the peninsula. But this internecine strife assumed a more complex pattern; predatory tribes joined with villages smarting under cruel wartime taxation by

10

their masters; others remained loyal to Carthage. The veteran soldiers of Eryx (who had not been paid to their satisfaction) spearheaded the rebellion. The city had no trained army to oppose them. On the other hand the rebels lacked capable leadership. They resorted to terrorism. Sensing her peril, Carthage withdrew authority from the Hanno family and recalled Hamilcar Barca to sole command.

Hamilcar summoned up new forces. Throngs of Numidian horsemen rode in to his standard; an elephant train sheathed in leather armor plodded out the gate toward the smoke of burning villages. With such heterogeneous forces Hamilcar's cunning tricked the hordes of rebels and rounded up the last of them in a blind gorge from which no bands of survivors escaped.

When the roads were open again upon the African coast that nursed its wounds, they were lined with crucifixes on which the leaders of the rebellion died. Among the bodies where the carrion birds swarmed hung that of the giant Libyan who had been vain of his earrings. The eight-year-old Hannibal must have seen something of this vestige of the "inexpiable war" as Roman historians named it.

Perhaps as early as this he conceived his aversion to warfare and the reluctance to send men out to battle that marked his later ears.

"Hamilcar Ordered All the Others to Draw Back . . ."

Exhausted, Carthage was assailed by a new dread. And this made the year 238—237 one of imperative decision by the city.

A new demand came from Rome, which had pledged peace so recently. The demand was for the Carthaginians to withdraw from the islands of Sardinia and Corsica, and to pay over again the indemnity of 1200 talents' weight of silver coin that had been agreed in the terms of 241.

Those terms, accepted by Hamilcar as envoy of Carthage, had been between states as equals—Carthage

11

yielding up all of Sicily, paying the indemnity for the cost of the conflict to Rome; both states confining themselves to certain spheres of trade control upon the sea, and pledging themselves not to molest the allies of the other. Then, too, Hamilcar had refused the request of the northern commanders for the surrender of all deserters and escaped slaves. Now in the African rebellion barely ending, there had been conflict between the Carthaginian garrisons of the ports in the other islands hemming in the Tyrrhenian Sea—Sardinia and Corsica, which were in reality near to the Italian coast. Unexpectedly now the Roman Senate intervened, to take advantage of the exhaustion of Carthage, to demand the withdrawl of these garrisons—which meant the surrender of the ports—on penalty of a new declaration of war against Carthage.

To the minds of the Council upon the Byrsa the yielding of Sardinia and Corsica meant more than the loss of some imports of timber and ore; it meant the loss of the ports that gave access to the western Mediterranean. The yielding of rich Sicily midway between the toe of Italy and the peninsula of Carthage barred them from the eastern Mediterranean as a sea power. After a supremacy of nearly three centuries, the merchants of the African city would have no single sphere of influence left to them—unless something unforeseen could be contrived. The matter of paying a double indemnity was merely a nuisance compared to the surrender of the strategic islands.

Those of the Council inclined to religious fatalism beheld in this a handwriting upon the wall, like that upon the palace of Babylon; those who were most angry declared that Hamilcar should never have left Eryx; the majority understood the impossibility of renewing the warfare against the forces of Rome refreshed by the three years of truce.

The record of history makes clear that Carthage withdrew her garrisons, abandoned the islands, and raised the silver coin for the new indemnity. But the anger of the leaders who bowed to the ultimatum, and their instant search for a new area of endeavor upon the Mediterranean appears in the record only in the action they took that year.

In this way and at this time was taken the first step

12

toward the greater conflict for mastery of the Mediterranean world known to posterity as the Hannibalic War.

Hannibal, at nine years of age, saw the first preparation. On the land side of the city stakes were driven for the erection of triple walls. The innermost wall would be Cyclopean in its dimensions—twenty paces in width, and in height seven times the height of a man. From this unbreakable rampart towers would rise at intervals of a bowshot. On its inner side would be built pens for herded elephants, stalls for thousands of horses, with storerooms to hold feed for the animals. The broad stretch of the wall's summit would serve as emplacement for the newest missile machines. When completed, it would render the city impregnable to attack by land. Or so they hoped.

Before the work was fairly begun, Hamilcar prepared to migrate to a new land in the west beyond the reach of Roman power. With Hamilcar would go the husband of his eldest daughter, certain officers, and veteran African men-at-arms. Hannibal learned that there was no longer an army of mercenaries such as he had known at Mount Eryx. Their route lay toward the setting sun, out between the Pillars of Hercules, to the shore of the Ocean. The journey was to be made quietly by separate vessels bound for an undisclosed destination.

Long afterward and far to the east at the court of Antiochus the Great Hannibal recalled how his father had called upon all nobles and officers to take an oath if they chose to accompany him. To do so they went to the temple of Melcart on the Byrsa summit, where the doves of Tanit swooped about them, and they went from the glare of the thronged courtyard into the darkness of the sanctuary. At the altar Hamilcar prayed to his name-god and slew the sacrificial lamb, holding a goblet in his hand.

"My father poured the libation to the god," Hannibal related. "I was standing near the altar. When he finished the rites, he ordered all the others attending the sacrifice to draw back a little way. Then he called me over to him and asked very gently if I wanted to go with him on the journey. Like a boy I accepted and even begged to be allowed to do it. Then he took me by one hand, led me up to the altar, and told me to put my other hand on the sacrificed lamb. He asked me to swear that I would never be a friend of the Romans, and I did so."

This oath of the Barcas at their departure for Spain has become noted. Constantly repeated by the chroniclers, it took on a significance it did not have at the time. We often read that Hamilcar made all his sons swear never to cease their enmity against Rome. And that the lives of the sons, particularly Hannibal's, were dedicated henceforth to carrying out this boyhood oath. Yet other Carthaginian officers gave that same pledge. Hannibal himself seems to recall it as an incident of their departure on the new undertaking already decided upon. Moreover his wording of the oath has a definite and somewhat different meaning. "Never to be a friend of the Romans" says nothing about lifelong antagonism, nor is it merely a weak phrase. The term "friend of the Roman Senate and People" had distinct political meaning at that time, as had the term "ally." If you became a friend of Rome, you submitted to Roman rule; as an ally you did that, too, but you had some privileges left. Polybius puts it this way: "When men come to terms after their spirit is broken ... they may be trusted as friends and subjects." What Hamilcar demanded and Hannibal swore was that he would never submit to Roman rule. Their anger was the cause, not the consequence, of this oath.

Polybius puts this also in a way of his own: "We must observe the first cause of the war between Rome and Carthage [the Hannibalic] in the indignation of Hamilcar, surnamed Barca, the father of Hannibal ... When the Romans announced that they intended to make war anew on Carthage, that city was ready to negotiate all points at issue; but as the Romans refused to negotiate, the Carthaginians had to submit to the circumstances. Although deeply aggrieved at this outrage, they were powerless, and evacuated Sardinia, besides agreeing to pay twelve hundred talents in addition to the sum exacted from them before ... This we must take to be the second and principal cause of the conflict. For Hamilcar felt the anger shared by all his countrymen."

And the Greek historian adds, with afterknowledge: "The third cause must be held to be the success of the Carthaginian project in Spain."

At the coming of spring sailing weather, the pilots gave the word. Hamilcar's great ship was warped from the admiralty basin through the canal to the commercial harbor. Ritual lamps were lighted before the teraphim in the cabin, and deck hands raised the sail yard to catch the offshore breeze. Where they clustered on the end of the mole, robed councilors and magistrates raised their arms in prayer for a safe passage.

Then the penteconter—the liner with five rowers to a long oar—turned off the Sacred Mountain. The gleam of marble on the Byrsa height faded into the blue of the sky above the red line of the shore. The boy Hannibal, watching from the canopied aft deck, could not have believed that thirty-six years would pass before he saw Carthage again.

For six days and nights the penteconter headed due west against the prevailing wind. The ship kept out of sight of Carthaginian staging ports on the African side, and far out of sight of the Pine Islands and Balearics on the European side. Then she entered the swell of the outer Ocean, and passed the twin Pillars of Hercules (Gibraltar and the height of Ceuta). Then, while strange dolphins sported in the thresh of the long oars, she swung north to an islet off the European coast.

The city crowded upon the rocky isle was Gades (or Gadir, the Fortress, now Cádiz) more ancient than Carthage, yet resembling the mother city in many ways. A narrow, curving peninsula reached out toward the temples and merchant houses of Gades, like a natural mole, sheltering a magnificent deep water bay. But the vessels moored here were heavy sailing craft. The robed magistrates who greeted Hamilcar at the landing merely offered hospitality in formal phrases while they waited to learn the reason for his coming. No women watched from the temple stairs as at Carthage. The surf that broke on the rocks beneath had the roar of a storm although the sky was clear. On his part Hamilcar greeted the Gaditans with politic courtesy. True, he had the sealed tablet that attested his rank of Shofet (Protector) of Carthage, yet he displayed with it a letter of credit, which assured the Gaditans that he would pay the cost of carrying out his mission.

His task was to subjugate the land of Spain. In the shortest possible time this western end of the European continent would be transformed into a new base for Carthage; so transformed, it would serve to expand trade along the western shores of the Ocean.

That explanation of Hamilcar's had much truth in it, but not all the truth. The great peninsula of Spain lay beyond the influence of Rome; inland the mountain wall of the Pyrenees sealed it off; new wealth could be drawn from its mines, and fresh armies recruited from its barbarian manpower. In this way the land of Spain would become a defense for harassed Carthage—a Mount Eryx on a vaster scale. Hamilcar's title of Protector might be read two ways.

Little time, however, remained in which to complete his task.

The Treasure in Spain

The Atlantic Ocean was no mystery to the Carthaginian seafarers, although they had taken pains to conceal that fact. In almost forgotten times Phoenician voyagers had circled the continent of Africa at the command of an Egyptian Pharaoh. For half a millennium, Gades (or Gadir) had been the mother city of an Atlantic trade that brought in dried fish, ambergris, and tin—all-important in the making of bronze. Rivals of the Phoenicians could never discover where the valuable tin came from. When Carthage rose to power in the sixth century, the secrets of the Atlantic trade were kept by force. Gades became the watch post of the strait leading to the outer Ocean. Apparently this blockade of the western outlet was well kept because when one rival sea captain, Pytheas of Marseille (Massilia) ran the blockade and returned to report the truth of what he had seen, Greek scientists believed his tale to be a fable. And this land's end of Europe became known as Hispania, "The Hidden Country."

16

Behind the screen of secrecy, however, Carthaginians probed the Atlantic as far as the Canary Islands, and perhaps the outlying Azores. One of them, Himilco, led a government survey to the north, skirting the actual coasts of the tin trade, Cornwall and Brittany, along the "white cliffs" of the great island called Albion, and the smaller "Holy Isle" (Ireland). In this fact-finding voyage, Himilco's fleet encountered a windless stretch of sea in which fish as well as ships became entangled. Although this resembles the Sargasso Sea off the American continent, it was probably a stretch of the Bay of Biscay, where floating algae weed entrapped the tuna shoals, always an object of interest to the Carthaginians. Himilco's account of the stagnant sea was added to the terror tales by which the Carthaginians guarded their secrets.

About the same time, 500 B.C., another Carthaginian, Hanno, captained a fleet that voyaged down the shoulder of Africa. This was no simple exploration. The 50 penteconters of the fleet carried 30,000 humans, crews and colonists. Hanno was carrying out a definite project because he dropped colonists at fertile river mouths as he fared south, and picked up interpreters to serve him in meeting the natives of the next stage. His Carthaginians heard the distant roar of native tom-toms and learned the name of an almost human beast, the gorilla. Before he turned back Hanno—who, like Hamilcar, was a Shofet of Carthage—built a town on an isle near a river mouth. He called it Cerne, but where it was no one can tell today. If Cerne lay, as many believe, due south of Carthage, Hanno's vessels may have probed up the Niger River. Just possibly his coastal colonies linked up with the inland caravan tracks that brought the elephants, gold, plumage, and slaves north to the mother city.

Be that as it may, by Hamilcar's day Carthage had her trading ports on the west coast of Africa—where European navigators did not appear again for nineteen centuries.

Moreover the Phoenician-Carthaginians had been the first people in the record of history to establish colonies across the seas. They did this by free enterprise. In doing so they had taken a first step toward a new era, a *modus*

17

vivendi between a city of culture and the outer barbaric peoples. Hitherto the course of empire had been by conquest, whether by the merciless subjection of the Assyrian or the milder domination of the Egyptian. Carthage herself actually ruled only the stretch of coast between the Cirta of the nomads and the desert of the Little Syrtes. Like the Dutch dominion long afterward, the Carthaginian held no more than a nucleus on the mainland, sustained by far-flung colonies. These trading centers did not attempt to rule the hinterlands. They did aid and often control the mining and agriculture of the surrounding land. The words of Ezekiel describe one such ancient trading port: "Tarshish was thy merchant by reason of the multitude of all kind of riches; with silver, iron, tin and lead they [the Tartessians] traded for thy wares." These Tartessians remained apart from the traders, following their own way of life near Gades on the Atlantic coast.

So Hamilcar was called upon to change this ancient system of extraterritorial relationship for the first time and to subject all of the peninsula of Spain with its numerous inhabitants to the government of Carthage.

For nearly nine years Hamilcar Barca drove himself and those who followed him without pity. He could not afford the luxury of delay to consider the affairs of individuals. The drip of the water clock in the Shofet's pavillion was like the clang of a tocsin, warning that time was passing. His dynamic force achieved much; his impatience lost as much.

Astute Hasdrubal, husband of his oldest daughter, realized both the ability and the failing of the Barca who had always been a leader of armed men. Hasdrubal the Splendid—as they called him—owned mining enterprises and managed wealth. The youthful Hannibal, kept at the Barca's side, became aware of the difference between the two. At that age he gave blind loyalty to his father.

They found a base of operations awaiting them in Spain. Sailing up the Betis (Guadalquivir) River from Gades, they entered the fair southland of teeming pastures and tranquil towns. The inhabitants greeted them with jars of wine and silver bowls of fruit, while dancers leaped

18

until their black capes flew to the sound of flutes and their shouted song.

These were the Iberians of the south, half cultured, and half Carthaginian in customs. Their ancestors had been Berber stock, migrating from Africa across the narrow strait. Their ports of Malaca and Abdera were Carthaginian-held. Outside their gates stone sphinxes kept guard with bearded bull men—strange guardians that had found their way in a forgotten time from the Nile or Tigris.

Journeying through the smiling valley of the Betis, the boy Hannibal may have red in the verses of Homer how here in the farthest west there was the Elysian Plain, where heroic men outlived death. "The gods will escort thee to the Elysian Plain and the ends of earth, where is Rhadamanthys of the fair hair, where life is easiest. No snow is there, nor yet great storm . . ."

Something of that might be true in reality.

When he had inspected it, Hamilcar made demands upon this Iberian plain. Mines to be sunk where salt deposits showed, canals to be run between the riverheads, timber hewn from the oak forests, and the young men who played at battle games to be trained in regiments.

Hamilcar had brought engineers and officers to aid the Iberians to build a greater state.

Up at the headwaters of the Betis rose the Silver Mountains. These mountains (the Sierra Morena) held within them the treasure of Spain, a treasure so great that envious Massiliote captains swore that a Carthaginian vessel rowed away from the coast with oars of pure silver. Hasdrubal's engineers marked out deposits of natural electrum. Under their commands new smelter chimneys rose, and mountain streams were channeled across gold-gleaming earth to wash the sediment away from the gold.

The citadel of the mountains was Castulo, crowning a ridge built up with massive stone blocks. Hamilcar entered it as guest of the lords of Castulo, and remained to rule them.

To the north of this mountain barrier stretched the more arid central plateau, where ranged the descendants of Celtic invaders. Iberian culture had touched them where they dwelt in round thatched houses among herds

19

of small cattle. Yet their Celtic blood drove them to raid more than trade. Hamilcar appeared among them like the thunderbolt of his name, taking hostages from village chieftains, storming the ancient stone citadels on solitary heights, occupied by Celtiberian kings. To the warlike he showed himself ruthless. These barbaric Spaniards rode with reins to their horses; they lacked the skill of his Numidians, but they had in them the making of better cavalry. The long esparto grass of their valleys could be gathered for ropemaking. Their horse herds could be bred for strength if not for pace.

A distant king mustered a formidable army of horsemen to drive the Carthaginian overlords back to the sea. Hamilcar advanced to meet it, with spear streamers whipping and the pipes of his Numidians wailing. He sent forward a score of his working train of elephants, sheathed in leather for battle. Such beasts always had a psychological effect on men unused to them, and they frightened the horses. In this instance, the Celtiberian horde melted away. Its king was pursued, caught, and carried before Hamilcar, who ordered him to be blinded and crucified. But the other captives were enlisted in the growing army of Spain.

Nine years passed. No more than a third of the country had been subdued. Then Hamilcar Barca was slain.

Tradition tells how he rode with Hannibal and another son into an ambush laid by tribesmen who summoned him to make a treaty. It was not far from Castulo—the White Castle. Hamilcar got away with the boys, but pursuit followed close down the hill. At a bend in the track the Barca ordered Hannibal to turn off with the younger son. The Spaniards followed after Hamilcar who managed to reach a river, only to be killed there.

Hannibal rode headlong to the coast. There, at army headquarters, the brood of the Barca gathered. After the charcoal fires of mourning had been lighted at the shrines, the Carthaginian officers elected Hasdrubal the Splendid to command them, in the place of Hamilcar. Then the army of Spain marched with elephants to avenge the well-loved Hamilcar by laying waste the villages and enslaving the inhabitants who had brought him to his death.

Again, eight years passed.

Now, however, a change took place within southern Spain behind the curtain of secrecy raised by the Carthaginians (within the waters forbidden by treaty to Roman ships). Hasdrubal, a natural diplomat, abandoned the aggressive subjection of Hamilcar for a moral conquest. He cultivated the friendship of the Iberian chieftains, ministered to their pride with honorable gifts, and took a bride from an Iberian family. In a modern phrase, Hasdrubal set himself to consolidate the gains made by Hamilcar—and to avoid the old soldier's mistakes.

Sails of light leather boats studded the rivers; the green of growing wheat spread through the valleys; the loading of precious metals brought down from the mountains by donkey panniers and ox carts to the head of navigation increased threefold. Iberia sent its gift of silver plate to the treasury of Carthage, and Hasdrubal prepared to mint a coinage of his own.

More than that, this creator of a Spanish state abandoned the ancient Gades on the western coast to open a new port on the eastern, the Mediterranean shore, no more than four days' sail from the mother city. On a fine natural bay sheltered by a promontory, Hasdrubal's surveyors laid out a site more than two miles in circumference. It was a site called Massia by the Iberians, who had an old temple there. The Carthaginians, laboring against time, ran a canal past the temple height into a lagoon of stagnant water, and raised shipyards along the protected lagoon. On the height of the city-to-be they built a temple to Eshmoun, and over the inner harbor a small palace for Hasdrubal, and they laid the foundations for a defensive wall. As soon as the quays were working, a mint stamped out the new coins.

However, a port of such dimensions could not escape observation from passing vessels. It bore an odd resemblance to Carthage in Africa, and watchful traders of

21

Marseille reported it to Rome as a new Carthage, *Nova Cartago* (Cartagena). Obviously new shipping would emerge from its yards.

Now these same Massiliote merchants (descendants of Phocaean Greeks—"skilled in oars") had a trading port far to the north above the mouth of the great river Ebro on the east coast of the Hidden Land. They had, as well, a vivid imagination of the deceptive Carthaginians stealing the coastal trade. Because the city of Marseille was an ally of the Roman Republic, she appealed to her protector. In due course of time—the Romans never took such action without previous debate in the Senate—envoys from the Tiber appeared before Hasdrubal. They requested from Hasdrubal a pledge that Carthaginians would not cross the line of the Ebro with weapons in their hands.

The politic Hasdrubal gave the pledge, on behalf of Carthage.

By so doing, Hasdrubal cut off his state-to-be from the natural defense of Spain, the Pyrenees. He virtually acknowledged the authority of Rome to exist 650 miles from the Tiber, here on the Ebro. He gained, of course, invaluable time for his own preparations. "He showed marvellous skill," spies reported to Marseille, and thence to Rome, "in tempting the native tribes to join his empire."

But time was running out. Five years after the covenant of the Ebro, Hasdrubal was assassinated.

A tradition relates that a Celtic henchman with a grievance slew the overlord of southern Spain. Such an act would be quite typical of a brooding Celtish warrior. There remains the possibility, without evidence to support it, that the assassination was inspired by the Carthaginian's powerful enemies.

Thereupon the officers of the army of Spain assembled in New Carthage and elected Hannibal to be their commander. "They saw in him the image of the well-loved Hamilcar."

This election occasioned some debate in the Council at Carthage. The project of Spain had turned out well, and already yielded surprising resources to the mother city. The Hanno faction, antagonists of the Barcids, claimed

22

that Hasdrubal the Splendid had made himself a king in all but name across the sea. He had never been a Shofet of Carthage. As for the boy Hannibal, as the elder magistrates thought of him, no one knew anything. Before being entrusted with command in the new country—so the leader of the Hannos argued—he should be recalled to Carthage, observed, and at least cautioned. The elders of the Council listened patiently—the triple land wall stood finished, an impregnable defense for the city itself—and acceded to the choice of the distant army. That is, they referred the question to the popular assembly of citizens, who had always favored the Barcas. This assembly voted viva voce for Hannibal, who was quite unknown to it. That decided the matter, especially as commemorative gifts arrived at the merchant harbor, gifts of silver ingots, hides, and grain in new-built vessels from New Carthage.

Still the question remained: what was to be expected from the youthful son of Hamilcar Barca?

In that year, 221, Hannibal was twenty-six, and old enough to have formed the mold of his character. Those who beheld in him the likeness of Hamilcar related how he had thrown himself into a flooded river, swimming across through rolling boulders, to call others after him. They said he disliked the comforts of a pavilion, and often slept in a lion-skin robe on the ground where the sentries watched. He was quick to act when difficulties arose; he kept his head in emergencies. He endured heat or hardships without showing fatigue.

So much might be said of many physically strong men. But Hannibal revealed some peculiarities; he ate sparingly, drinking little wine, and he wore mantles and headcloths of common dark wool and the loose leather riding boots of the Spaniards. His appearance was marked only by the splendor of inlaid weapons, and horse trappings. That was hardly characteristic of Carthaginians, certainly not of Hasdrubal the Splendid. But it was like the Iberians, eager horsemen and hunters upon their rugged hillsides.

Hannibal had, too, a gift of laughter, a sense of irony that included himself as well as those around him. Again this trait was shared by the southerners of Spain, expansive men, a merry folk riding far to festivals, unawed by ancient gods. Even their quick speech had its kinship with Hannibal's Punic. His adolescent years had been passed in the Andalusian valleys; he had known bold women with shining caps set upon their dark, bedecked tresses, their ears hidden by jeweled lappets. He took one of them, a princess of Castulo, among the Olcades people, for his wife. Only her name is known, Imilce. A poet said that theirs was a love of memories. This marriage, like Hasdrubal's, might have been of policy, because the Olcades held the frontier between the Silver Mountains of the Iberians and the midland plateau of the barbaric Carpetanians who acknowledged no overlord.

Still, there are hints that Spain itself may have influenced Hannibal's character more than the bare record of history reveals. Undeniably the Hidden Land laid its hold upon him; he favored the Iberian armed forces in the years to come. Perhaps at the tidings of Hasdrubal's death he thought of this land as his own, apart from Carthage and the enmity of the Middle Sea. His first move was swiftly made, to extend his authority to the north.

The peninsula of Spain was divided, like the Gaul of Julius Caesar's later conquest, into three parts. That is, the human inhabitants were of three kinds. Someone has remarked that the celebrated Caesar showed so little understanding of the Gaulish peoples that it is a wonder he ever mastered them. That was not the case with Hannibal, son of Hamilcar, who had grown up among the Spaniards, had married one of them, and had taken pains to find out—as will soon be apparent—as much as he could about all the others of the peninsula. And they were numerous indeed.

The first and smallest third of Spain was made up of the Tartessians and Iberians of the south and east coasts. The second third consisted, roughly, of the later Celtish invaders who had settled down, blending their tribal customs with ways and means learned from Iberian culture. These long-limbed, emotional, and heedless barbarians had been accustomed to burn the bodies of their dead; the Iberians had buried their dead with gifts for the spirit life,

24

often in elaborate tombs like the superior Carthaginians. Now the Celtiberians followed both customs; they continued to burn their dead but buried the ashes in elaborate urns with gifts of all the weapons owned by the deceased. The Celtiberians occupied, in the main, the Meseta plains around the headwaters of the Tagus where Toledo stands today.

The last third of Spain, in the north, was held by late-arriving Celts. Some of these had crossed the barrier of the Pyrenees as late as the fifth century, and they were still in motion, mixed with elements of the fierce Germanic folk who had driven them down from the Baltic rivers. These warlike Celts—called Gauls or Galatians by Roman observers—sported tartan cloth, soothed themselves with bagpipes, and summoned forth ancestral forest gods, including an odd boar-man, by the trumpets of their priests. Somewhere along their march they had left their druids behind, but they held to tribal councils of elders and guided themselves by omens. On the night of the full moon they danced clumsily around ceremonial fires fed by the living bodies of war captives. They had a power in their numbers and a fierce energy when aroused.

Scattered through the three parts of Spain, the silent Basque folk, the oldest inhabitants, had sought refuge in mountain fastnesses.

This much and more must have been known to Hannibal, who had so little time to complete his conquest of Spain. With his skeleton officer corps of educated Carthaginians, backed by trained African infantry and half-trained regiments of Iberians, and the imposing array of elephants, he was advancing from the light of civilization among the coastal cities toward the darkness of the primeval highlands. In doing so he had to play a duel role; as head of the reigning Barca family, he was the supreme commander serving the Council of Carthage; in the eyes of the Celtish folk he was obviously a king with a mighty treasure and a fair-sized host of warriors. Of necessity Hannibal had to play the part of an ironage king whose word disposed of life and death. Otherwise he would not have been understood by the tribal Celts, who, doubting him, would have slain him with their long swords as Hasdrubal had been slain to ease their perplexity. Long years passed before Hannibal could abandon this duality of personality, and to the end he had to act a certain part, as Julius Caesar did after him.

His own eyes beheld Spain as a kaleidoscope of widely dissimilar peoples, feuding together, raiding the others' harvests to increase their own, lacking any concept—even his Iberians held aloof in their Betis Valley—of a central government. That was precisely what Hannibal meant to impose upon them, explaining it afterward.

Moreover, he had to lead his advance at every point in person. It is said that he was the first to throw himself into a battle. In that age a ruler needed to lend his presence to any group undertaking; even Hannibal's Africans expected to follow him rather than proceed somewhere by his order. Hasdrubal, it is true, had delegated the recruiting of the new army to Hannibal, and the soldiers readily obeyed the son of Hamilcar. But Hannibal had no such alter ego as yet, certainly not even the veteran Maharbal could bring an undesired law and order into chaotic Spain.

"By his cunning he won the friendship of the chieftains," observers related. "By force and by bribes, he won them to his will."

Within a year, playing the dual part of a king who could punish or reward at will, Hannibal was across the middle Tagus. Recruiting as he advanced and storming hostile towns, he threaded his growing host through the Sierra Guaddarrama, to appear among the surprised Vaccaeans, remote kin of the Carpetanian horsemen. He demanded of these highlanders only three things: a token payment of tribute, provender for his forces, and the enlistment of the hardy youth in his command, which enjoyed the obvious benefits of daily meat in the cooking pots and payment of silver in strange coined money.

But he had too little time. The primitive folk could not comprehend such a change in their ancestral customs; they needed an interval of years in which to meditate upon what they would do. They could not understand why this restless man of power walked out of his tent to talk with them, and they took him by the hand to guide him back to his quarters where they could sit on the hide carpets, to meditate on the strangeness of his words. (He had learned the speech of the Celtiberians.) And within a year, as had happened to Hamilcar farther south, the tribes of the north made up their minds to combine to resist him.

The Vaccaean-Carpetanian warriors especially began to muster with formidable numbers of riders. Hannibal was advised by his officers to offer battle without delay. This he disliked to do, and it would have been no easy matter to move out his infantry against free-roving horsemen on those sedge-grown plains. Instead, he led his forces in retreat, back to the swift-flowing Tagus. The Celtiberians swarmed after, in increasing numbers, to find the Carthaginians drawn up along the southern bank of the river. When the barbarian riders rushed to swim or ford the river, they found themselves floundering in deep water while trained spearmen drove them back from the shore, and the awe-inspiring elephants hurried along the bank to flail the riders and send the horses plunging in panic.

The tribal army, disheartened, fled away. The Carthaginians pursued, to put an end to further armed resistance. Without a stand-to battle, the prestige of the Carthaginian invader spread from the central plain to the east coast as far as the Ebro.

On that coast a center of resistance formed around an old walled city on a preciptious height, called Arse by the Iberians who had built it, and Saguntum by the Romans who now took notice of it.

The months of maneuvering in the hinterland had cost the anxious Hannibal what he could least afford to lose—time.

Encounter at Saguntum

In this Hellenistic age the leaders were men of many abilities. After Alexander and the Macedonians had opened routes as far to the east as the mountains of India, new concepts of science and agriculture flowed back from the great cities of Asia into the area of the Mediterranean. Trade expanded along the new routes, and fed the growth of such junctions as Rhodes, Ephesus, and the new-built Alexandria at the outlet of the Nile. Thence commerce and ideas alike reached western ports such as Syracuse in Sicily—"the glory of Greece." The koiné of Greek speech became known from Marseille to India. Aristotle had been one of the first to feel the impact of the new discoveries. Alexander, his protégé, had sent back to the philosopher of Stagira more than specimens of animal and plant life; a hint of ancient scientific knowledge had come as well. In the time of Alexander's successors, the age called Hellenistic, men in the Mediterranean became conscious of universal ideas that dwarfed the philosophy of the earlier schools, even of the outward-looking Stoic, Zeno, chief of the Stoics, had been part Phoenician.

In Syracuse the aging Archimedes labored over problems of leverage and specific gravity of metals. Probably he never said that he could move the sphere of the earth by leverage if there existed a place to stand outside the earth; but at the insistence of Hiero, tyrant of Syracuse, Archimedes made designs in his idle hours for gigantic sailing craft and mechanical monsters to defend the harbor of Syracuse at need. In Alexandria, where the Musaeum housed a universal library, another expert mathematician, a certain Eratosthenes of Africa, prepared astronomical tables from data of the Chaldeans, and a geography of the known world as well. Eratosthenes settled the long-debated question of the true size of the earth by experimenting with the shadow of the sun at midday within a deep, dry well. They said of him that he had five minds in one body.

Hasdrubal the Splendid had shown the same diversity of ability in carrying out his mission of mine developer, city builder, statesman, trade manipulator, and governor as well. All these varied responsibilities fell upon the shoulders of Hannibal, a much younger man, who had been confined to army encampments for the last dozen years. And at once we sense the working of a different mind.

Hannibal wasted no thought, apparently, on building projects or fostering of trade. Such matters he left to his brilliant younger brother. In his own mind, Hannibal explored the shores of the seas around him. Perhaps he studied the *Periplus* or coastal survey of Charon of Carthage, or the record of Himilco's voyage. He might have read the lost work of the other African, Eratosthenes, *On Means and Ways*—on physical resources and their scientific development. Eratosthenes came from Cyrene, the ancestral home of the Barcas. (Eratosthenes of Alexandria jeered at Homeric myths, saying: "You will find the route of Odysseus when you find the shoemaker who sewed up the bag of the winds.") Hannibal summoned a medical director, Synhalus, from Alexandria, not from the island of Cos, where physician healed by thaumaturgy. Hannibal also showed a deep interest in the history of surrounding peoples, especially in the Romans who had little history available as yet. Almost certainly he studied the career of Pyrrhus, the crowned soldier of fortune who had gained nothing by victories over the Romans.

However, there were not many written books to read. Like others of that time, Hannibal burned the oil of his night lamps while he listened. Returning sea captains, incoming merchants, itinerant poets, and his own far-wandering spies related what they had found on other shores. Hannibal's curiosity seemed to be insatiable. What were the customs elsewhere, what manner of harvests gathered, and when? What were the traditions of Marseille, what metals forged, in what way? Where and when did the Celtish tribes find their way through the mountains called the Alps?

Hannibal's curiosity extended to mysterious people like the Etruscans and to obscure animal-keepers like the Ligurians. He was piecing out in his mind a picture of realities in all the Mediterranean. At the same time, during these precious months of 220, he was traversing the central plains and considering the possibilities in the half-subdued Celtiberians. Not as powerful physically as the Libyans, yet capable of enduring more if they were minded so to do—short, dark and volatile, active as panthers—they would make matchless cavalry if they could be trained and led.

And to the north grazed the Uxama herds of long-barreled horses, powerful and easy-gaited. There the people worshiped Epona, goddess of horse-breeding. Hannibal called for these herds. He had a mind alert to minutiae. The Celtiberian sword, two feet long, double-edged and slightly curved, could be used with a free sweep on horseback. These warriors had invented an unusual lance, some five feet in length with the pointed end of iron, no more than a half-inch thick. This immense needle could be thrown from the saddle, to pierce shields and crude armor as well. If the Celtiberian horsemen could be led—

Spanish mercenaries, as Hannibal well knew, had been highly unreliable. Payment could not bind them, nor would they conceivably serve as conscripts. The varied Spaniards had one thing in common with Carthaginians, their freedom of life. Their peculiar pride cannot be rendered into an English word—Spanish historians of today call it *altivez,* a certain innate arrogance-but it had a touchstone. If a Celtiberian *devoted* himself to a leader, he did so by oath and kept the oath, even to killing himself if his sworn leader was killed. In some way Hannibal managed to get this oath of devotion from the Celtiberian horsemen.

Having won over these fighting men, he made serviceable supply trains out of their light wagons—unknown in Africa—drawn by small, quick-paced oxen.

Then, before good sailing weather in the spring of 219, envoys of the *Civitas Romana* appeared at the port of New Carthage seeking him. There they met with him—two older men in simple togas. They requested that he keep the covenant of Hasdrubal not to cross the river Ebro, and that he refrain from approaching Saguntum, which had become an ally of the Roman People.

Saguntum itself was a fortress on the coast about halfway between New Carthage and the Ebro, and accordingly well within the Carthaginian area of the covenant. It had a colony of Greek traders as well as a faction favorable to Carthage. So this citadel on the sea was torn by intrigue and counterintrigue, and what actually happened within it will never be made clear. Apparently the Saguntians had killed off Tartessian settlers near by, and certainly they had appealed to Rome for protection as an ally. It was a slight matter, as slight as the assassination of an Archduke of Austria on the obscure coast of Serbia in modern times. What mattered hugely was Hannibal's response.

By the covenant, he said, the Roman People had no authority south of the Ebro. As for the Saguntians, they had oppressed the Tartessians, and must answer for that. "For it is the hereditary custom of Carthage," he added, "to aid an oppressed people."

That sounds like irony; yet possibly the young Hannibal was voicing a purpose forming in his mind. At any rate the request of Rome had been refused. The envoys returned to their ship, to take the issue to the Council at Carthage as they had been ordered to do. Hannibal sent his own report of the situation to Carthage.

(As happened almost invariably with the internal affairs of Carthage, no record of Hannibal's message of 219 has survived. On the other hand Roman records were preserved, and often rewritten. Two centuries later the diligent Titus Livius, a Paduan, composed his monumental history, *From the Founding of the City,* and by then—in the great Augustan age—the first meeting of New Carthage suffered a drastic change, in Livy's writing. The question of the true cause of the Hannibalic War had become momentous. In Livy's pages, Hannibal was already besieging Saguntum [which he actually did the following year], and when the two ambassadors arrived "he sent men to the shore to meet them and say that it would not be safe for them to come to him ... nor had he time to listen to them at such a crisis." Yet Hannibal did see and talk with the envoys at New Carthage. As for his report to Carthage, Livy explains that even if he did not see them, he must have assumed they would go on to Carthage, and he wrote himself to advise "giving no satisfaction to the Roman People.")

For that is what actually happened at Carthage. There the envoys demanded the neutralization of Saguntum.

The Council on the Byrsa refused to interfere with Hannibal.

(In the pages of the *Founding,* Livy makes Hanno the Great, leader of the party opposed to the Barcas, speak eloquently in rebuttal of the will of the Council. This recorded speech is eloquent of Livy's afterknowledge and afterthought. Hanno begs his fellow councilors "not to provoke a Roman from the Saguntine war." Hanno, it seems, had warned them against sending the offspring of Hamilcar to the army because "neither that man's ghost nor his brood of sons would ever cease from troubling the treaty with the Romans. You have sent to your armies a youth who lusts for power and sees the only way to obtain it, by sowing the seeds of a war. Your armies now invest Saguntum, which the treaty forbids them to approach. Soon the Roman legions will be encircling Carthage. You have fanned the flames that now blaze up around you."

(Now this apparently naïve forecast by a Carthaginian of events to come is not at all naïve. It is the prologue of a fable written down by Titus Livius and his countrymen, to account for Hannibal son of Hamilcar and the catastrophe of the ensuing eighteen years. Already the outline of the fable begins to take shape: that the boy pledged to enmity against Rome, as a man sought to gain supreme power by precipitating Carthage into the war against the will of her wisest leaders.)

That summer Hannibal's army attacked Saguntum.

Testimony of the Sea

The waters of the Middle Sea itself might have told the true cause of what began in the year 219. For this was the climax of the struggle of 120 years for mastery of those waters by two avid and pitiless human powers.

An invisible line, of course, had always divided the south of the Middle Sea from the north. It divided the continental mass of Africa from Europe, the Libyan-Semitic-Egyptian inhabitants from the Aryan invaders who swept over the Greek peninsula and the lovely island of Crete. Phoenicians of the south had joined with Persians of the east against the Dorian Greeks. There was still little in common between the dwellers on the southern coast and those on the northern. Eratosthenes (as geographer) had just drawn his main axis of the Mediterranean, through the Strait of Gibraltar and Sicily above the island of Rhodes. The coasts themselves were entirely different.

In the north miniature seas lay between peninsulas; great rivers drained the hinterland; sheltered bays invited ships, while island chains led toward distant shores. On the south the forbidding African coast stretched interminably, with almost no harbors and with the outlet of only one great river, the Nile. On the north heavy rainfall fed the pasturage of animals, except in Greece, and nourished increasing masses of humans; on the south the Carthaginians had to improvise agriculture, and remained dependent on the sea. The Latin people of the Tiber thrived on agriculture and for a long time appeared content in doing so.

The Middle Sea had one junction point where the divided coasts all but touched, where the long peninsula of Italy extended across the narrow Strait of Messina to Sicily, the western tip of which lay less than 125 miles from Carthage. This land barrier in turn separated the large eastern half of the Mediterranean from the western half. From time to time refugee peoples migrated from the east into the still barbaric west, as the Etruscans journeyed from Asia Minor to northwestern Italy, and the Phocaeans to the mouth of the Rhone at Marseille. Adventurous colonists of Greek mother cities brought their quarrels and their triumphs in artistry to the tranquil harbors of the heel of Italy, to Tarentum (Taras) and luxurious Sybaris, and around the toe of the peninsula as far as the New City (Naples), where in time they encountered Etruscan traders. Very early indeed they built Syracuse on a land-locked harbor, thus creating out of sun-warmed southern Italy and eastern Sicily a Magna Graecia.

With the migrants came the growing trade of the eastern shores. Vying against each other for the new wealth, Etruscan, Massiliote, and Syracusan ships explored more distant routes and fought combats at sea, only to have Carthaginian shipping seize the mastery of the western Mediterranean. (Barred from the straits, the traders of Marseille drew the valuable tin from the Atlantic shores overland, down the Rhone.) By their posts on Sardinia and Corsica the African seafarers controlled the Tyrrhenian and Ligurian seas, off the west coast of Italy. Although the enlightened tyrants of Syracuse contested their shores bitterly with the Carthaginian fleets, they could not keep the Africans from the deep sea routes of

33

the west. And these became more important as the now precious gold and silver began to fail in the mines of the eastern shores. The cultured eastern Mediterranean had growing need of the raw materials of the barbaric west. After the turn of the third century, the attempt of Pyrrhus, soldier-king of Epirus, to carve out an empire through southern Italy and Sicily—the prosperous Magna Graecia—was a consequence of economic need, although it was occasioned by the first appearance of Roman ships off the free city of Tarentum.

When the brilliant Pyrrhus was at last defeated by Roman legions (275) and left the shores of Italy, legend makes him say: "What a fine battlefield I am leaving to the Romans and Carthaginians." Probably he never said it, but it turned out to be true.

Hannibal had been studying all that happened in these years.

He must have understood more clearly than we can understand today how most of Italy had been mastered by the obscure city—not even a seaport—in the hills of the lower Tiber River. How the accomplished Etruscan people had been subdued by the still dynamic Greeks of the south, and how Magna Graecia went the way of the Sybarites, softened by luxury. The stolid Latin folk had taken their first step when they managed to capture Etruscan Veii on the upper Tiber. Then the league of Latin cities dissolved in stubborn conflict, to emerge either as allies or subjects of the *Civitas Romana* alone. By tenacity and unceasing conflict Rome with her allies gained the mastery of central Italy, and the submission of Capua, wealthiest and most cultured of the southern Greek cities. Then when her iron tenacity drove Pyrrhus back to his ship, her march to the seas quickened—renowned Tarentum falling in 272, Rhegium on the Strait of Messina (Messana) in 270. Six years later a few of her cohorts followed some mercenaries, self-styled "Men of Mars", across that treacherous narrow strait, and found a Carthaginian general installed in the citadel of Messina on the Sicilian side.

Unperceived by the participants in the Messina affair, a change was coming over the extent of the Mediterranean.

Ancient city-states were ceasing to be dynamic forces; the supremacy of individual tyrants, or dictators, was ending. Pyrrhus would be the last of them. The rule of empire, still embryonic, was taking form.

Hitherto Roman expansion had been overland, while Carthaginian hegemony lay along the waters. The proverb that a lion will not quarrel with a whale held true in their case. Amicable in their separate orbits, they often entered loose political alliance, and as late as the Pyrrhic victories, Carthage offered a fleet to aid the Roman Senate (and to keep the army of Epirus out of strategic Sicily.)

Now the two orbits had touched at the Strait of Messina. The skirmishing at that town spread inland, and intrigue prepared the way for armies; Hiero II, last tyrant of Syracuse, decided that the Roman legions would prevail, and offered them his impregnable city for a base, his fleet for transport. The Carthaginian hold on the west half of the island was broken. Belatedly the Council on the Byrsa awoke to the fact that the island key of the Middle Sea might be lost.

Until then the African city had followed a policy of limiting wars. Fitting out fighting fleets only at need, Carthage had relied on foreign mercenaries to form an army which could be paid off when it had served its purpose. Once an objective had been gained, Carthage ended the conflict. A scholar of today remarked that her army served the state policy, while Roman state policy served the army. Roman independence had been won from more powerful neighbors only by the strength of her legions, a remarkable national army. Pyrrhus observed with some bitterness: "In warfare these barbarians are not in the least barbarous." Now for the first time, in Sicily, Roman commanders found themselves opposed by the astute leadership and the resources of a foreign power.

For Carthage and Rome were foreign to each other; the one had grown out of Africa, elder in culture, following the older gods of the east; the other had emerged from European tribal folk, forming their ancestral customs into laws, intolerant of any other way of life. Because of that, the clash of arms at Messina had grown into what history calls the first Punic (Phoenician) War,

35

but what was in reality the beginning of the irreconcilable struggle for mastery of the Mediterranean world.

Regulus Offers his Terms

In brooding over this, two things must have been uppermost in Hannibal's mind. The first was the defeat at sea.

During the first three years it became increasingly evident to the unimaginative commanders of the Senate and the Roman People that you could not capture an outlying island unless you could master the waters around it. Faced with this practical problem the Romans, with characteristic energy and skill, set about building their first battle fleet. (At the outbreak of hostilities an exploring squadron had been captured entire by the Carthaginian ships in a bay, the reason—never publicly explained—being that the inexperienced crews were seasick after a storm, when they took refuge in the bay.)

Within a year Rome had assembled and manned 100 quinqueremes (five rowers to a long oar) and 20 scouting triremes (three rowers to a smaller oar). This feat on the part of landsmen who disliked the sea has the appearance of a miracle and it has been explained by a fable, still repeated today. By this fable, some Romans found a stranded Carthaginian quinquereme and copied its design in building others, while fellow citizens learned to row by machines set up on land.

Now a war galley of that time was a fragile affair resembling an oversize racing shell topped by an oblong framework that seated as many as 300 oarsmen. Only the larger craft were "covered"—that is, decked . The galleys fared badly in a rough sea, and had to seek shelter from a storm. Their armament consisted of an iron or bronze ram. Often these rams appeared in a vertical pair on the prow, to crush into a hostile galley above and below the water line, or to break the oar bank on the enemy's side. Then, too, the galley might lay along the other vessel to allow its armed men—who were not the rowers—to

board and master the enemy. In action its mast was lowered, to avoid breakage in the shock of collision. All in
all, the war galley required handling by experienced mariners. Nor could it keep the open sea for long. Sailing
craft that served as transports and merchantmen might
run through or away from the galleys in a strong wind.
But usually in a calm they were helpless against the attack
of the oared galley with its ram.

What the Roman commanders actually did in conjuring
up a battle fleet was to call upon the subject seaports
which already possessed the galleys—Tarentum, Naples,
Pisa of the Etruscans, not to mention the fleet in Syracuse. Such ports bore the title of *socii navales,* allies of
the ships. These Greek- and Etruscan-built vessels already
had experienced crews. As for the picturesque rowing
machines, they never existed. By law—and the laws of
the city of the Seven Hills were rigid as those of the earlier Medes and Persians—no citizen could serve under
arms except in the legions of infantry, and noncitizens
could not serve under the standards of the legions.
Freedmen and slaves might join the crews of the ships or
the rowers on the benches.

The armored legionaries, however, did go on the new
fleet. Their methodical commanders planned to use them
as boarders, and to aid them in doing so giant grappling
hooks, the *corvi* or beaks, were furnished the galleys, cou-
pled with wide boarding bridges over which a half dozen
men could run shield to shield abreast. The plan was to
grapple the enemy craft, to allow the trained Roman soldiers to engage the hostile crew in hand-to-hand fighting
on the deck.

The plan paid off. The battle fleets met for the first
time off the peninsula of Mylae, not far from Messina
(260). The Carthaginian fleet was accustomed to maneuvering, and carried only small contingents of soldiers.
Probably surprise played a part in the result. Most of the
Carthaginian galleys were captured or sunk. The Roman
commander carried off bronze rams of the enemy to be
set up as trophies of a triumph around the Forum. It was
their first victory upon the sea.

Of course the triumph at Mylae did not establish Roman sea power in a day. Other Carthaginian fleets fared

better and even harried the coast of Italy. Then, too, Roman commanding officers never learned the lore of the sea; their stubbornness and inexperience combined to lead them into shipwrecks that lost tens of thousands of lives to the waters. But what happened at Mylae did something to the will of the Carthaginian leaders at sea; thereafter they seemed to fear a battle test of their ships against an Italian armada.

Hamilcar realized that the naval supremacy of his city no longer existed, and Hannibal must have realized that her army could no longer expect to make a voyage across the open sea.

Another memory became a factor in his thought. The words of one man, Regulus, who happened to be a Roman Consul. The triumph at Mylae had opened a new horizon to the dwellers in the Seven Hills. It offered them a way to other shores than their own. Inevitably the Fathers in the Senate perceived that the Sicilian struggle could be ended by taking Carthage. Three years after Mylae—a notable feat in organization—a flotilla of 330 vessels left Messina with four legions aboard; it fought its way through the Carthaginian fleet south of Sicily, and carried the war safely into Africa. The two Consuls, Regulus and Vulso, commanded the expeditionary force. There appeared to be no equal force to stand between it and the city, which had no land wall at that time. When envoys of the Council sought the Roman entrenched camp to temporize, Regulus greeted them almost with contempt. (The sudden appearance of the European army had stirred up the restless peoples of the African coast into tumult; remembering this after fifteen years, Roman authorities would allow Hamilcar Barca to take with him from Mount Eryx the deserters and escaped slaves who added fuel to the flames of the civil war of the mercenaries.) "If you call yourselves brave," Regulus said, "you will either conquer or accept the lot of the conquered."

Regulus spoke as the war commander of European tribes—who still kept the organization of the Thirty-five Tribes—and a man with a simple code of courage impelling him to go forward to slay or be slain. The cultured

38

and much more complicated Africans desired neither alternative.

Then bluntly Regulus offered them terms for the safety of their city. These were:

The cession of Sicily and Sardinia.

Surrender without payment of Roman prisoners, and ransom of Carthaginian prisoners, with reimbursement to Rome of the cost of the war, paid in annual installments.

Carthage to pledge herself not to make war or declare peace without the consent of the government of Rome.

Carthage to agree not to outfit a fleet for battle; except that one galley might be kept in service.

Carthage to be bound to furnish, upon request, fifty triremes for the use of the Romans.

What befell after that was as unexpected as the reversal at Mylae. These terms meant the ruin of the city that had been mistress of the seas. And the city roused herself to meet a danger unperceived until then. Ships went out to bring Hamilcar Barca with his veteran mercenaries back from the Sicilian front. (The Roman galleys were beached in the Tunis bay, their commanders encamped on the shore.) Another trained soldier, Xanthippus, leader of Spartan mercenaries, was given the Numidian horsemen and elephants that he asked for to encounter Regulus' legions on the open plain with new battle tactics. Against the Xanthippus-Hamilcar heterogenous force the legions marched, overly confident, to disaster. Regulus was made captive with about half his command; the remnants were driven back to the beachhead and transports. Other galleys arrived to take them off. But on the homeward voyage the Roman officers insisted, against the advice of the experienced pilots, in laying a course by the southern shore of Sicily. A storm caught them on the lee shore. The galleys went down with most of the transports—284 vessels lost with all on board.

Characteristically, when the extent of the disaster was known, the Roman Senate ordered the requisition for the building of a new fleet. Within three months, it is said, 220 ships were equipped and ready on the Italian coast. And permanent winter pens for that number of galleys were erected.

After long years the rival powers, mutually exhausted,

agreed on the compromise peace that ceded Sicily to Rome with payment of the 1200 talents in indemnity.

This was the peace of 241, made by Hamilcar while he defended Mount Eryx. It left Carthage a sovereign power, without restrictions on her fleet. It was broken by the Romans within three years.

But Hannibal had engraved the terms of Regulus on his memory. The oath of the Barcas pledged him with his brothers never to submit in that fashion.

"I Hold Within This Fold of My Toga War or Peace—"

Wherever he rode, Hannibal carried a map with him. He kept it for his own use, while his Greek scribes filled in upon it the shores, mountain chains, and harbors of the north of the Mediterranean. A map at that time usually gave distances between places with a notation of the surrounding people. For the last nine years slight yet significant changes had taken place on the map around Italy. Word of them reached Hannibal from well-disposed merchants, or his agents in disguise.

Advices from Rome told how the doors of the temple of Janus had been closed, after generations of strife, because the great Republic was at last at peace. Yet a fleet had crossed the Adria Sea (Adriatic) to the far side on a mission to punish "pirates." (Pyrrhus had come out of that other coast of the Adriatic.)

After 226 (the year of Hasdrubal's covenant) the changes had increased in tempo. In the north of Italy Celtish tribes revolted along the river Po. Armies marched from the Tiber to subdue them and to build frontier posts on the Po—a frontier that stood in the same relation to Rome as the river Ebro stood to New Carthage, now becoming a thriving port. In 224 these armies crossed the Po, and two years later captured Milan, the central city of the Celts. Simultaneously another expedition crushed the last resistance of the islanders in Sardinia.

Then, in 219 armed galleys left port with urgent speed to cross the Adriatic again, land their legions and pro-

claim the Dalmatian (Illyrian) coast a Roman protector-
ate. The native rebel in this case was Demetrios of
Pharos, who fled to safety in Macedonia. No doubt the
Roman forces had been provoked in various ways. Yet
Demetrios and the Celts—called Gauls in Italy—and the
Sardinian mountaineers had taken to arms on their own
soil.

The changes on the map made a picture that Hannibal
could not have mistaken. To the east, the Adriatic had
been made a Roman *mare clausum;* to the west of Italy,
the Tyrrhenian Sea behind Sardinia and Corsica had been
mastered. How far outward would the move continue into
the Mediterranean? Carthage still held to the western end
of that sea, where the African and Spanish coasts came
together. Midway within that end lay the Pine Isles and
the small Balearics and the port of Saguntum.

Then the Roman envoys entered Spain to claim a pro-
tectorate over Saguntum. Behind these envoys large land
forces mobilized within Italy, and some 200 fighting galleys were launched from their winter pens. Was not this
power mobilized against Spain?

In early summer of 219 Hannibal made his decision to
act. His army, composed largely of Spanish recruits, attempted to storm the citadel on the height of Saguntum,
and failed. It had neither siege engines nor skill in engineering an approach up the rock slopes. Hannibal encircled Saguntum and waited for its defenders to yield. He
even left Maharbal in command and rode off to the unsettled Celtiberian plains. During those months his wife
Imilce gave birth to a child.

Within Saguntum the inhabitants waited for aid to
reach them from Rome, their acknowledged ally. But no
such aid appeared. After eight months the Carthaginians
broke into the ancient Cyclopean wall of the city, and
resistance ended. Hannibal ordered rewards to be given
his followers and a treasure of silver, as well as captured
merchandise to be sent to Carthage.

Then by the hand of desperately speeding couriers came
the news from Carthage.

What happened in the senatorial chamber at Rome
during those months of 219 remains somewhat obscure.

After the fleet returned from the Adriatic there must have been increasing debate on the question of Carthage, and argument spurred by Hannibal's move against Saguntum. Some of the great nobles, the Claudii and the Scipios, spoke for a total mobilization against Carthage, while the no less powerful Fabians held out for negotiation. One of the elder Father, Fabius Verrucosus, is quoted as warning: "It is one thing to debate warfare in this chamber; it is something very different to encounter it on the field of battle."

This seems to have been one of the times when the authoritative Senate disagreed with the Roman People. The new horizon of the sea fascinated many leaders; beyond their shores waited untapped resources, and a share in the overseas trade that had been denied patricians until then. (A law of 219 permitted men of senatorial rank to engage for the first time in such trade.)

On the other hand the assemblies of the Tribes—the *Populi Romani*—seemed to remember too well the terrible loss of life in the war years of 264-241, and the deterioration of the farms during the absence of the men. They wanted to raise wheat of their own and cared nothing about its import by shipowners from newly acquired Sicily. These workers of the soil had found a slogan: "Farming and Italy for the Italians!"

The operations against the dreaded Gauls had been supported by the popular assemblies—the *comitia centuriata*—and their tribunes, because they yielded more public land as well as an increase in security. (Every citizen remembered the dark days when the Gauls of Brennus had ranged through Rome itself.) But in their opinion another conflict with "the Punics" offered no tangible profit and warded off no visible peril.

So the debate went on, while the gates of the temple of Janus remained closed, and no fleet was sent to the aid of Saguntum. The news of the fall of the city to Hannibal gave the Claudian-Scipionic faction of the Senate a telling argument for declaration of war. An ally of the Senate and the Roman People had been attacked. As for the matter of profit and loss, the silver mines of Spain could pay the cost. So argued envoys from the distressed Saguntians and aroused Marseille, also an ally.

Early in 218 the senatorial factions agreed on a compromise and the popular assemblies accepted it. A delegation would be sent, as the Fabians wished, to negotiate with Carthage. If negotiation failed the delegation would declare war.

There was a great possibility that the Carthaginians would yield to an ultimatum. They also had a party resolved upon peace. They had asked for terms in 241; then they had yielded up Sardinia and Corsica with further tribute; no more than eight years ago they had agreed to the treaty of the Ebro. Now, again, they might take refuge in negotiation, at which they were so adept.

Five envoys (*legati*) sailed from Rome in March of 218. Three of them belonged to the Claudian-Scipionic faction, but the eldest—and in consequence the spokesman—was a Fabian, although not, apparently, the Verrucosus who had warned the Senate that matters looked quite different on a battlefield.

On the height of the Byrsa within the curtained chamber of the Council of Carthage, Fabius, chief of the legates asked the question: would the Republic of Carthage now surrender Hannibal son of Hamilcar and his staff to Roman authority?

The Council gave its answer: no.

Fabius asked then, through his interpreter: did the Republic of Carthage authorize the action of its general, Hannibal son of Hamilcar?

The Council would not disavow Hannibal's action. In turn, it asked questions, fiercely legalistic. Did the Senate of the Romans hold to alliance with the city of Saguntum rather than to its ancient accord with Carthage? Since when had Saguntum been an ally of Rome? If before the covenant of Hasdrubal, then that covenant disowned the Saguntians, who were south of the Ebro; if after—

Fabius rose. "These phrases weary me." He closed both hands on the breast of his robe. "I hold within this fold of my toga war or peace. Carthaginians, choose which you will have."

The elder Shofet requested permission to withdraw with his councilors. Fabius assented.

When the Carthaginians filed back into the chamber,

43

the Shofet made an answer that was quite unexpected. "Choose yourself."

Fabius said, "Then it will be war."

Several voices cried: "We accept it!"

The news that Rome had declared war went at once to Hannibal by couriers speeding along the African coast trail, to the ferry at the straits.

When the five envoys returned to the Tiber, they made their report to the Senate. The gates of the temple of Janus were swung open, so that the two-faced god might look out toward the sunrise and sunset, and the Roman People would know that they had entered a state of war.

II. Journey Over the Alps

Mystery of the River Rhone

After the Ides of March ushered in the new year for officials, Publius Cornelius Scipio became the patrician Consul. He was a drab-looking man without honors to his name but with a hard core of common sense. However, the family of the Cornelii and that of the Scipios ("The Staff") had given the state successful leaders for many generations, and this circumstance probably brought about the election of Publius. He drew lots with his fellow Consul for command of the two armies, and the army readied for the invasion of Spain fell to him. This was quite fitting, in public opinion, because the Cornelian-Scipionic party in the Senate had sponsored overseas expansion with the objective of acquiring Spain as a province—the project that had been delayed nearly a year by the resistance of the popular assemblies.

In fact, that delay had made it necessary to change the war plan. Saguntum no longer awaited them, as a base for landing on that coast. It was decided, therefore, to open the war on two fronts. The large expeditionary force would sail from the base of Sicily to land on the African coast and proceed as quickly as possible to besiege Carthage itself. The smaller expedition would sail under command of Publius by way of friendly Marseille to seize the barrier line of the Pyrenees. In any case, it would hold in check the single field army of the Carthaginians somewhere in Spain. This plan quite obviously put the Carthaginian army on the two horns of a dilemma—whether to go back to Africa to the aid of the mother city, or become separated from Carthage.

Recent advice from the observers in Marseille was that the Carthaginian army was coming up across the frontier river, the Ebro, with Hannibal leading it.

What with this changing of plan and last minute preparations, Publius Scipio did not get to sea until summer. He sailed from the new port of Pisa, built by the ingenious Etruscans, with two legions and twice as many allied forces—24,000 in all—and 60 rather aged galleys escorting the transports. Perhaps because it clung to the coast the fleet was badly tossed about by heavy winds and most of the legionaries, unaccustomed to the sea, became sick.

This nuisance added itself to others in the consciousness of the Roman Consul. Up in the north the intractable Gauls had surged back into their fields along the river Po that had been allotted to Latin colonists; ahead of him to the west, Roman envoys—the same five who had behaved in such dignified fashion at the Council in Carthage by refusing to bandy words with the Punics—had met with a hostile reception when they tried to win the friendship of barbarian chieftains above the Pyrenees. The barbarians had laughed at them, saying it would be stupid to offer their fields to defend the fields of the distant Romans. Moreover the Pyrenees themselves bore the name of the unknown goddess Pyre, reputedly proud and of great power. It was as if intangible forces opposed the advance of the Roman command. Beyond taking them into account, Publius wasted no further thought on them. He was a very practical man.

He was glad, however, to seek shelter for his fleet in the nearest mouth of the great river Rhone. There, as he expected, anxious officers from Marseille awaited him on the watchtowers of the shore. They cut short his ceremonial greeting by shouting astonishing tidings. Hannibal was here at the Rhone.

46

"You mean at the Ebro," Publius ventured to correct them.

He could not believe that the Carthaginian army of Spain was actually on this river of the Gauls, two days' march from his landing place. However, he dispatched a squadron of noble-born riders to investigate the situation, and he entrenched the camp where his seasick legionaries recovered their legs. In five days his horsemen returned to assure him that there was in fact a great Carthaginian camp up the river. They had driven a number of strange, cloaked riders, undoubtedly Africans, into it, and they had sighted elephants among the wagons as well as gangs of men with axes making rafts.

Their tale of such unusual phenomena did not banish Publius' skepticism. What could have brought Carthaginians among the lands beyond the Alps? He summoned his regimental tribunes to discuss what should next be done. It was clear to all that Carthaginians, their declared enemies, were doing something up the river. The right thing to do was to offer battle to the enemy. Accordingly Publius gave orders to advance the legions in readiness to deploy for combat. They moved cautiously upriver. And they found the enemy encampment deserted, with a horde of intoxicated Gauls pounding their shields and singing around the ashes of the fires.

The battle could not be fought. Three days before, the Carthaginians had crossed the river and vanished toward the north. But whither?

The new Consul faced a situation without precedent in his brief military experience. The enemy, instead of giving battle, had departed toward an unknown destination. The river flowed out of the mountains called the Alps, and beyond those Alps lay his homeland of Italy. Publius found himself between the horns of dilemma, whether to turn back on his own initiative or to carry out his mission by going on with his fleet.

The Consul settled this problem by common sense. Ordering his army to proceed to Spain on the transports, escorted by Massiliote guard ships, under command of his brother, he returned with the fast galleys to Pisa, there to carry out his responsibility as Consul. This decision of the practical Scipio would have momentous consequences.

His primary duty was to defend the frontier of Rome. And if that could no longer be done on the Rhone, Publius Cornelius Scipio would do it on the Po. It must have occurred to him that he was going back rather a long way. But it is doubtful if he realized that he was beginning to follow where Hannibal went.

Fable and Reality of the Great March

The steps taken by Publius are clearly revealed in the records of the year 218. On the other side of the events, silence covers the proceedings of Hannibal son of Hamilcar. He took pains as well not to let his intentions be known. Yet here and there traces of his planning can be discerned.

First of all, he had anticipated the declaration of war for a year, ever since the two envoys of Rome faced him at New Carthage. During the winter that followed he had made a shift in armed forces, sending some Spanish recruits to Africa, and summoning some garrisons from Africa; he had given unusual leave to his Spaniards to pass the winter in their homes. He had sent envoys with gifts to the remote peoples beyond the Pyrenees, all the way through the Alps to the Celtish chieftains in northern Italy. These envoys were to report on the extent and time of the harvests along their route, the characteristics of the peoples, whether warlike or not, whether hostile to Rome or not.

Then, too, Hannibal had made a tour of southern, or Iberian, Spain during the winter. He even visited Gades at the land's end, and there again beheld the surge of the outer Ocean along its remote horizon. Consider him there for a moment, on the temple steps where no women came. Taller than ordinary Carthaginians, stooping a little under the black mantle of Spanish *sagum,* his curling hair and beard close-clipped, his eyes enigmatic in a thin, weather-browned head, the nose high-bridged over tense lips. A man not marked from others by his attire, physically restless, yet held by contemplation.

48

Hannibal rode back through the Andalusian valleys, fair in early spring. Archaeologists have found evidence of his handiwork in the adobe brick watchtowers built the length of the coast, and known afterward as "Hannibal's towers," and in the hurried building of citadels just then, out of ancient squared stones fitted together in new designs. Then, too, the authority of Iberian princes was strengthened along the endangered east coast.

There was no sign as yet that he had any intention of leaving Spain, which had been the homeland of the Barcas for twenty years.

Now the Roman fable of the Barcas, related afterward, explains that the sons were oath-bound to become the enemies of Rome; that the father migrated to Spain against the will of Carthage; that Hannibal himself kindled the great war into flame; that Hamilcar prepared Spain for the jump-off of his son's march overland across the Alps to attack Rome. The fable fits together neatly, and it is dramatic as a tragedy of Euripides. Yet it is not the truth.

The Barcas were sent to Spain by, and on behalf of, their city of Carthage.

There exists no evidence that Hamilcar planned the incredible march through Europe and bequeathed it to his son, like a von Schlieffen plan of modern times, to be handed down from the one generation to the next. There is a rather firm tradition that before his death Hamilcar warned Hasdrubal the Splendid and his sons that their task in Spain had barely begun, and that they lacked the strength as yet to withstand the armed forces of Rome.

Hannibal ended his winter's ride of inspection at the palace above the teeming port of New Carthage, where trade was increasing yearly. Wagon trains from the mines brought down to the port a yearly yield of silver sufficient to pay the revenues of Carthage itself. His oath at the altar of Melcart bound him and his brothers never to submit to Roman rule, and where else than in remote Spain would he be better able to do that?

Moreover, in whatever action he took, Hannibal had to depend upon the manpower of his Iberians and Celtiberians. No leader of his sensitivity could have failed to realize the dominant characteristic of the Spanish people, with their *altivez* complex. These men of the Silver Mountains and great plain would fight like fiends for their homes and towns; taken elsewhere, oath-bound or not, they would lose heart and become moody. He was very soon to make proof of that characteristic of the Spaniards, the mainstay of his new army.

At this point it is apparent only that Hannibal was preparing to defend the Spanish coasts. Then in April the couriers from Carthage brought word of Fabius' choice of war. Hannibal ordered the soldiers on leave to return to the encampments around New Carthage.

Soon after that he must have learned from Carthaginian agents in Sicilian ports that a fleet was assembling there for the invasion of the African coast, 100 miles to the south. In fact hostile war galleys made probing raids on the coast near to Carthage.

Regardless of any oath, Hamilcar and his sons were dedicated to one thing, the service of the Republic of Carthage. Had not the Thunderbolt left his stronghold on Mount Eryx to negotiate a peace desired by the Council? Had he not then returned to serve his city in the catastrophe of the mercenaries' rebellion? Hasdrubal the Splendid had made his covenant with those same enemies at the bidding of the mother city. Whatever Hannibal may have hoped to achieve in his new homeland—even the independent kingdom proclaimed by his antagonists in the Council—he now faced the grave danger to Carthage of invasion from Sicily.

And Carthage had no fleet capable of warding off the invasion. Carthage had a garrison within strong walls but no army—except his own—able to withstand a trained Roman expeditionary force. If Hannibal returned across the straits to defend the mother city he would abandon Spain to the enemy.

There is no evidence of his thoughts. He acted without delay. He embarked Imilce, his wife, and his year-old son in a fast vessel bound for Carthage. He watched the vessel sail from the harbor, past the lighthouse point into the darkness that would screen its crossing to the African coast. Had he sent his family away to protect them from danger, or to be hostages for his future conduct? In either case, they were a tie, holding him to the African city.

In May Hannibal rode after his army, already moving north along the coast.

It moved in separate divisions without haste In fact, it seemed to be grouped by nations differing a great deal from each other. The Numidians and Moors rode without reins, with their pipes wailing as the slender horses grazed the countryside. These desert riders kept to themselves; fastidious in trifles, they spent their spare hours in braiding their hair, cleansing their teeth, and polishing gold ornaments. They rode swathed in white mantles, seated on leopard skins; when they charged the throw of their long javelins outranged enemy missiles; fighting knee to knee they wielded small shields of elephant hide and long knives, using both arms against a foeman who had only one arm free if he guided his horse with reins. But the threat of the Berber folk lay in their speed; they could overtake clumsier horsemen, or escape from them at will. The Libyan and Berber infantry marched at pace, closed up on the trails, wearing their iron plates of armor, but with leather helmets and long shields slung to the spears on their shoulders. They were under the rigid command of Lord Maharbal, who had served Hamilcar.

Near the heavy infantry columns wandered light-footed bands of Balearians—"The Throwers"—with leather slings of three different lengths coiled over shoulders or waists. Like the Spaniards, they were fiercely independent of rule. One of their missiles consisted of a fireball of flaming pitch, and another of a heavy lead ball that could break bronze shields.

Horsemen made up an unusually large part of the moving host. Massylian warriors covered their heads and necks with leather hoods, studded with iron. While the swift-paced Numidians relied on a quiver full of javelins, to be thrown with either hand, the heavier horsemen counted on the shock of lances; the Celtiberians wielded the terrible iron shafts before using their short, curved sabers. In battle their cherished horses were protected by leather breastplates.

While the African regiments formed the core of the army, the heart of it lay in the Spaniards—the highlanders of Castulo and the Meseta, the clans of Vaccaea and Uxama with wolf and lion heads for helmets, who danced around the fires through a night when they had wine. Other tribes joined the Balearians with the light weapons of skirmishers. Only the Iberians, who responded to discipline, marched as regiments under standards of the rayed sun and crescent moon. They escorted the wagon trains.

For Hannibal, who allowed these dissimilar war bands to hold their native festivals, took care to load the trains with spare weapons, tools, grain, medicines, and an enormous reserve of silver in chests. Although few of the wild Basque folk appeared in the march, a supply of their peculiar double-headed axes—for forestry—went along.

As an army this moving host sadly lacked discipline and cohesion. All in all, it might have numbered fifty thousand humans and forty elephants. Yet as a whole, it was gathered together for the first time. It could cover country well and endure hardships—to which it was accustomed, between the feasts. But how would it act together?

Only small portions had come from Carthage, chiefly the detachment of engineers and a body of horsemen, noble-born, marked by picturesque red cloaks. These served actually as a pool of young officers at need. They also acted as interpreters in the polyglot host. Hannibal himself was followed by no standard-bearers; he might be anywhere among the marchers—he could address them in their varied tongues—unrecognized until men could mark his face or the gold inlay upon his weapons, or the silverwork of his reins. His shrine and teraphim traveled in a small tent.

Later, his enemies paid tribute to this army. "For sixteen years . . . he never broke up his forces or dismissed them from the field. Yet, holding them together, he kept so large an army from sedition against himself or within its own ranks, although the troops were not of the same nation or even race—for he had Libyans, Spaniards, Carthaginians, Ligurians, Celts, and Balearians as well as Italians and Greeks all together.

"Still the ability of their commander compelled men so radically different to obey his single will."

Unwittingly in saying this the Roman writers touched

upon the secret of the army. It was manned by the peoples of the Mediterranean shores, from the Syrtes to the straits, and—at this point as far as the river Ebro. They were gathered into national units going with him from motives of their own. (He had no Ligurians, Italians or Greeks as yet.)

The army crossed the broad mouth of the Ebro without hindrance. It must have seemed ironical to Hannibal that Carthaginians should cross the treaty river "with weapons in hand" after the treaty of peace had been ended by the Romans.

"To Those of You Who Wish to Turn Back—"

After the army crossed the Ebro something very strange happened. Something very strange, that is, if you believe the army was en route to cross the Alps before winter. For three months and a half it lingered between the river and the passes of the Pyrenees, a distance of some 180 miles, which this army could have covered in six days.

The coast was rugged, the inhabitants—Ilergetes Celts—strange to the Carthaginians, and the chief ports, Emporiae and Tarraco (Tarragona), hostile because they were trading posts of the Massiliote Greeks. But all this offered no serious obstacle to a march through. Hannibal himself must have been responsible for the delay.

The cause of it is quite evident, upon reflection. Hannibal had made no decision to enter Europe further as yet; instead he was doing what had to be done. This last third of Spain across the Ebro, with the barbaric beer-drinking Ilergetes and the hostile ports, had to be brought under Carthaginian control, to complete Hamilcar's task. The coast road needed to be opened to traffic and the eastern pass of the Pyrenees secured, if Spain was to be defended.

Already his brother Hasdrubal had been left in charge of New Carthage and the southern garrisons. Although only twenty-three years of age, Hasdrubal had a genius for improvisation and a quick imagination of what needed to be done. Impetuous in action, he lacked Hannibal's inflexible determination. The youngest brother, Mago, was a fire-eater, a favorite of the soldiers. Mago sped about in a light chariot, his crimson cloak flying. Hannibal left him in the city, to be held in check by Hasdrubal. The three brothers were very young in comparison with Roman commanders.

Hannibal himsel was not a Shofet of Carthage; he commanded the army in Spain, self-supporting, obedient to the will of the Council—which had sustained the action of the Barcas, so long as Hannibal himself obeyed the Council in Africa.

Carthaginians made up Hannibal's staff. Maharbal and Hanno, son of a former Shofet, Bomilcar, were veterans of the last war, cunning in battle and inexorable in hatred of the Romans. Another veteran, the aged Hert, sat in their conferences. Lesser officers were former chieftains of Spaniards or Libyans. The specialists also came from all nations—Synhalus, the Egyptian, being physician-in-chief; and two Greeks, Sosilos and Silenos, serving as chief secretaries; while Bog, the astrologer of the expedition, came from Asia. Sosilos, a Spartan, had taught Hannibal Greek.

This unorthodox staff had the aid of men who remained nameless because they gathered intelligence from the Mediterranean ports and the hinterland of Europe. Only one is known, Carthalo, who carried out undercover missions. Hannibal was to depend greatly on these faceless officers who eked their way into merchant's conclaves, arranged omens and prophecies—perhaps counseled by Bog—in strange cities, listened to the chatter in barbershops, and felt the pulse of common folk in the fields.

While he moved slowly toward the Pyrenees, these intelligence agents added to his anxiety, with word that the Roman invasion fleets were fitting out in Syracuse and Pisa.

So at this point Hannibal learned that an invasion of Africa was preparing.

Then, abruptly, a change took place in the army. A division, 10,000 strong, was detached to carry out the subjection of the trans-Ebro highlands and ports. An advance force started north to hold the nearest pass of the Pyrenees, called the Pertus. The balance of the army began to climb the foothills, where fugitive Basque tribes gathered to watch, amazed.

What had caused the change in plan? There are no indications except one. By then, or earlier, the Carthaginian emissaries had returned from the far north of Italy. Moreover, they had brought with them Celts who included the chieftains of at least two tribes, the Boii and Insubres. These Gauls from the valley of the Po must have stirred the curiosity of their remote kinsmen from south of the Ebro; they came for conference, which meant that they wore battle dress of helmets with mock horns, of shields adorned with emblems of their exploits, arm rings of weighty gold to display their wealth. Sword-bearers guarded their backs, and priests warned them of portents. They brought unlooked-for tidings to Hannibal.

In their ancestral fields, said the Boii and Insubres, they had taken weapons in hand to drive out the intruders, servants of the strange War-god. Grieving for their city of Milan, the Celtish people had attacked the Roman fort towns; they had made captives of praetors; they had driven out the colonists; their horses drank again from the clear waters of the Po. They would not sheathe their swords until they had taken back the last of their fields.

Hannibal had to weigh the boasting of the Italian Celts against the eyewitness accounts of his agents. These told him that Roman legions destined for Spain had been called back to meet the insurrection in the north. The insurrection might not last long.

At some moment during his long sittings with the oracular Celts the son of Hamilcar made his decision. He accepted their gifts and offered his own, in friendship. He pledged them aid in the name of Carthage, and this aid he would give them himself in Italy.

That decision to lead his army to Italy must have been wrung from days of mental agony. With the certainty of hardships and danger, it offered only one possibility of success. By reaching the Po in time he could gain allies, who would furnish supplies. By so doing he could hold the Roman armies of invasion within Italy itself, and keep the war at a distance from Carthage. For the first time the cost and the pain of it would fall upon the Romans and their lands. Beyond that, nothing was clear except the need of haste.

The anxious Boii and Insubres were well satisfied.

Whatever had been discussed beforehand with Hasdrubal and the far-off Council, Hannibal acted alone on his decision at the shore beyond the Ebro. When he rode north into the pines of the foothills he turned his back on twenty years of life, on New Carthage and the people who had come to be his own. To remain in Spain offered the ease of wealth and delight in personal matters, the horses of his stable, the books he relished. He had no joy in warfare, and if he went on he must sustain, alone, the thousands of his followers by warfare. He could expect no easy peace from the Romans. He remembered too well the warning of Regulus the Consul: conquer or accept the fate of the conquered.

It was a silly alternative.

One night in the foothills 3,000 Carpetanians deserted the camp.

Instead of sending other Spanish troops to compel the return of the Carpetanian regiments, Hannibal called their officers to talk with him. Knowing their temperament, he explained that the war now beginning would reach them wherever they were. The Romans had demanded the surrender of Hannibal and his brothers, and they did not intend to surrender (an echo of the Barca oath).

The Spanish chieftains retorted that they were not afraid. They did not wish to enter unknown mountains, in the power of strange gods. They had a longing to behold their plains again, not to go farther on a journey.

Hannibal understood them; he was dealing with their *altivez;* no order could compel them to go where they did not want to go.

"To those of you who wish to turn back," he said at length, "I give my permission to go. To those of you who will accompany me I give my welcome. I will share the rewards with them."

Seven thousand more of the Celtiberians elected to go home. Hannibal sent them to Hasdrubal. In the granite ravine of the Pyrenees he left an officer with sufficient force to hold the pass and keep open the route to Spain. Beyond the mountains he called the heads of the tribes to meet him. (Carthaginian agents had passed among them with gifts.) With them he arranged a sworn truce swiftly: no Carthaginian weapons would harm these Basque people if they did no harm to the army.

It was mid-August then, with little time remaining before the autumn snow would close the passes of the Alps. In four days the army reached the bank of the wide Rhone.

Once Hannibal had made his decision to march on Rome he wasted not an hour.

"These Mountains Do Not Touch the Sky."

The far bank of the river was covered with hostile tribesmen, hurrying to resist any attempt to cross it.

The army felt a new uneasiness. Rain fell from a gray sky; the gloom of the dense forest oppressed the Africans and Iberians, accustomed to arid earth and a remote clear canopy of the sky. When these men of the southlands kindled fires of damp wood, they scattered ashes far around them, to hold off the evil spirits of the dark sky that pressed down, incredibly, into the treetops.

Hannibal, studying the river and its noisy defenders on the other bank, sensed the melancholy of the men and drove them to work. The encampment became a focus of preparations to cross the river. Boats of every sort were brought in from the villages of the near bank. When the families of these villages found themselves paid with silver for the boats, they set to work eagerly to rig coracles and put together rafts, to get more silver from the foreign soldiers (and to hasten their departure). Hannibal's men took to their forest axes, to add dead trees to the floats. They searched for goatskins in which to stow their equipment when they swam the current. They had made their way over many such rivers.

Hannibal quietly detached Hanno son of Bomilcar with

a column of Iberian horse, to ascend the Rhone to a ford at an island.

By noon of the second day enough had been done to rush the river. Black smoke rising in the north showed that Hanno had crossed, unseen by the war bands of Gauls waiting expectantly on the bank. Hannibal set horns blowing through the encampment; flutes shrilled as the regiments raced down to the bank with piercing war cries. Thus challenged, the Gauls chanted their bravery in response, clashing spears against their long wooden shields, tearing off their body garments to strip for an affray that would be memorable in their traditions.

Nothing of the kind, however, befell the Gauls. When the uproar was mightiest, and the Carthaginian throngs entered the water, swimming the horses over, protected by missile throwers in the larger skiffs, Hanno's armored horsemen appeared in the forest behind the tribesmen (who had been roused to do battle by agents from Marseille). Valiantly the Gauls faced about, only to be driven from the bank by the rush of armed men from the boats. Disheartened, the Gaul warriors fled where the way was open, downstream. The Carthaginians ceased their play acting and proceeded to ferry over the bulk of the army and its supplies. The temperamental elephants were brought over by another artifice. Their drivers led females down to a massive raft covered with earth. Some male beasts followed, and the great raft was pushed out into the current, while other beasts swam or waded after it.

Except for one prized elephant, the herd was made up of African animals, no more than nine feet in height, and more agile than the eleven-foot Indian species. These elephants were accustomed to work in water, but disliked the chill of the glacier-fed Rhone.

This successful crossing, almost without loss of life, did not end the uneasiness of the men. Those who had climbed the taller trees reported that far ahead in the east the hills rose to dark summits hidden in the gray veil of the sky. Surely it seemed that the road ahead was barred by mountains that entered the sky itself! Besides, the men could neither dry nor warm themselves in the dank forest. What actually frightened them was the distance they had traveled from their familiar shore, and the strange aspect of this northern land that seemed to ascend to the realm of unknown gods.

Then Numidians rode in, nursing their wounds. These were the survivors of the patrol that had clashed with the well-armed Roman horse from the mouth of the Rhone.

Hannibal lost no time in calling the officers of all the national units together, to meet their growing malaise with his anger.

First he presented to them Magal, the eldest chieftain of the Boii, who had shared the quarters of the Carthaginian commanders. Magal stood before the others armed. He said that he and his companions had come by way of the Snow Mountains in the east: that Celtic tribes often made the journey over the heights, and while it was not an easy road, it was practical for men and beasts of burden. Then Hannibal faced his followers, to compel them to think of realities instead of fears. He tongue-lashed them in anger, because he knew the nature of the ordeal that awaited them.

"What *are* these Alps—except rather high mountains? These mountains do not touch the sky; you will pass over them beneath the sky. Families of Celts live upon them, and cultivate the fields."

He reminded them of the length of road they had traveled. "From New Carthage to this river you have marched sixty-four hundred stadia. Go on for twenty-six hundred stadia more and you will come to the valley of the first Italian river."

He bade them think about the Romans.

"You say a Roman army has appeared here, arriving from the sea. It is true. Go back to the Betis valley, or seek shelter with the Iberians in New Carthage. You will still see Roman armies approaching from the sea. Go to Gades. They will follow. Will you sit down in huts to cook food and wait for the coming of the legions that will conquer you? Your wives and sons are waiting for your return. How will you return? As fugitives from an enemy you have not seen?"

Hannibal put into hard words what was in his mind: that if they could overcome these armies at Rome itself, they would destroy the Roman power to make war. After that they would be free to live where they willed and as they wished.

He no longer asked if any of them elected to turn back. Instead, he dismissed them to prepare for a long march. Instead of keeping on toward the rising sun as they expected, he led them north along the left bank of the Rhone, with guides from the villages. The first march was, as he had predicted, a long one with few halts. (And Publius Cornelius Scipio with the Spanish expeditionary army found the encampment deserted near the site of Aigues-Mortes today.)

Hannibal did not attempt to follow the coast route where the highlands came down to the edge of the sea; that route led by hostile Marseille to the coast of the Ligurians, beyond which waited the garrisons of the Roman frontier. A northern route through the higher Alps would bring the Carthaginians out on the headwaters of the Po, among their new allies the Boii and Insubres. So much Magal and his fellows had made clear. (In their eagerness, these chieftains of the Gauls had promised greater aid than they could actually offer.)

A third route led direct by sea to the Italian coast. Hannibal, obviously, had not considered that. Upon the Spanish coast the Carthaginians had 32 galleys in service, against the 200 reported outfitting on the Italian coasts. If the transport vessels for such an army with its animals, supplies, and vehicles had been available, a voyage to the east would have taken the Carthaginian convoy past the enemy posts on the islands of Corsica and Sardinia and run the almost certain risk of meeting a Roman battle fleet that could destroy the entire convoy.

Yet Hannibal had not put the sea routes out of his mind. Time could bring a change in the situation; in time the inner harbor of Carthage might launch a greater strength of ships. If the great city could turn its resources into armament without molestation by the Romans . . .

Early in September Hannibal's host showed its heels to the first Roman expedition, and vanished up the Rhone.

At the same time an order from Rome put a stop to the embarkation of the second expeditionary force in the southern Sicilian ports. The legions destined for Africa were ferried back to Italy. Under the second Consul, Tiberius Sempronius Longus, they began the long march north to the river Po, where Hannibal was now expected to appear.

The Way to the Ascent

The Alps do not rise into a single great barrier. Many ranges intertwine, often descending to lakes and sometimes rising to the great heights of everlasting snow. Wherever you approach them, however, there is a certain similarity. First an outer ridge must be ascended to a higher valley. Since water always takes the easiest way down, the rivers mark the most practical way through. You follow such a river past the settlements in the higher valleys, and you keep to its bank after it becomes a gray rushing torrent fed by melting snow and glaciers above it as well as rain. Now ahead of you rises the inner fortress of the Alps, the higher snow-crowned ranges. And there your river fails to be a guide because it bifurcates into streams and waterfalls dropping from the crests and hidden, besides, within dense forest growth.

At this point a guide must lead you up to the notch in the skyline that offers a "pass" through—or you will blunder into blind ravines, or come out on the edge of an unsuspected precipice. The human settlements lie behind you, and the cold at night, except in mid-summer, becomes dangerous. In autumn, however, there is still pasturage for animals on the late-growing grass beneath the snow line. Above the timber line and the last moss and heather, rise the boulder screes and granite walls of the summit pass. Snow slopes close in on you, and a storm may end all visibility in cloud and lashing hail. A climber must carry his own food over the high pass, and cross as quickly as possible to the corresponding slopes and the headwaters of the river route down the far side.

Before Hannibal's coming, tribal peoples had migrated through the Alps, and the Celts along the Rhone must have been familiar with the nearer passes. But no army of foreigners of record had made such a crossing. The Carthaginian army numbered some 30,000 on foot and 8,000 on horseback; it was supplied by a wagon and pack animal train that had to be brought through; it was accompanied by about 37 elephants that needed to be coaxed over unfamiliar ground—and the Alps were quite unfamiliar to captive elephants.

The approach march and the ultimate descent offered no great problems to this particular army, accustomed to the barren heights of Spain. But success at the critical summit pass depended on two things: guides to point out the right track, and a rush to get the animals across, for two or three days, to grazing on the lower levels beyond.

In addition to this Hannibal needed to keep open the route behind him from the Pyrenees to the Italian rivers; if he failed to do so, his army would be cut off from its base in Spain.

Which route did the hard-pressed Carthaginians take?

The riddle of Hannibal's way through the Alps has intrigued scholars and geographers for the centuries after his day until now. It is still not definitely solved. Immense pains have been taken to narrow it down to a very few possibilities. The Great Saint Bernard Pass could not have been mastered in the time of the Carthaginians' march through; nor, for the same reason, the Little Saint Bernard. Then, too, the Latin writers of that early day— Polybius, the Greek, retraced Hannibal's route sixty years after him—seem to believe that he crossed more to the south and nearer the coast; that is, between Mount Genèvre and the sea. For instance, Strabo describes his way as "the pass to the Taurini," and he certainly came out among the Taurini on the headwaters of the Po (near modern Turin). The closest river-to-river connection to the Taurini would be south of Mount Genèvre. But which river did he follow up, to meet with the Po on the far side?

The riddle of where he went, however, is fairly dwarfed by the puzzle of *how* he got the army over. There exists clearer evidence as to how that was done.

For four days the Carthaginians pushed north along the left bank of the Rhone, leaving the Roman scouts far behind. Their march began in a mood of apprehension that was not helped by heavy rains. They came then to a fork where another smaller river flowed in from the Alps— from the right hand of the Carthaginians. In this fork of the rivers lay a fertile plain bestudded with Celtic villages—the Island, as the soldiers named it—and just then crowded with tribesmen who had gathered to dispute or fight out (the two things were much the same to the Celts) a question of rule. Hannibal seems to have lost no time at the Island in making two arrangements: acting as arbiter of the dispute, he settled it by naming the Carthaginians overlords of the Island territory, and getting from the inhabitants a stock of woolen overgarments with leg wrappings and hide shoes. These provided winter garments for his own men in their passage of the mountains. He took guides as well as supplies, and probably repaid the natives with the assurance that his army would leave their territory at once. By so doing he kept his return route open as far as the Island.

Then he did something puzzling to the inquisitive scholars of future days. "Now in seeking the Alps he did not make his way straight in to the right, but turned to the left." The explanation may be quite simple: that he did not follow up the right fork coming from the mountains but went up the left, which was still the main stream of the Rhone. In other words he by-passed the first river entry to the mountains to go to one farther on. That seems to have been the Drôme. As the valley narrowed, the trace of a roadway vanished, and the Carthaginians were forced to ford the river in spate. They hauled the wagon train up the boulder-paved gorge. Chilled by the unnatural cold of the heights, they sighted the crest of the ridge guarded by granite pinnacles. And these bastions of stone were thronged with shaggy, unkempt men, weapons in hand.

These mountain Celts evidently had no knowledge of the Carthaginian army, other than that it bore within it the wealth of civilization, horses and goods and silver-inlaid arms. Hannibal and his officers surveyed the scene above them and halted the army. The last thing they wished was to assault strange barbarians on the mountain ridge. Accordingly they sent up spokesmen from the escort of tribal Islanders, with some veteran Carthaginian officers to observe the situation above them. The parley was held under truce.

The Celt-Carthaginian envoys returned to report that the defenders of the mountain were Allobroges, given to looting and hardy in combat. Their chief market town lay in the valley beyond. On his part Hannibal ascertained that the Allobroges took to arms during daylight and were accustomed to retire to their hovels at night.

Time pressed, because the constant rain might turn into snow that would bury the trail. The stormy season was at hand. That night Hannibal ordered the fires to be kept up in the camp regardless of the shortage of wood. Apart from the fires, he assembled a column of Celtiberian heavily armed foot. Leading them up the side of the gorge, he brought them into the vantage points on the crest deserted by the Allobroges during the darkness. It was done at a cost of many injuries and deaths by falls. Then by the signal of a waving torch he set the army below in motion toward the crest. But the wagons made slow progress in the dark, and by dawn the supply train and horsemen were still threading through the pass. The descent on the far side narrowed to a track along a sheer slope.

Before sunrise the Allobrogian warriors appeared, climbing toward their posts. Finding these occupied by Carthaginians, while the supply train wound down the descent, the mountaineers had a moment of stupefaction. Then they rushed down to the track, swarming against the carts that carried rich spoil. The pack animals surged in panic, and wounded horses bolted along the trail, sending men and beasts over the precipice.

Hannibal held back his guardian force on the height until he could make certain what was happening in the mist-veiled tumult below. Then he led his light-armed Spaniards to clear the tribesmen from the slope. Once attacked, the mountaineers fled like goats to the valley below.

There the Carthaginian horsemen were able to act. The angered riders cleared the hamlets of the hill pastures and swept into the palisaded town on the valley floor. The inhabitants had deserted it, leaving behind stores of corn and herds of slaughter animals sufficient to feed the army for three days.

Hannibal brought the precious supply train down to make camp in the town. But he no longer had guides. The delegation of Boii and Insubre chieftains had gone ahead to prepare for his arrival on the Po. In the town the escort from the Island turned back, explaining that they knew no landmarks beyond this point, while the Carthaginian army needed only to keep on toward the sunrise (that is, southeast). Hannibal began to have a new understanding both of the imagination and unreliability of these European Celts.

It was not possible to halt in the midway valley, nor would he turn back. The next day the army was in motion across the level basin, watchful of the bleak uplands where thatch huts clung to ledges and men in animal pelts showed themselves furtively. On the third day a band of elders appeared up the trail, waving branches in token of amity, and offering cattle and guides to aid the apparition of an army on its way. The Carthaginians accepted all this with reservations. Their new guides brought them, on the second day, to the bank of a small river, foaming down through its bed of boulders, overhung by narrowing walls of granite cliffs. Here the amicable elders disappeared, and rocks crashed down on the trail, while bands of mountaineers struck like wolves at the guarded wagons. For a time Hannibal with the rear guard of infantry was cut off from the supply train. He managed to put an end to the wild assault by climbing the rock wall of the gorge and clearing it of the marauders. On this table top he waited to protect the last climbers with the disorganized pack animals, and for another reason.

From this height the Carthaginians could survey the citadel of the Alps. Ahead of them the inner heights rose in gray rock surfaces to snow summits, blinding white in sunlight, hidden by driving cloud in a storm. With each dimming out of the sun the cold increased. Where lay the pass through the summits?

Perhaps by leaving the river's channel and keeping to the south of east as the Islanders had advised, the Carthaginians might have found a way through on the lowest level. If so they would have escaped the snow. They decided to keep to the gorge of the roaring river, and so they began the last ascent toward the north of east.

"These Are the Walls of Rome."

Because they knew nothing of the way ahead, they never gave a clear account of it. They remembered unusual incidents and the exhaustion that increased as they climbed. Hannibal had the elephants put at the head of his cortege, perhaps to frighten away the mountaineers who had never seen such beasts, perhaps because the instinct of the great animals might keep them all to the easiest going. In any case the elephants had to be coaxed to climb, and human enemies soon disappeared because their habitations had been left behind. So had the tree growth and the last of the grass. One daybreak the astrologer sighted the Pleiades setting in the sky (which meant that the day was late in October).

The Carthaginians were forced to cross the cascading water from bank to bank, and to manhandle the carts after them. The chill of the icy water did not leave them. And after a while wind drove swirling cloud upon them and snow drifted into their faces. The small river vanished into separate streams descending in falls out of obscurity. To keep the elephants going their attendants wrapped them in woolen tent cloths. There was no more wood for fires.

On the ninth day, by their count, after leaving the ridge of the Allobroges, they found themselves walking through snow on level ground where the wind struck them from all sides. When the cloud cleared they looked down into the sky. They had reached the summit of the pass.

Here Hannibal ordered a halt for two days. It was necessary. All that time, units that had lost their way rejoined the camp. Injured men hobbled up, and horses that had slipped their packs came up to the army herds. Many of the sick died here in the snow.

On the third morning the sky cleared. The white bastions of the Alps stood on either side. The survivors got into motion again reluctantly when officers called them to the unit standard poles. Their stiffened bodies ached with hunger. Hannibal, who had ridden ahead with the scouts, turned back to summon the leaders of the different peoples to him. He had mastered the speech of the Balerians as well as the Celtiberians. As soon as they joined him, he took the leaders on to a rise of rock.

From this rise they could see far to the east beneath the sunrise. There below them lay dark forest growth and the green of cultivated fields gleaming like jewels in the distance—the fields of Italy.

Hannibal gave them a moment to realize what this meant. The black storm on the summit had held for him the ill omen of the cloud rack over Eryx in his childhood. He had hoped to keep the route to Spain open behind him. Now he could be certain that the way was closed between the ridge of the Allobroges and the summit pass. After another storm, the army itself would be cut off from Spain.

Aware of this, he threw back his black mantle to display the jewels in his sword, and pointed around him, smiling. *These,* he told the leaders, *are the walls not only of Italy but of Rome. You have surmounted them. There,* he pointed down, *are the cities of wealth with many women. You have only to ride down to reach them.*

The leaders carried his message back to their exhausted men, and quickly it grew in the telling until the guards of the rear heard: *The worst is over . . . we're heading down now, to the cities below, for meat and wine and fires, and spoil of gold . . . and—only think—women to pour out the wine.*

The army stirred itself, to follow a new hope.

The way down was steeper than the ascent; the track was often lost beneath the snow. The new snowfall covered a hard crust of old snow. For three days the animals had gone without grazing, and in their weakness they slipped and fell, or struggled helplessly when they broke through the hard undercrust. Afterward the men of the army remembered only certain obstacles. Once a landslip sheathed in snow blocked the trail on a steep slope where a new track could not be made around it. The long line of marchers scraped away the snow where they stood to wait out a night while a timber walk was built across the slide.

And when they had left the snow slopes behind, the way to the forest below was blocked by an immense fallen rock. Engineers set to work to remove this by burning brush and trees upon it, and then pouring a vat of vinegar on the calcined stone. After that men with heavy picks could crumble the stone away, and men and beasts could run down into the shelter of the tree growth. They came to flowing water and brush that offered feed to the starved horses, and that night they lighted fires in the forest.

Hannibal's army had crossed the Alps from the first crest in 15 days. The greater part of it was still alive—12,000 Africans on foot, with 8,000 Spaniards, and 6,000 horsemen. So 26,000 in all followed Hannibal down a stream that ran into the headwaters of the Po. Perhaps 12,000 had strayed or been lost on the way from the Pyrenees.

When they reached the first hill settlement of the Gauls they did not find it to be what they had expected.

Skirmish at the Headwaters

The Gauls of Italy within the Alps—as the Romans named these Celts—were a long-bodied race, proud in spirit and exceedingly uncertain in mind. Diodorus of Sicily, who lived in the time of Julius Caesar, says they wore neck chains of pure gold to mark their dignity, and they combed their long hair back like a horse's mane and let their mustaches grow to strain the soup they drank. They gave the choicest meat and wine to the guests of their halls. "And it is their custom even during a meal to begin to argue over some trivial thing, and then to challenge one another to single combat without any regard for their lives."

That heedlessness of life came not only from the Gauls' physical hardihood but from the teaching of their druids that their life spirit would not die but would change to another body, which might be an animal's. These warriors were also fond of relating all their own notable deeds. "They break out into a song of the valiant deeds of their ancestors as well," Diodorus observes. "They enlarge the bronze helmets they wear with horns, to give an appearance of great size. They carry shields as long as their bodies, embossed with the bronze head of some beast. They speak in riddles, hinting darkly at their meaning, while always extolling themselves. Terrible in aspect, they appear threatening; yet they have sharp wits and are often clever in learning."

Diodorus sees in them a resemblance to their distant kinsmen the "Britains of Iris" that is, to the Irish. Cunning, and highly emotional, the Gauls left learning to their druids, who read omens, gave out amulets, and prophesied events to come. They were egged on besides by their strapping, lustful women who craved the fine woven cloths and superior hearth implements of the Etruscan dwellings in the south. The women watched the yield of the farmed fields jealously, while their men, now settled in tribal life in the towns, remembered vaguely the greater glory of their warrior ancestors who stormed across Europe sword in hand. The Gauls in fact still carried long swords of an ancient type, clumsy except in hewing at an enemy's body. These were chained to their belts, which were ornamented with silver plates and blue Etruscan enamel.

These Gauls, then, were still primitive, clinging to the farm lands of the fertile Po (Padus) Valley, while covetous of the better living of the upstart Latins of the Tiber from whom they had learned nothing. "Even Hannibal," envoys from Marseille had predicted to the Romans, "will not find it easy to hold in check the fierce spirit of the Gauls."

When Hannibal entered Cisalpine Gaul in November of 218 he must have been appalled by what he found awaiting him. There was no sign of his sworn allies, the Boii or Insubres. The nearest tribes were preparing to winter in their towns, there to debate their feuds with others. No two seemed to be joined in any resistance to the Roman occupation. On the other hand the Roman forces, without any idea of hibernating, were strengthening their new garrison posts along the great river below. In Hannibal's path the Taurini Gauls flocked together with weapons to survey without favor the strange army of Carthaginians debouching from the heights. Certainly that army, wrapped in the dark mantles of the Rhone Celts, riding sodden horses, escorting a herd of swaddled elephants, did not appear as imposing as the spokesmen of the Boii had pictured it. Moreover, since the Taurini were at feud with the Boii that year, the Carthaginians were technically foemen, to be treated as such.

The Carthaginians reacted sharply to this hostility. They swept into the chief town of the Taurini (at modern Turin?) and drove the occupants out. Here for a little space Hannibal gave his men rest to overhaul their equipment and restore the vitality of their cherished horses. The elephants, however, did not recuperate in the winter cold of the north that would soon kill them off.

Very quickly Hannibal led his army west across the headwaters toward Milan and the towns of the Boii and Insubres. The Carthaginians marched through chilling rains, feeling their way over a strange land, trusting in no more guides. When they neared the Ticino (Ticinus) River they discovered that a Roman army was coming up its bank toward them.

Publius Cornelius Scipio had lost no time in meeting Hannibal again. The patrician Consul (after leaving his expedition at the Rhone) had landed at Pisa and made his way north to pick up the legions on march to put an end to the sedition of the Gauls.

Probably neither Publius nor the citizenry of Rome expected that the young Carthaginian would manage to bring his army over the Alps at that season. Still, it was the Consul's responsibility to bar the way if he did so. So Publius hastened toward the passes, only to learn that Hannibal was already on the open plain of the Po. Surprised, he turned north along the Ticino where it flows into the great Po. It was common sense to bring his trained legions at once to grips with this elusive enemy. Hannibal could not very well escape him this time.

The spirit of the Consul's command was good. The younger levies knew nothing of the conflict with Carthage in their fathers' time. Some older veterans of the *triarii* (the third and last rank of the legions) recalled that "the Punics" had yielded up Sardinia and Corsica for a bought peace. They said and believed that "the Punics" had no heart for a proper, stand-to battle. The centurions (company commanders) added that this particular host of Hannibal had lost a meeting engagement to the Consul's *equites* somewhere on the Rhone, and then had fled away.

Publius felt his way north cautiously, entrenching the nightly camp with more than usual care. When he called his tribunes and officers together for a last conference, he said something rather odd. "Do not think that this enemy commander showed boldness in crossing the pass of the Alps. He did that unwillingly, being fearful of not doing it. And it lost him a great part of his command. The survivors are still suffering from cold and lack of food; their horses are in worse shape. It is the good fortune of the Roman People that you have that advantage over them."

Now in saying that, Publius came close to the truth. He must have been well informed, because he did not tamper with words to his troops.

The weight of anxiety lay on Hannibal, who had not faced legions before. Behind Scipio lay the reserve manpower of the Roman Republic, 770,000 at the last census of men able to bear arms. Behind the son of Hamilcar in Italy there was nothing. Snow had closed his road over the Alps. And a Roman army had cut his route at the Pyrenees. At either side the sea barred the way, and the sea was open to the movements of his enemies. By the same token intelligence of outer events came to them from all the coasts, while it no longer reached him. In Spain he had been in touch with the sea routes and in communication with Carthage by courier, if not by messenger pigeon. Visibility here had narrowed to his immediate surroundings. Probably that was his greatest anxiety.

In the valley of the Po the Carthaginians found themselves in a situation still obscure, where their hoped-for allies, the Gauls, had failed to join them. Many Gauls, they began to suspect, served in the Roman ranks for pay. "One thing is certain," Hannibal told the elder commanders, Hert and Maharbal and the son of Bomilcar, who gave him advice so eagerly. "We can't go back."

Instead of speaking to the army as a whole, he staged a pantomime for it. When the detachments were assembled on the slopes of a hollow, he had a band of captives led out into the center space. These were Gauls of the mountains, chained and filthy with dirt and weak from hunger. Before them officers threw down two sets of costly arms, with shields and panoply beloved by the Celts. An offer was made to the prisoners in Hannibal's name. Any two who volunteered would be given the arms. They would then fight together, the survivor to carry away his weapons to freedom.

All the captives volunteered for the trial, and two of them were led out loosed from chains. The intently watching Carthaginians noticed how the two stood with pride when they were full-armed. They felt the eyes of a multitude on them, and they fought savagely until one sank down to die. Even so in death the warrior made a finer showing than the chained slaves.

The watching thousands understood the pantomime. They also had the choice of carrying off the spoil of victory, or of dying.

That evening officers of the peoples went among the campfires repeating a message from Hannibal: *From this day all nations in the army will have the same privileges as Carthaginians. All slaves who accompany their masters here will have freedom and the price of it will be paid by Hannibal to their masters.*

This action leveled the ranks within the army. It also gave the underprivileged a reward in hand. It stirred expectancy of more to follow. And very soon it did: *Hannibal pledges his word that all who desire to return home may go back after victory is gained in Italy.*

On a morning when mist hung over the banks of the Ticino the armies came into sight of each other. The disciplined Roman forces moved forward automatically, the legions ranged out for combat, horsemen screening the flanks. They moved toward the indistinct mass of Carthaginians but they did not go far.

Celtiberian and Berber horsemen appeared at the far sides, swift masses moving upon the mounted Romans. And that was all.

Outnumbered, the detachments of Roman horse broke

apart under the charge of the Africans. They were soldiers mounted on horses while the Spaniards and Africans were experienced riders. Then, too, the Consul fell wounded among the horsemen. It is said that his young son and a Ligurian slave saved the Consul's life, but in any case he was severely hurt.

Then the Numidians appeared at pace, circling wide to the rear of the halted legions. The *triarii* of the last rank faced about, bringing down their long spears. The Numidians merely flashed by them with a discharge of javelins into them. Then either Publius or his legate (adjutant) gave a sensible order. Since they were deprived of the cavalry wings, the legions withdrew to the entrenched camp of the previous night. They retreated in tight formation, carrying along the wounded. The Africans merely followed at a distance as if watching a novel spectacle, nor did they attempt to attack the palisaded camp of the Romans.

It was an odd affair, this skirmish at the Ticino. Clearly, Hannibal had held his forces back from battle.

In doing so he had gained his first opportunity to study the characteristics of the Roman legion in action. Probably while he watched, Carthalo, his intelligence chief, and some of the experienced Gauls explained details and interpreted the commands given by trumpet and horn.

The Gauls said the legion was the gift of the War-god to the tribes of the Tiber. Into it at one time or another went all youths who were citizens, hardened by intense training and drilled until they reacted mechanically to orders. Each legion had its Eagle of silver or gold, carried by the favored Thousand Cohort, always to be found at the right of the front, and always watched by the men of the other cohorts, who carried standards of their own. During his years of service the recruit went from the last cohort to the chosen Thousand, and perhaps from a leader of ten to become the envied Centurion of the Thousand. Even within the cohorts—of 550 fighters— men moved, like marionettes, in fixed positions. Those of the *principes* or front line, were the ablest; the weaker held the second line of the *hastati* or spearmen; the elder veterans kept the line of the *triarii*, or rear rank. They moved in to the support of the others at need. The legion itself had a reserve of chosen *triarii* as a support.

Although the legion numbered only some 6,500 fighters on foot, it also had a force of about 400 horsemen, and more light troops to harry the enemy and pursue. On its wings it had more than these numbers of allied forces of Italians who might be stronger physically but lacked the iron discipline of the Roman legionaries.

In that discipline, Hannibal knew, lay the strength of the Roman machine of war. The legionaries had been trained never to break formation to flee or to pursue— whatever the light troops or auxiliaries might do. The legionaries, moreover, were all armed in a pattern; they carried their entrenching tools and food and camp coverings on their backs. They made camp in readiness for battle and they marched in the same way. The baggage train carried the mechanical aids of dismounted boat bridges, of catapults to project stone missiles or spears, of the dangerous scorpions, with mantlets and beams to construct wooden towers. So that a Roman encampment was always prepared to give or to stand a siege.

Apparently the Romans had developed a mechanism for battle that had no weakness. Yet Hannibal understood at once that the legionaries could hardly do anything they had not been trained to do. They depended on the orders given them—and that meant on the minds of their commanders. What would those same commanders manage to accomplish if they were faced by a situation entirely strange to them? And how would they behave if they were deceived into making a mistake?

The Ambition of Tiberius Sempronius

Hannibal managed to accomplish several things at the Ticino. His volatile Numidians had recovered confidence in meeting Romans, after the beating some of them had taken at the Rhone. Hannibal himself had studied the disciplined legions in action for three days. And, most im-

74

portant of all, the Carthaginians had gained prestige in the eyes of the Gauls. Delegations of these inhabitants of the Po had been interested observers of the retreat of the Roman standards before the Carthaginians.

That night 2,000 Gallic warriors serving in the Roman ranks broke out of the encampment after killing some of their officers and stealing useful horses. They sought Hannibal, to offer him their swords. He gave the deserters meat and wine with gifts of silver and suggested that they return to their villages, there to explain that spoil and honor could be gained by others who wished to drive the Romans from their lands. Some of the wittier Gauls he kept by him to slip back to their comrades still camped with the Eagles and inform him—and them—of whatever happened. This gave him the nucleus of a spy service.

Soon after the Ticino affair spokesmen arrived from the Boii, to welcome Hannibal in long speeches and offer him three captive Romans of praetorian (area commander) rank. Courteously Hannibal returned the greeting and suggested that the Boii keep the hostages to exchange against Gauls who were captives of the enemy. The prisoners taken by the Numidians proved to be mostly allied skirmishers—light-armed men of people subjected by the Romans. These Hannibal released without payment to return to their various homes and relate what they had seen. (They were the first of a multitude set free by the unexpected mercy of the Carthaginians to carry propaganda back into Italy.)

Among themselves the Gallic chieftains debated this unwonted manner of making war and wondered what it might achieve—if anything—against the dreaded legions. Readily enough they brought Hannibal tidings of the approach of the other Roman army from the south. The Carthaginians showed no sign of alarm at this; they continued to forage through the fields newly cultivated by colonists, and to seize the military depots of grain—sometimes bribing the keepers of the depots to give up the grain instead of dying in its defense.

The second Consul, Tiberius Sempronius Longus, had been elected by the popular assemblies and he was ambitious. Perhaps he felt himself inferior to the patrician Publius Cornelius, whose family had been awarded age-old honors including at least one triumph. Down in Sicily Sempronius had scored certain successes, in taking the island of Malta (Melita) and raiding the African coast. Success had given him confidence. He brought in his large command by forced marches on the Rimini road, eager to go into action against the far-wandering army of Carthaginians. He found his fellow Consul wounded and sheltered within the lines of Placentia (Piacenza), the outermost of the new garrison posts on the Po. It was a strong place, although at the moment belying its name of "The Pleasant," being crowded with refugees and the moody legions of the other army, which had come back from the Ticino camp. Moreover Publius Cornelius, wounded and confined to his cot, was not willing to take the field again.

In fact, as he rubbed his bald forehead uneasily, Publius looked like a sick man. He kept saying that most of their levies were not battle-tried. They could hold the fortified points from Placentia to Cremona safely through the winter, until reinforcements arrived with the spring levies. He did not relish the behavior of the Gauls.

Publius did not explain, because it would not be fitting, what troubled him instinctively. In the moment at the Ticino before he was knocked bodily from the back of his horse, he had seen the strange riders closing in around him. He had never seen horsemen like those before.

The plebeian Sempronius found the arguments of the sick man exasperating. Here, he complained, two Consuls of the Roman *Respublica* sat behind walls, with a strength in legions of 14,000, and 22,000 armed levies of the Latin name, and all the garrisons of the northern frontier, while African riders foraged the fields around them. In Italy itself! Such conduct, argued Sempronius, was against all Roman tradition.

He did not say that it was then the winter solstice (December) and the eve of a new election, when other consuls would be chosen to replace them. Unless—so Sempronius reasoned silently—one of them earned a full-blooded victory over the Punic invader. By degrees his reasoning arrived at a further conviction. Since the stub-

76

born patrician was still confined to his cot, Sempronius alone might command the army in its victory. If he could take the field before Publius recuperated, and before the elections were held in Rome! He visualized himself arriving alone at the Collina Gate, in duty bound to conduct the election, but with word of his triumph over the Carthaginian Hannibal going before him and the popular assemblies uniting to demand his re-election. That could not possibly happen if Sempronius waited out the winter ignominiously behind fortification.

So it befell that the combined armies did take the field inasmuch as they moved out of overcrowded Placentia a short distance up the river Trebia (Trebbia), there to dig a comfortable-sized encampment. And there Sempronius, no able soldier, watched for a chance to take command while Publius, a soldier by instinct, fought against the weakness of his wound.

The chance to act came quickly enough. A mounted scouting force blundered into Numidians foraging the fields near by, and pursued the Numidians to the protection of heavier Carthaginian cavalry. Roman horse moved out to support the scouts, and Sempronius led two legions out of the camp gate. He offered battle, but the Carthaginians drifted away beyond the flooded reaches of the Trebia. This convinced Sempronius that the elusive Punics would not stand against his legions.

The winter solstice came with rain and icy cold. The camp streets turned to mud, while Sempronius fretted at the weather, which seemed to end any chance of action. Thus it happened that he was overjoyed to be awakened in the last hours of a night by his lieutenants with word that Numidians were raiding up to a gate of the camp. Roused abruptly from sleep, he did not pause to wonder why the Africans had appeared at that hour. Nor did he think of breakfast. He gave order for the cavalry wings to mount and sally out, and all legions to form under arms in the camp streets, while he went himself to see the lifting of the standards.

Outside his quarters a flurry of snow shone around the torches. It was bitter cold.

"He never felt he had done enough in preparing his men," the Latin writers said afterward of Hannibal.

And it is clear now that he had begun his preparations for that winter night on the Trebia quite a while before-hand. He had weighed the stories of the spies from the Roman camp across the river, and probably he had formed his own opinion of the ability of Sempronius. Then he had ridden over the flooded plain on the Car-thaginian side of the river—which Sempronius had never seen—and had dismounted to climb over a line of brush-grown hillocks far to one side. Within the hillocks lay a narrow gully of some size. On his ride of inspection he took a young officer, Mago by name. He called Mago into the gully. Mago, he said, would pick out ten men, from different units who could be relied on under the worst conditions. Then these ten would each pick out a hundred like themselves. The resourceful thousand would be placed under Mago's command, and their post would be this gully.

Mago agreed that the sunken way made a good hiding place.

Hannibal had a habit of jesting before an ordeal. "Yes it will, for one reason. Because nobody will be looking for you here." After that he gave the eager young officer some explicit instructions.

Half a mile from the gully toward the Carthaginian camp the muddy plain rose to a slight slope of hard earth. Here Hannibal superintended the digging of a shallow trench with a firm dirt parapet that would not be visible from any distance. From his childhood he had heard Hamilcar insist, "Make the ground fight for you." Pyyrhus the Epirote, the master of strategy, had said that in his day, but Hamilcar had made a fortress out of a mountain at Mount Eryx. Here there was nothing but a soggy plain beside the rain-swollen arms of a river. On the last evening Hannibal devoted himself to talking over all they might do with the leaders of his heterogeneous command. Never breaking the concentration of his own mind, he sat among them at such a time listening to their opinions, seizing on apt suggestions.

That night, after the five hundred Numidians had started toward the river and the Roman camp, and Mago had marched out his thousand chosen fighters toward the sunken way, Hannibal told his lieutenants, "After tomorrow the roads to the Latin cities will be open. Do you really think they hold such wealth in them? Or is that barbershop gossip?"

The older commanders said they knew it to be truth.

"Then tell your men."

They understood that, whatever Hannibal himself believed, he wanted the men in the ranks to be thinking of some reward from the battle.

That night, in the worst of weather, the son of Hamilcar had decided to give battle to the legions of the Wargod, to the disciplined ranks that moved like a machine at a command. He had done what he could to make the ground itself difficult for the legionaries and helpful to his followers.

Before the Carthaginians armed themselves by the warmth of built-up fires, they took oil from waiting jars to rub down their limbs as a protection against chill. It was still dark when they ate hungrily from bowls of stewed meat and barley gruel. At the first light the missile throwers moved out into the plain, the Iberian and Libyan heavily armed foot moved forward to the prepared trench. There they sheltered themselves under goat-hair cloaks. The elephants, with drivers and javelin casters astride their leather-draped backs, trundled out to the sides with the heavy cavalry. The Carthaginian horses, well accustomed to the smell of the great beasts, were not disturbed by them.

What followed is known as the battle of the Trebia; but it was actually decided by the preparations that were made, or not made in both encampments before the dawn of that day.

The Roman legions that followed the cavalry pursuing the elusive Numidian raiders had to make their way in the dark for several miles. The regiments had eaten nothing before the hurried march from the cold barrack huts; they wore only battle dress, and they forded the arms of the swollen river sometimes in water up to their armpits. They were chilled to the blood stream when the centurions halted them on the muddy bank to redress ranks. When they moved on after the retreating enemy skirmishers they found it hard to keep direction in the gray light, under the pelting of hail and snow flurries. They trudged on another mile, at last to find the African infantry waiting, sheltered by a parapet of earth. From behind the parapet hissed the stones from the slings of the Balearians.

What the advancing legions might have accomplished if left to themselves cannot be ascertained. Their defeat began elsewhere on the flanks, where some of the Roman horses bolted away from the oncoming elephants, and most of the horsemen scattered or were smashed back into the lines of infantry by the weight of the charges of the Spanish and African horse. The lines of the unbroken legions curved back like a bow that is bent by hands gripping each tip.

By midmorning hunger began to increase the weariness of the Roman swordsmen, straining for a footing in the mud. When the trumpet of the commander ceased to be heard sounding the orders, the legions faced enemies on three sides. Then Mago's thousand emerged from hiding to throw themselves against the rear of the legions.

By then the anxious legates and tribunes of the regiments began to call for formation of columns, to break out of the encirclement.

At this point all reports are silent. Apparently 10,000 Romans regained their encampment in formations. More than half the army of Sempronius the Consul was fugitive in the drifting snow, or captive, or dead. Of the captives, Hannibal sent the men of the allies back to their homes. The legionaries, which is to say the Roman citizens, were held by the Carthaginians for ransom.

Sempronius himself sent a very dubious report south to the Senate. Quite briefly it stated that his army had entered battle with the Carthaginians, but bad weather had prevented a victory. The survivors left the river Trebia to take shelter in the fortifications of Placentia, which were no longer overcrowded.

In January, the month sacred to the god Janus, who presided over the beginning of the year, Tiberius Sempronius rode south as duty prescribed, to conduct the new election. He was not re-elected. Ironically, the only honor derived from the battle on the Trebia went to his fellow Consul Publius Cornelius for advising so urgently against it. Moreover, being incapacitated, Publius had not been present at the stunning defeat.

(When his wound healed Publius asked permission to take command of his old army in Spain. Not that he wished to avoid a third meeting with the mad Carthaginian—as Hannibal was coming to be called. The commonplace Publius had a silent conviction that the conquest of Spain would decide matters for the Roman state. His fellow senators of the Cornelian *gens* agreed that it was common sense to look for victory in a land where Hannibal could not be present.)

A sense of foreboding lay over Rome as the new year was ushered in. The augurs—who had heard the full details of the retreat of the army into the security of Placentia—reported that omens clearly revealed the anger of the ancestral gods. Phantom ships had been seen crossing the sky; lightning had struck the temple of Hope; javelins in the temple of Mars had taken fire and the waters of Caere had run with blood. To purge the city, a gift of a gold thunderbolt weighing 50 pounds was made to Jupiter, and a banquet served to the images of lesser deities. When the ritual sacrifices had been completed, all citizens turned their attention to the north to discover what manner of man Hannibal might be, and what action he would take next.

Winter Quarters on the Po

For the two midwinter months the Carthaginians rested under roofs. It was the first break in their march since they had sighted the Pyrenees. They also divided up the spoil of weapons, money belts, and gear taken from the battlefield. The Latin historians said long afterward—it is so easy to be wise after the events—"Hannibal never felt he had done enough in giving his men definite rewards to fight for."

The word "definite" is significant. It suggests more than a pledge of reward. The army already felt itself to be enfranchised. It had gained privileges. A Libyan water carrier bred to hatred of his Carthaginian masters in Africa now had the status of a free man who need not bow his head at the approach of a Carthaginian wagon inspector. Actually the dark Libyan continued to carry water as before, but he felt different. A Celtiberian horseman who longed to set eyes on his Meseta again, had acreage in Italy pledged to his possession, or—if he refused it—the price of the new land paid into his hand in silver. Already the ragged Celtiberian felt himself to be a man of affairs, like a superior merchant. If the words *esprit de corps* had been invented then, this would be it. The intelligent Latins described it—afterward—"They were soldiers who had confidence in their general, who in turn relied on them."

Hannibal had not asked too much of them in the storm at the Trebia. After giving them all the advantage the ground offered, he had simply called on the infantry to hold a line in front of the battle line of the Roman legions. As for his horsemen, they made up a third of his army, while the Roman cavalry were no more than a tenth of the enemy array. Man to man his African and Spanish riders outmatched the Italian riders. Once these last were out of the way, the legions could not manage to keep their accustomed frontal line and fight off masses of horsemen at their sides. It was as simple as the equation that 1 equals one third of 3.

But the equation had not worked out quite as it should. The legions had a hard core in them; their men were not easily killed. The greater part had fought their way bearing all the Eagles back to the entrenchment that Hannibal was too wise to attack. "He never risked a battle," said the chroniclers, "unless there was a decisive advantage to be gained by it."

82

The advantage that Hannibal gained at the Trebia was the firm alliance with the Cisalpine Gauls.

They came in to him from all the lands of the Po as far as the marshes of the Veneti in the east. Chieftains of the savage Ligurians rode in from the western coast. While Hannibal feasted them in careful order of their rank and heroism record, and separated them according to their feuds, they extolled his victory in speeches for most of the two months. All of them took note of one of the fasces— the bronze-bound rods and ax, symbol of the authority of a consul—which Sempronius' bearers had dropped in his flight. The chieftains, gleaming in heavy gold, could not avoid noticing it because it lay on the lion skin that happened to be under Hannibal's leather-booted feet. The proud Insubres, allied to the Boii, renewed their oath of fealty to the Lord Hannibal and their pledge to send their swordsmen with him wherever he went.

Patiently Hannibal explained that their alliance was not with him but with the state of Carthage—although he bound himself to protect their lands. Neither he nor Carthage desired any territory from them. And he showed them a record stone carved in stiff Latin letters that some of the Gallic chieftains could piece out. The letters in the stone spelled out a law. The law stipulated that the Romans ruled the Gauls on the Po not as *foederatae et immunes* but by the *lex provinciae:* that meant the Gauls were not allies for mutual defense, but subjects under the law of a province, as in western Sicily or Sardinia or Corsica. In a province the Roman Republic held title to the land and held the inhabitants under the laws of war.

Hitherto, Hannibal told them, they had fought against the intrusion of the Latin tribes of the Tiber. Now they could end the invasion and do away with all laws of subjection. They could do that by helping him to destroy the Roman power to make war. Then the name of Rome would be no more than it had been three centuries before, when the Gallic people first came to the river Po.

Enthusiastically, the Gallic chieftains agreed. They were his sworn allies; they would march against Rome as their heroic ancestor Brennus had marched in the days of their greater glory. Bards of the Boii began to chant of Gallic victory-through-strength; young druids circled the hearth fires sounding their long horns with bronze boar heads. With difficulty Hannibal restrained them from burning alive some Roman prisoners as a sacrificial offering before setting out.

For the Gauls demanded that he set out at once. Their impatience drove them to seek victory on the Tiber as they had beheld the Carthaginians achieve it on the Trebia. Besides, the large Carthaginian army was eating up their lean stock of provisions at the winter's end. They begged Hannibal to take his army away to live off Roman fields.

All in all, the Gauls added from 9,000 to 14,000 men to Hannibal's command. Probably the number was actually less than 10,000. More important, he had a new base in the valley of the Po, with a new reserve of highly undisciplined manpower. It cut off the remainder of the Italian peninsula from the Alps and the continent beyond. The garrisons at Placentia and Cremona were left to their own devices, watched by some swift Numidian horsemen.

While Hannibal might have remained in security in Cisalpine Gaul, there were reasons why he could not do so. The northern winter had been hard on his men, accustomed to the milder climate of Africa and Iberia. Most of the elephants, too, had died in the cold. They say that one stricken beast had picked up a green bough in its trunk to wave it at passing Carthaginians—as it had seen human beings do in appealing for mercy.

There is also an odd story told about Hannibal himself at this time—that he kept by him several wigs of different colored hair, with garments of varied kinds to go with the wigs. By these he disguised his age and appearance, to go about unrecognized. This oddity the Roman annalists explain, as usual, in the way least creditable to the dreaded Carthaginian. They say he disguised himself because he feared assassination. That could be true; it had happened in Spain to the older Hasdrubal. But the probability is that Hannibal was merely playing his dual role. Fittingly robed, he appeared in public assembly as the commander in chief of Carthage; disguised, he carried out his tours of investigation. He made every effort on entering (Roman) Italy to see what lay ahead with his own eyes. That could

84

hardly be done by a commander riding across country with his staff.

And on the Po in that month of March he had anxieties which Carthalo and the spy network could not relieve. Only rumors reached him from Carthage and the intervening seas; probably he had no information from Spain except that a sizable Roman army had landed there. He needed to regain contact with the old and new Carthage at the earliest possible day, when the seas were open to navigation.

He could be certain as well that, after their defeat on the Trebia, the Roman commanders would be drawing in their great resources to resist him. With each month of good weather, stronger forces would be mobilizing along the paved roads of the south. Perhaps then Hannibal made his bitter comment on the waging of war: "If you gain a victory even those who hate you will hold to you; if you are defeated even your friends will leave you."

So Hannibal struck south with the Gauls at the mobilizing armies of Rome. This early start before the end of winter exacted a heavy price from him.

Passage of the Swamps

The mountain chain of the Apennines runs slantwise down the Italian peninsula. From the coast above Genoa this mountain spine tends to the east of south until it all but touches the other coast on the Adriatic. Narrow valleys offer passages through it, but the mountain chain runs unbroken to the toe of Italy. The Carthaginians might have taken the longer and easier route toward Rome by following the range down and crossing it near to Rome. Instead of doing so they struck straight south through the range.

It was a little like crossing the Alps again. The first valley they entered rose to a crest where hail and driving rain checked them. They retraced their way to a shelter camp to wait out the storm. Apparently they made their next try elsewhere, and this time got through to the western slopes. They descended to lowlands turned to silt and mud by floodwaters. Beyond lay swamps hidden in mist. This direct way was a hard way.

Hannibal did not wait to search for a dry road. In the swamps the pack animals fell under their loads, and carts had to be manhandled through. For four nights and three days the men did not find a dry camp site. They perched on their kits to sleep at a halt.

The veterans of the Alps were sent ahead, and the Gauls kept between them and the Numidians, who gathered up the stragglers and the sick. The Gauls, physically the strongest, shirked the mud march. The Spaniards, uncomplaining, must have wondered where were the rich plantations and the stone-paved roads and marble-white cities of the fabulous Rome. Chilled by the crossing of the Apennine crest, they were weakened by attacks of swamp fever and malaria.

Again the horse herds had no grazing. The remaining elephants died in the chill of the waters, except for one of the largest—it might have been the solitary Indian elephant of the herd—that kept its strength.

The physicians of Synhalus could do little to check the fevers in the swamplands. The mist dampened their garments; it seemed as if the gods in the sky had set this evil in the way of the army. Hannibal was in the grip of malaria, suffering from head pains. The physicians could only wrap him up and insist that he ride above the wet on the back of the surviving elephant.

Hanno, son of Bomilcar, feeling for a way out of the inundated area, came to moving water that led toward trees on his left. Turning the Berber horsemen in that direction, he found a mass of hills taking shape in the mist. Skirting these, the horsemen entered a valley leading south. Here the mist cleared and the sun shone on green pasture land dotted with the white of houses. The Carthaginians named it the Valley of Light; it was in reality the lovely valley of Fiesole (Faesulae).

There it became known how Hannibal suffered from the head sickness. An optical nerve had failed and he was blind in one eye.

In the valley he abandoned the elephant to mount his horse again. He rode forward on a wide dirt road. Where tufa cliffs rose at the valley's side dark apertures showed, framed in ancient corroded stonework. Slaves plowing the fields with oxen said that these doorways of the cliffs were tombs of the Etruscans broken into and plundered a long time ago.

The road led the Carthaginians to the river Arno. At the fords of the Arno waited nondescript peddlers who, however, had costly incense and ivory in their packs. These were spies of Carthalo's network, and they sought Hannibal to sell him their rarities openly and to murmur their tidings to him in Phoenician. They told him that the valleys ahead of him offered good grazing and plentiful foodstuffs; the people were not warlike. But up in the eastern hills, a half dozen marches farther on, a strong Roman army watched for his coming.

Hannibal increased the pace of his columns. He struck south to pass by the Romans in the juncture of the hills. That way led toward Rome.

It took the Carthaginians through the heart of ancient Etruscan lands. Again, as it had happened at the river Po, they did not find what they had hoped for.

III. From Trasimeno to Cannae

"I Have Not Come to Make War on You."

A nation does not die like a man, at any single moment. It has its language, its way of doing things, its religion, and, above all, its purpose or vision that impels it onward. Even if conquered by others, the nation will not perish unless these sustaining forces are lost.

The strong and imaginative Etruscan nation had ceased to exist not long before Hannibal's coming. The Latin speech prevailed in its valleys; its cities, even Veii and sacred Tarquinii had become *municipia,* ruled by the laws of Latium—the Broad Plain. The sun worship that had followed the Etruscans in a dim age from the shore of Asia, had yielded to an Apollo in graceful human semblance.

Oddly enough, in submerging the Etruscans the barbaric peoples of the Latin league had taken to themselves much of the Etruscan culture. Roman engineers built bridges and aqueducts in enduring stone after the manner of the northerners; the army that filled its ranks by *legio*—drawing of lots—copied the earlier Etruscan, even to details of equipment such as breastplates, greaves and serviceable shields. The gladiators who had performed in

Etruscan funeral games were beginning to act their mimic combat in Roman colosseums for the entertainment of the crowds.

But more had been taken from the culture of the north: the ax and staves of a consul's authority (the *fasces*); the art of the augurs who foretold the future by the Sibylline Books; the ritual songs of the *vates,* and the orations at the funerals of those who had descended into the shadow life of Hades. In such intangible matters the hardy folk of the Tiber had relied on the wisdom of their new subjects, and they had adapted themselves to the *Etrusco ritu.*

Etruscan art had been the last to die. As late as the fourth century it had left tomb walls painted with dancers of more than human beauty, swirling in half-seen garments. That dance of theirs was a brilliant flame rising from embers. Now Etruscan artists exhibited their skill in fleshy portraits of bejeweled nobles on convivial couches. Metalworkers forged surgical instruments and practical braziers, still with a trace of ancient imagery in ornaments of winged griffons, or the four white horses that had drawn the chariots of forgotten kings.

The Etruscans themselves had lost any will to resist. They made excellent wine for the Romans, who brought authority with them and held back the savage Celts in the farther north.

On entering a Roman-Etruscan town, Hannibal must have noticied in the baths and theaters signs of a culture that he had missed since leaving the Iberian palaces. Yet he met with no response from the few officials who awaited his coming. He told them: "I have not come to make war on you but on the power of Rome alone. You can be free from that power." They answered evasively in Latin, and they sent report to Rome that here was the apparition of an army not even African in origin, but dragged from the limits of the world. They neither resisted Hannibal nor heeded him.

Now until then, except in the passage of the Alps, the Carthaginian had won over portions at least of the peoples on his route. Behind him in that month of June Ligurians were ambushing Roman officers within their boundaries and sending weapon men to Hannibal. Presently Roman garrisons, isolated on the Po, would mutiny.

Ahead of him waited a population of some 6,000,000, speaking Umbrian, Etruscan, and Greek as well as other tongues, and the Latin of offcialdom. In the roster of manpower of 770,000 of that population, no more than 358,000 had been citizens of the *Civitas Romana*. (And by now he had eliminated a portion of the latter.) To throw his army against such a force would be a gamble of desperation.

While Hannibal might not have known these exact numbers, he understood the proportions that made up his problem. He would need to win the support of many of the allies of Rome to have a chance of success. And he had merely neutralized, as it were, the inhabitants of Etruria through which he was passing at speed. He was leading his ill-conditioned divisions toward another battle which must serve, beyond the loss of life, to destroy the prestige of Rome as far as possible.

When he by-passed his enemy's camp in the hills—wherein he had no wish to go against the legions—he threw his horsemen across the valley to plunder and burn the villages. That brought in certain supplies, and it might well serve to bring the enemy command down from the hills. Apparently the Carthaginians were moving on Rome. If Sempronius had been the commander in the hills he would have lost no time in marching down to confront the Carthaginian.

Hannibal, half blind, was in no patient mood. When spies reported to him what they had leared of the nearby Roman forces, of the new Consul Gaius Flaminius, he snapped at them: "What use is this parroting of numbers? Give me one look into the mind of Falminius."

The spies accordingly repeated what they had learned of the character of the new Consul.

Gaius Flaminius, the plebian Consul, was a remarkable man, who earned the lively hatred of the heads of the great families, and accordingly of the annalists who described him after his death. Livy says that "he had no experience of affairs and no military ability whatever." But had he not?

As Tribune of the People Flaminius carried through a farsighted agrarian law against the will of the Senate; as praetor he governed Sicily well enough to earn the gratitude of the Roman Sicilians; as Consul in 223 he led an army into battle with the Cisalpine Gauls against the orders of the Senate, and gained a victory that subdued the Insubres until the coming of Hannibal; as Censor he began the building of the great Flaminian Way to the north—the paving of which can still be seen beside the modern motor speedway. Reelected Consul in 217 by popular demand to succeed the unhappy Sempronius, he did not linger in Rome for ritual sacrifices but hastened north—against the will of the Senate—to join his command in the field.

Although detested by the noble families, especially by the Fabian, Falminius, then, was a self-willed man of unmistakable ability. His weakness was overconfidence.

Consider his actions in the field. With his colleague, Servilius, he decides to abandon the province of the Po for the time being, and to await Hannibal on the threshold of Roman territory. This plan of waiting for the enemy draws the indignation of the Senate. The Romans have two armies moving up. Shrewdly, Flaminius goes to the west of the Apennines at the heights of Arezzo. Servilius waits in the east, at Rimini, at the end of the Flaminian Way. When the Carthaginians are discovered moving past him in the valley, Flaminius does not catch at Hannibal's lure to hasten down into battle on open ground. Instead he sends urgent advice to Servilius to march south at speed. Then, when he hears that Servilius is on the road with the eastern army, Flaminius debouches from his hills to follow the track of the Carthaginians. It is marked, clearly enough, by burning villages.

The track turns east, and Flaminius hastens the pace of his legions. The road leads by the site of Cortona, toward Lake Trasimeno (Trasumennus). In two or three days at this pace Hannibal will cross the Flaminian Way, down which Servilius is hastening. Then, inevitably, he will be caught between the two Roman armies, and this meeting in rugged, hilly country will favor the Romans. Accordingly Flaminius presses on to be certain of closing the jaws of the trap.

Flaminius did not lack military ability. But he knew nothing of the mind of Hannibal.

Numidian skirmishers kept to the rear of the Carthaginians, almost within sight of the patrols of the pursuing Romans. They came in at night to report and to screen the camp. In the afternoons Hannibal habitually rode on with a small escort to look over the country ahead. When he rode down the long valley to Cortona, he sighted the deep greenish-blue line of a lake ahead. The lake extended to a great width (more than its size today). On the north side, close to the Carthaginians, it was framed in a half circle of broken knolls, hardly as large as hills. The labyrinth of knolls was rocky, scummed over with brush and olive trees. At intervals steep promontories pushed out into the water.

Here the road led around the lake, as roads do, by the easiest way. This was the narrow strip of shore at the water's edge. So the shore really made a small wilderness, with the larger hills behind it.

After he had seen all he wanted of it, Hannibal left the shore of Lake Trasimeno to return to the Carthaginian camp. Before the short June night had ended the greater part of his army marched out and wheeled left into the hills above the lake, vanishing in the early morning mist.

A division of tired African spearmen kept to the road around the water, the Numidian riders shepherding their rear as usual. It was the twentieth day of June.

Daylight came early on the morrow, the twenty-first of June. But before light the army of Flaminius, more than

93

WESTERN MEDITERRANEAN - 218 B.C.
Showing peoples recruited by Hannibal
on his march to Rome

■ CARTHAGINIAN TRADING PORT

40,000 strong, was on the march from its camp at the end of the valley. Legionaries and allied recruits carried their equipment slung to spears and belts. It was a well-disciplined force. As usual the advance legion forged ahead, following the tracks of the Carthaginian horsemen on the road by the lake.

The main body followed in good spirits. The Consul commanding them had won a victory over the savage Cisalpine Gauls now retreating before them. In another day and a half, their tribunes said, they would reach the junction with the Flaminian Way and gain contact with the other consular army. Slave dealers and peddlers following the camp had brought along empty carts to be loaded with spoil taken from the Carthaginians, as well as chains to put on the captives.

The darkness continued after the hour of sunrise; a heavy morning mist lay over the lake; the column felt its way through a gray murk. There was some confusion when the cavalry wings pressed in on the marchers as the way narrowed; there was something of a scramble to get around the first steep promontory point. Although crowded, the cohorts straightened themselves out, found their ranks and kept up the pace. The mist began to thin overhead, but it still veiled the lake on their right hand.

They noticed first the roaring that rose over the clatter and thud of the marching. It did not seem to come from any one place unless from the air overhead. Veteran *triarii* realized that they were attacked, but their assailants remained invisible, and the veterans could not think where another army might be in reach of them. The mist hid everything beyond stone's throw. Through the mist hissed missiles, changing into the close-packed ranks.

Discipline is like a clamp. It holds trained soldiers in set motion, obedient to the last given command. For a space, unable to see what was happening, the legions attempted to keep their pace forward in the marching column. Then they began to shed their kits and get the shields on their arms.

"In such a fog, their ears served them better than their eyes, and they heard the groaning of the wounded with screams and shouts that made them peer first one way and then another."

95

The standards could not be seen. Instead of legates galloping up with orders, riderless horses plunged through the ranks. Centurions shouted to form front to the left, and the ranks pushed that way, to take accustomed places. There was no room to wheel properly. Front rank men stumbled up through brush and boulders to find the hillside swarming with men leaping down on them. Many Roman legionaries swore afterward that an earthquake had shaken the shore of the lake at that moment.

The shock of the attack threw the laboring ranks into confusion. Companies that pushed up the slope were surrounded. "While they tried to think what to do they were slain without realizing how."

Hannibal had sent his divisions simultaneously into the surprise attack from the crests where they had been held waiting. The heights were clear of mist after sunrise. Apparently the divisions of Africans, Iberians, Celtiberians, and Gauls could see each other, and from his post above the far end of the lake road Hannibal had them all under observation. The Gauls, and the Insurbres in particular, went to attack with berserk rage against Flaminius, the Roman commander who had devastated their lands and driven them to surrender. So witnesses relate.

Their attack never lost its force because they came down into the marching column that could not manage to form front against them. The fighting swirled over broken ground between the slopes and the water, in a way well suited to the agile Spaniards and forest-bred Gauls. It was held to that stretch of shore because the formidable Carthaginian heavy cavalry came into action at the rear of the Roman column. The horsemen emerged from a hidden valley within the hills. However bad the condition of their horses may have been, there was no disciplined force to stand in the way of the cavalry. At Hannibal's end of the crescent shore (most probably this half-moon extended between the promontory point of Passignano and the slopes of Monte del Lago) the advance force of African infantry under Maharbal closed the exit. Flaminius, not Hannibal, had been caught by the closing of a trap.

Even while some of the companies backed together to make a stand, panic spread through the broken legions.

There was no way open to escape; throngs of fugitives blundered into each other and broke up formations that were still firm. "A great part, finding no road to flee, waded out into the lake until only their heads and shoulders were above the water. They were cut down by the horsemen who rode into the water after them."

By ten o'clock in the morning the battle of Lake Trasimeno was ended. The sun had burned away the mist. The advance legion of the Romans, which had pushed on, unmolested in the obscurity, to the high ground in the east, could see that the shore of the lake below was occupied by Carthaginians, and that the rest of the Roman army had vanished.

Hannibal Turns to the East

The surviving legion tried to escape. It was caught up and surrounded by Carthaginian horse under Maharbal. Then something unwonted happened. The legion surrendered its standards and—6,000 strong—became prisoners of the Carthaginian, under terms.

In fact, the entire conflict at Trasimeno was something without precedent in Italy. The Carthaginians, sick men on weak horses, had almost annihilated a stronger Roman army. No remnant of it was got together again. Its 15,000 survivors were captives of the Carthaginians.

When Hannibal rode over the field that evening, he beheld the evidence of the rout—the sacred silver Eagles on the ground with standards on the maniples, the captured equipment piled with stores and sections of portable bridges and engines. He ordered the burial of slain Carthaginians. They had lost 2,500—for the most part Gauls—in killed and wounded. Hannibal made careful search for the body of Flaminius to bury it with fitting honor, but it could not be found. Insubre horsemen chanted in triumph that they had struck down their foe the Consul. Probably the body had been stripped of trophies and thrown aside.

It mattered less than that the dreaded legions had been

dissolved into fugitives clawing their way to escape. The legionairies rarely lost their courage, but when they did they could be cut down like sheep.

That happened when ranks were broken. In this age of the heavily armed infantry—whether Greek hoplites or Roman legionaries—men in formation protected each other. They presented a front of helmets, shields, and greaves, bristling with hand weapons. Missiles of that day, before firearms and power bows, could cause little injury to such an armored front line. It is said, probably truthfully, that no more than 192 Athenian hoplites lost their lives at Marathon. They kept their ranks intact. But if ranks were broken, heavy casualties ensued. Fugitives usually dropped their shields and were struck down by thrown javelins of slingstones, or the lances of pursuing horsemen. In the hands of the swift-moving Carthaginians such weapons were deadly. (On the stricken field of Cannae a great part of the Roman infantry would lie helpless, with their knee tendons slashed by a cut from behind.) Never before the battle of Lake Trasimeno had Roman legions failed to form their fighting front.

That night the Carthaginian priests spread ritual cakes and poured sacrificial wine before the teraphim in the shrine tent. And Hannibal had a heated quarrel with the downright Maharbal. The latter had pledged the captured legion that its men would be released after surrender of their arms. Hannibal refused to approve the pledge. No Roman citizens might be released. Maharbal's prized legionaries were destined to be sold to Greek slave dealers. Meanwhile, with other citizens, they were given short rations and hard treatment. In visible contrast to this, the prisoners who had come into Roman service from the allied peoples were well fed and released to seek their homes. Hannibal assured them that he held no enmity toward them: his enemy was the city on the Tiber, and that alone.

"I have not come to make war on Italians," he told them, "but to aid Italians against Rome."

Then, as usual before setting out, he had a conference with his commanders and the spokesmen of the nations that made up his army. Some of the Gauls, intoxicated with their success, must have pleaded with him to hasten

98

south to besiege or harry that same city of Rome. No doubt Maharbal and the veterans of Hamilcar longed to do that.

After hearing them out, Hannibal rejected their advice and agreed with the younger commanders and the Spaniards who urged that the army had journeyed to the limit of its endurance and must rest. He said that, more than rest, the army needed to be welded into a new whole. It would take the remainder of the summer to do that, in a secure place.

Where, demanded the veterans of Carthage, would they find a secure place under Roman rule?

Hannibal took them on the road to the east. They turned their backs on the drowsy Etruscan towns, and their faces toward lofty Perugia and the broad valley of Assisi. Thus they were on their way again to cross the Apennine barrier, to gain the distant coast of the Adriatic. They were leaving the malarial lowlands to pass through fertile grazing with a convoy of captives and a wagon train bearing the equipment of a Roman army.

At the start of their march to the east they came to the junction with the Flaminian Way and ran into 4,000 Roman horsemen. These were the advance of the army of the other Consul, Servilius, coming from Rimini. Perhaps as surprised as the Romans at the encounter, the Carthaginians encircled Servilius' cavalry and took 2,000 survivors captive.

About the same day crowds gathered in the Forum of the city of Rome. Rumors of disaster spread from the northern gates to the homes of citizens, and they waited to hear announcement of the truth by the Fathers of the Senate. Only a few months before, the same throngs had been reassured by a message from Sempronius the Consul after his withdrawal from the river Trebia, and the events there had proved to be worse than the Consul stated in his message.

The doors of the Senate remained closed to the anxious crowd. At length a single praetor, Pomponius Matho, came out to the tribunal stand. After waiting for silence, he said a dozen words.

"We have been vanquished in a great battle. A Consul is dead."

99

"Singly or all together," Polybius observed afterward, "the Romans are never so much to be feared as when they have real danger to fear."

This tenacious courage was, as the Greek historian pointed out, peculiar to individuals as well as to a disciplined mass of Romans. They had been bred to hardships. The city they had built so laboriously within the Seven Hills possessed no natural advantages, and several serious disadvantages. Unlike the great cities of the eastern Mediterranean, it had no seaport. On the marshy plain of the Tiber it lacked any natural defense. It was not even healthy until Roman engineers drained the marshes as the Etruscans had done before them. For defense the early Servian Wall had been built between the seven hillocks.

At that time Rome was smaller and much less imposing than majestic Syracuse or enlightened Alexandria of the city library and monumental lighthouse—a wonder of the world. (Carthage, although smaller in size and population, possessed the advantages of the other two famous centers, a strategic site and an established culture.)

The Roman social body still consisted of the Thirty-five Tribes, still rudimentary in culture. Roman oratory, not Ciceronian as yet, limited itself to influencing voters and extolling the records of the dead. Music was confined to Saturae medleys, imitated from the Greek. Literature appeared only in written tradition and translations of heroic poems such as the *Iliad*. In fact the people of Romulus, vague about the origin of their ancestors, liked to fancy that they were descendants of the storied Trojans. Actually their race had migrated from the unheroic shores of the Danube, and it retained the lack of imagination and patient endurance of the dwellers beneath the north wind.

The stoicism of the Roman people owed little to the philosophy of the Greek *Stoa,* it was in their nature. For the most part they remained deeply superstitious. The temple of Fortuna, designed by Greek architects, had offerings from plebeian families as well as the wealthy, who may not have been convinced that a supernatural destiny shaped their lives. The average citizen never stepped out of his door in the morning without looking for the omens of the day in the flight of crows overhead or the pattern of leaves underfoot. The taking of omens became an official duty, and a flock of sacred chickens served the consuls in deciding upon great undertakings. The general worship of war-gods stemmed from inherent superstition, enhanced by the belief that such gods had favored the efforts of the Romans. The two-headed Janus might have power over others, but Mars was a tutelary deity of the descendants of Romulus; even his sister, Bellona, possessed a costly temple served by priests and women who slashed blood from themselves in savage ritual dances.

Warfare, which had preserved the city, was enlarging its power to the *imperium Romanum*, the new dominion peculiar to the people of Mars. For the Roman ability to organize had devised the system of annexation of territory never attempted by the less practical Greeks. Colonists were moved outward into a freshly conquered province; the conquered people were uprooted and shifted inward to serve in useful ways. As for the average Roman—keeper of a small farm and a large family—he looked on a campaign, at which his people had been strikingly successful, as a welcome source of money and spoil to eke out his working of the soil. There was hardly a merchant class as yet. The great patrician families, the Fabians, Claudians, Scipios, Aemilians, and Valerians, formed a strong military aristocracy, accustomed to the dangers as well as the profits of battle. One of them remarked quite seriously: "In times of peace we lose the benefits we have gained by war." Tradition required military service of them, as it had of Flaminius. Roman achievement was won by blood and sweat but without tears.

Roman discipline, unequaled in its efficiency, really sprang from traditional self-discipline. The heads of families—the *patres*—had become the inexorable judges of their families. No great time had passed since they ruled outsiders as *reges*, kings. As a Roman citizen of the highest order—the *optimo jure*—possessed privileges beyond lesser citizens and unknown to outsiders, he had also a standard of conduct so rigid that it disregarded human life in its performance. Military commanders executed their sons for a breach of discipline. Such hardihood was more than pride; it was an ethic of conduct that no one might change. It was the Roman reaction to danger, and the Romans were never more to be feared than when they had most to fear.

The disaster at Lake Trasimeno was accpeted as another "black day" of defeat, although greater than any *dies atra* in the record of the past. Curiously enough, the news of the loss of Servilius' cavalry several days later caused more consternation. Tense nerves seemed to give way under the slighter misfortune. Women, especially, who were denied participation in public gatherings, made outcry in the streets. Rumor arose in the streets that the city would be evacuated at the coming of the Carthaginians.

For once the popular assemblies were in full agreement with the leaders, the conscript Fathers of the Senate. The Consuls, everyone felt, had bungled the strategy of the war. Hannibal had made numskulls of Sempronius, Flaminius, and Servilius. In this danger to the city, a dictator must be appointed to defend it properly. Accordingly "they did what had never been done until that day; they named a dictator by popular election."

Characteristically, the united parties appointed the elderly man who had warned the Senate in the earliest days that warfare in the field was very different from discussion in the Senate chamber—Fabius Verrucosus, "the Warty."

This head of the Fabians seemed to earn nicknames throughout his life. As a boy his awkward silence and laborious studying made him "the Lambkin" of his schoolmates. He was to gain hatred and admiration very soon as *Cunctator,* "the Delayer," and to end up in the Roman heraldry of achievement as Maximus, "the Great." The silent Fabius had his own way of thinking through a problem before attempting to solve it, and of impatience with all interference when he was solving it. As a commander he had driven the savage Ligurians out

102

of Cisalpine Gaul. He had unlimited patience, a dislike of argument, a ruthless determination and a carefully concealed vanity.

In appointing him the Senate urged him to strengthen the walls of the city and defend its bridges. Old Fabius did nothing of the kind. After ordering the decemvirs to search the Sibylline Books of mystery, to discover the cause of the disaster, he announced that sufficient sacrifice had not been made to the gods—that, to purge the city, new temples must be vowed, and in particular 300 oxen must be sacrificed to Jupiter. This act of ritual penance served to distract the populace and instill some hope that by favor of the gods things might change for the better. Fabius also made impressive display of his new authority by appearing on horseback with twenty-four lictors—twice the prescribed number—carrying the fasces before him.

The mild-spoken Fabius then demanded a total effort from the city, a new tax and general enlistment—and as much from all the allied peoples. When he rode north to take over the remainder of Servilius' forces, he ordered the surviving Consul to dismiss his lictors and discard his toga of office and to approach Fabius as a common citizen on foot.

More than that, Fabius, as Dictator, ordered a scorched-earth strategy to be carried out. Wherever the Carthaginians marched, harvests must be burned, and cattle and people removed before their coming. And almost immediately he heard strange tidings. Hannibal's army was scorching the earth as it passed. For ten days during the crossing of the Umbrian mountains, the Carthaginians had burned and destroyed, carrying off captives and killing all males of military age. (In this region closely allied to Rome Hannibal made use of terrorism for the first time.)

A new wave of dread passed through the city. To allay it Fabius spoke to the leaders. "Why do you utter the name of Hannibal in fear? He is only one man, far distant from Carthage. He has left to him no more than a third of the army that followed him into the Alps. He must get his food from one day to the next. Each day will find him a little weaker, while we grow stronger."

103

Although Fabius' facts were not exactly true—and he may have known that—his reasoning was correct. Time worked to the advantage of the Romans. And Fabius resolved to gain time at any cost.

Hannibal's actions mystified the leaders of the Senate. Why did the victorious Carthaginian betake himself away from Rome to the east coast where the land was poor, without harbors, the cities few and the people almost beyond the sphere of Roman authority?

Fabius made no attempt to answer their questions. Leaving most of his experienced officers on the Tiber to train a new and greater army, he led his own command east to intercept and watch Hannibal.

Fabius Moves Against Hannibal

That summer the Carthaginians recuperated on the highlands of the Adriatic. Here the Picentine inhabitants had little thought of the conflict in the west, and, except for the Roman landowners, they accepted the coming of the Carthaginians as a dispensation of unpredictable Fate. After marching more than 1,800 miles in the last 15 months the Carthaginians were glad to go into rest camps. Physicians treated the fever victims. Ailing horses were turned out to graze, and their hunger mange treated by rubbing down with stronge wine.

Presently Hannibal began the renovation of the army. Its makeshift garments were discarded for Roman cloth and mail and leg greaves. The captured weapons Hannibal sold off to Greek traders for the most part. The shields could be issued to the Gauls, who were quite familiar with Roman weapons and tactics. But the Spaniards preferred their two-edged, two-foot swords to the straight stubby blades of the Latins.

Once equipped, Hannibal drilled them all in new tactics, as he had trained the barbaric Celtiberians in past years. He had learned much of Roman tactics, and he no longer depended on the advice of his older officers. The horsemen were given heavier armor, and formed into handier units of 500 and 150. Hannibal devoted himself especially to the undisciplined Numidians, placing them under the watchful command of Maharbal—and possibly removing Maharbal from the all-important African heavy infantry.

Even before finishing the new training, Hannibal moved south along the coast by easy stages into Apulia. The army of Fabius appeared on the skyline, observing the Carthaginians. It kept to the higher ridges, digging in each night. Although the Romans of this new command often sallied forth in strength to drive off Hannibal's foragers, they did not descend into open valleys. They neither offered nor accepted a greater engagement.

After watching them for some days Hannibal said abruptly, "We have won the war. The warlike spirit of the Romans is broken."

Perhaps this was meant, as so often happened, to encourage his officers. Yet at this moment the Carthaginian may have put his own thought into words. His ultimate purpose was to break down the Roman will and power to make war. And he sensed a change in the spirit of the command now facing him.

Hannibal marched south into the high plain around the crossroads at Luceria (Lucera). His horsemen grazed the level country, apparently oblivious of the enemy. Fabius watched from a distant ridge. As they continued on, the Carthaginians ravaged the estates of Roman landlords while doing no injury to the villages, poor enough in this region. They even gained recruits from starving hunters and shepherds. The Romans followed along the ridges, where they were not attacked.

"The Phoenician tried his enemy by ravaging fields within his sight; by marching off rapidly elsewhere and then lying in wait behind blind turnings of the road."

Fabius kept clear of such traps by scouting the way ahead. Every week swelled the numbers of the legions training behind him at Rome. In their mutual maneuvering, Hannibal crossed a small river, the Aufidus, near a stone-built village called Cannae. He was familiarizing himself with the country. But he was also accomplishing something unperceived by the Romans, something that has escaped their recording.

The secrecy that covered the planning of the Carthaginians is not easy to penetrate. Hannibal never wrote his commentary upon it, and it must be deduced from the events that followed.

For one thing, during this midsummer on the Adriatic he regained touch with the sea and Carthage. Small galleys slipped from Africa past the Roman fleets to the harborless Picentine shore. Seemingly here Hannibal sold off his Trasimeno prisoners to slave merchants from the east. For the first time captive legionaries appeared in chains at Greek ports, and they must have caused something of a stir. On their heels Hannibal certainly sent envoys across the Adriatic to Philip, king of Macedon, overlord of the Dalmatian coast that had resisted the Roman army of occupation recently. Carthage invited Macedonia to join forces against Rome.

For another thing, Mago, youngest of the Barca brothers, seems to have joined Hannibal on the Adriatic. With him Mago brought the eagerly awaited tidings from Spain. Those other brothers, Publius and the bald Gnaeus Scipio had landed there indeed but north of the Ebro (where Hannibal had expected the Romans at the war's opening), where the belligerent northern Spanish tribes opposed the invaders with arms. Hasdrubal watched them, comfortably enough, from New Carthage. Still, hostile fleets scoured the Spanish coast and the Pine Islands as well.

Most important of all, a battle fleet had put out from Carthage, 70 strong. I had intercepted convoys to Spain, and had even raided the west coast of Italy, putting in to Pisa too late to meet with Hannibal's army on its march from the swamps to Lake Trasimeno. In reaction the Romans had sent a powerful fleet of 120 quinqueremes out from their base in Sicily—under command of the demoted Servilius—to circle Sardinia and Corsica and search for the Carthaginian raiders off Africa.

The larger picture thus made clear was not encouraging to Hannibal. The two Scipios at the Ebro had severed the line of communication he had hoped to keep open with Spain. Although he himself was barely 400 miles by now from Carthage as the pigeon flies—and messenger pigeons may well have been flying back and forth—powerful Roman fleets barred that route by sea.

This large picture of the Mediterranean never left Hannibal's mind. It was at once his greatest hope and anxiety. He had no illusion that Carthage—one city with one tenth the manpower of the Latins—could match the resources of Rome, once they were mobilized in full. But the balance could be changed. That balance rested on the unstable fulcrum of the sea. If the mines of Spain could be held, and the forests of Corsica added, with the grain of Sardinia and the manifold wealth of Sicily, then the Carthaginian side of the balance would rise and the Roman drop accordingly. Thus the brief sally of the battle fleet from Carthage offered hope and disappointment as well.

About this time secret agents voyaged from Carthage to Syracuse, the citadel of Sicily, and at Hannibal's side Carthalo extended his spy network into Rome.

Hannibal led his army west, toward the fertile fields and walled cities of Campania, where the active port of Naples served that other coast. In doing so he failed to bring Fabius down to battle; instead he was caught in a trap laid by Fabius.

The Army of Oxen

Southern Italy forms a natural labyrinth of narrow valleys and deceptive ravines usually threaded by mountain streams and rarely opening into plains of any size. Spurs of the Apennines run down in promontories into the sea. Even the beaches offer only shelving banks beneath heights. In the last World War the Fifth and Eighth American and British armies—with all the aid of modern planes and motor transport—found their way barred by rivers in the ravines and rock pinnacles in the heights, from the beach at Salerno to the rock face of Mount Cassino.

Under such circumstances it was comparatively easy for the Roman army to make its way along higher ground, but quite another matter for the Carthaginians to get anywhere along the lower valleys. More often than not the towns occupied knolls above winding rivers, and the towns had stone walls. Then, too, the Carthaginians were passing through a linguistic blackout, wherein the natives understood neither Latin nor Greek.

At some time that autumn the Carthaginian officers bade the native guides lead them to the valley of Casinum (below the monastery of Mount Cassino today). The guides misunderstood the name as the Carthaginians pronounced it and brought them eventually to a town called Casilinum in the midst of blind valleys. In trying to extricate themselves from this labyrinth the Carthaginians entered a valley that narrowed to a steep ravine. There the army halted with its long wagon train of captured goods, while scouts explored the way ahead.

All this was observed by the Romans from their higher ground. The Roman officers led by Minucius, *Magister equitum* (Master of Horse) deputy to the Dictator, had chafed under the restraint of Fabius, who kept them marching as mere spectators of the ravaging carried on by the Carthaginians. Their growing anger was not eased by demands from their kinsmen within the Seven Hills to put a stop to the march of this enemy army "made up of the scourings of the earth, inhuman in its ferocity, feeding on the flesh of its victims." As usual in such cases, the "Punic atrocities" were more in evidence in the streets of Rome than in the Campanian hills. But the officers were angry enough at being compelled to conduct a campaign against the ancient spirit of the Romans. Already Fabius was called "the Delayer."

That afternoon Fabius beheld the possibility of carrying out a Trasimeno envelopment to entrap the Carthaginians. His officers were sent into action, with due caution. Portions of two legions, some 4,000 men, were hastened to the far end of the defile to hold the exit, while the main force descended to a convenient rise of ground commanding the entrance. There it entrenched. By sunset the Carthaginians were caught in the valley pass.

Hannibal learned as much from his scouts. It was like the Allobroges, all over again, except that the Romans would neither desert their posts during darkness, nor be drawn into a useful parley. Hannibal prepared to make a diversion that his enemy would not suspect. He had seen it done in the mountains of Spain. Drivers of the animal herds were ordered to lead a large number of oxen, perhaps a thousand, toward the head of the valley, to bind fagots of wood or pine torches to the horns of the beasts and to wait there. Then the army was fed and allowed to sleep.

About midnight Hannibal joined the cattle drivers with a small force of Celtiberians accustomed to hills. The oxen were started up the steep side of the valley. The Spanish detachment carried fire with it, and after ascending a way they began to ignite the fuel on the horns of the beasts, driving them forward and raising a wild shouting.

As the fires blazed, the oxen plunged up through brush and tree growth. The Roman posts at the far summit beheld a spectacle of hundreds of torches—so it seemed— and heard a multitude breaking away over the slope some distance from them. They hurried in that direction through the darkness, presently to encounter a baffling confusion of bellowing animals and taunting human voices. When they pressed on they were met by a discharge of missiles. They did not find the Carthaginian army.

That army was proceeding through the defile below to safety. By sunrise the end of the Carthaginian column was passing over the summit where the Romans had deserted their posts. Hannibal took care to send back strong detachments to bring off the Spanish skirmishers who had led the legionaries on a wild-goose chase.

From the entrance below, the main Roman forces had watched the spectacle of torches wandering through the hills and had been too puzzled to take any action. At least Fabius had refused to order them forward into the night's confusion. When the mystery was cleared up, his officers blamed him for inaction.

At Rome the story of Hannibal's escape aroused new resentment against the old man, the Delayer. Fabius paid no attention to the talk, but toward the end of the year he was summoned to Rome, ostensibly to attend to the ritual sacrifices, actually to answer his critics in the Senate.

On leaving, Fabius instructed his deputy, Minucius, under no circumstances to be drawn into battle with Hannibal.

"For Him There Will Be No Peace In Italy."

The great battle of Cannae did not begin on that fatal dawn of the third day of August, 216. It had its beginnings months before in the mind of Hannibal and in happenings in Rome that set irresistible forces in motion toward Cannae.

Minucius Rufus was young, born to the knightly order *(equites)* and a member of the Aemilian-Scipionic faction, antagonistic to the overproud Fabians. His officers shared his loathing of the bloodless delaying tactics of the old Dictator. So it is not at all surprising that Minucius accepted the opportunity that Hannibal at once offered the restless Romans. A wing of their cavalry, while driving off Punic foragers, came headlong against the Carthaginian outpost line on a rise of ground. The Romans entered into savage combat, and when Minucius hurried up with fresh troops, the Carthaginians were almost driven from their line. The next day the Romans found the hill deserted by its defenders. Hannibal was in retreat. (This slight engagement bears a remarkable resemblance to the preliminary success gained by Sempronius on the Trebia.)

Naturally Minucius used some glowing phrases in reporting it, and it caused a tumult of rejoicing in the streets of Rome, where the populace had heard of unbroken catastrophes until now. The people drew the quite logical conclusion that as soon as Fabius left the army it won a victory by attacking. Fabius himself said that he feared such a success more than adversity.

In turn Minucius was recalled for consultation, and honored by appointment to be co-Dictator. To have two dictators at the same time was without precedent in history, and inevitably it caused complications. As usual Fabius made no objection; he merely asked Minucius whether his new colleague wished to share the command of one army, or to command a separate half of the army. Minucius chose separate command. When they returned to the field their twin forces trailed Hannibal to a corner of Samnium, where Minucius again attacked, and was drawn into heavy combat out of which Fabius extracted him by a forced march across a river to the scene. Again Hannibal drew off, waiting.

Again the two Dictators went back to their hill camps. The time was at hand when, by inflexible law, the power of a dictator ended. The annual election would name, instead, two new consuls.

An anecdote relates that Hannibal said then: "That cloud on the horizon is breaking in storm at last." If true, this remark might be interpreted in several ways.

In fact his actions at this time present us with a riddle. Was he merely adapting himself to the Fabian tactics? Hardly likely. Did he realize during this second winter that, as Pyrrhus had discovered before him, he might never overcome the manifold resources of his enemy? Did he think of making a compromise peace and returning to Spain? (In Rome Fabius was declaring, "For him there will be no peace in Italy.") At sea, a Roman fleet had taken station in the Adriatic; on land Hannibal had failed to win over any people allied to Rome. His army, numbering some 35,000 at Trasimeno, might have grown to 40,000, hardly more. The army mobilizing at Rome was vastly larger. And that army became Hannibal's target.

Whatever the son of Hamilcar meditated, he kept his own forces intact while he went on moving by slow stages across the lands of Rome's closest allies. He took his provisions from them. And as the winter ended, this search for provisions led him to the Roman military depots, with their stored grain. His passivity, a riddle to us, puzzled the enemy as well. Rumors reached Rome that Hannibal planned to retire to friendly Cisalpine Gaul.

Moreover provision began to fail at Rome owing to the swath cut through the harvests by the Carthaginians. The stoutest of allies, Hiero II, aged tyrant of Syracuse, sent the Senate a gift of a shipment of grain and a statue of Victory, made of 220 pounds of gold. Usually for reasons of prestige the Senate, as head of the *imperium Romanum*

111

refused such gifts from lesser allies; in this case the Senate kept the gold statue and the grain. Short rations were shortening the tempers of the citizens, who were also the voters.

At the same time angry protests came from the usually silent Samnites, who had endured the ransacking of the Carthaginians while Rome itself and all the broad plain of Latium remained unscathed. The Samnite envoys, laconic men, observed the great industrial activity around the Via Sacra where contractors spent and gained fortunes in furnishing munitions to the new great army. There were even shipping magnates passing through the Forum followed by swarms of clients. The theaters and resorts had never been so crowded as during this wartime activity.

The anger of the Samnites was echoed by plebeians whose families suffered from hunger. These plebeians thronged around the street rostrums, demanding why the patricians who had started the war refused to take action to finish it. The solid party pledged to "Farming and Italy" had spokesmen in every rostrum to complain that agriculture and Italy itself were the chief sufferers from the Hannibalic invasion. Among the political orators perhaps the most effective was a certain Terentius Varro, a new man.

Varro had no particular ability, but he pleased the crowds. He had a way of saying things. "The Fabian senators tell us that their policy is preserving the Republic; but in preserving us they keep us from conquering Hannibal." It was only a step from accusing the magnates of prolonging the war to saying that he, Gaius Terentius Varro, would end it at the first chance, and only a step from that to promising that, if he held command, he would go all out for victory the first day he came in sight of the hated Punic.

That was exactly what the popular assemblies wanted done. Varro was swept into office as plebeian Consul, replacing the Dictators in the year's election.

When the omens were taken into account at the new year, the images of the war-gods were observed to sweat blood—a sign that the gods themselves urged the people to take arms.

Then, too, the election of the patrician Consul had

been delayed by the head-on dispute of the Fabian faction with its policy of attrition warfare, and the Aemilian-Scipionic faction with its policy of total mobilization for conquest. As far as Varro—already elected—was concerned, being a son of a father prominent in the meat-packing industry, he had a partiality for the Aemilian group, a power in that industry.

Fabius fought his political opponents ruthlessly. But the Delayer had lost all popular support, and he lost followers in the Senate when a report came in that Hannibal, making the rounds of the harvests, had spared an estate belonging to Fabius while he devasted all around it.

After that the Delayer had to bow his head to the storm. And it befell that the second, patrician Consul was an Aemilius Paulus, an elderly man of distinguished record but reluctant to take the post. By his election he became committed to act to end the war.

Aemilius Paulus had been one of the five envoys who had faced the Council at Carthage, to make known that Rome would begin the war. It was fitting, then, that he should end it. There is a story that Fabius warned Aemilius: "You will find Terentius Varro more dangerous an enemy than Hannibal."

The truth is that something like a crusading spirit swept all elements of Roman society toward Cannae in that summer of 216. More than one hundred Senators resigned their posts to enlist in the legions. The whole of the knightly order joined the cavalry decuries. The lower classes volunteered in the hope of looting the riches of the Carthaginian camp and gathering a new crop of slaves. The ranks of the new army swelled to a total of 85,000, and more than half were fresh recruits.

Even the military advisers of the Senate agreed at last upon taking the offensive. They pointed out that in the Trebia conflict the legions had not been broken, while at Trasimeno they had not been able to form for battle. The new, super army of eight legions—the greatest force ever mustered by Rome—with the allied troops could hardly fail of victory in the ancient Roman way with sword and shield. It would take many lives, of course, but Hannibal could not afford such bloodshed. By now the Roman commanders had learned all Hannibal's bag of tricks. No

113

Punic ruse could dissolve away eight legions on firm open ground in clear daylight.

No one agreed more than Minucius, who was to hold a high command. By now he was looked up to as the one most experienced in meeting Hannibal. Among the young dilettantes of society, Publius Cornelius Scipio, who had aided his wounded father at the Trebia, forsook his wine bowl and political argument to join up as a regimental tribune.

A slight incident started this volunteer army on the road to join the veteran forces in the field. News arrived in Rome that Hannibal had seized still another grain depot, this time in the half-ruined stone village of Cannae far away on the Adriatic shore. A slight matter, but it appeared intolerable to the Senate and popular assemblies alike that this Carthaginian should be allowed to work his will upon Italy for one week more. The Senate ordered all forces to march and unite against Hannibal. The new Consuls would take over the command.

After the departure of the new army all reports coming from the east were hurried to the Senate chamber and relayed thence to the throngs waiting at the rostrum in the Forum.

The early reports provided good omens. The new troops had stormed a Carthaginian outpost camp, finding rich spoil of silverware and jewels lying in the abandoned tents, almost as if waiting to be taken by Roman hands. The cooking fires of the camp were still burning, and the enthusiastic legionaries had broken from their officers' control to pursue the hated enemy.

A raid of the wraithlike Numidian horsemen had been driven off successfully, and the forces of the Consuls, Aemilius and Varro, pressed after the raiders.

The two Roman armies were united, pursuing Hannibal. He had abandoned his main camp at their coming, to retreat across the river Aufidus.

There, on the open plain of Cannae, the Consuls had brought him to bay.

It was the third day of August.

A witness watched Hannibal standing by his favorite horse during the sunrise. They were on a knoll, the highest point of the dry plain. Already wind whipped at his light mantle and the long mane of the charger, and the wind came from his back, from the west. The natives called it a Volturnus wind. It had a breath of furnace heat, stinging with dust.

From this post Hannibal's eye could see all the sweep of the gray plain, no more than three miles from the cool waters of the Adriatic. Between him and the shore the long line of the Roman legions advanced slowly behind its screen of skirmishers. It was really a line made up of rank upon rank of the disciplined infantry moving slowly to keep the standards of the cohorts properly aligned. When the sun broke through the haze, the ends of the line could be made out as horsemen—the inevitable attack formation of the Roman army. The glint of metal on the Roman right showed that the heavy cavalry occupied that wing. These armored horsemen, in fact, filled all the ground between the end legion and the winding river across which Hannibal had decided to move his last camp to the plain of Cannae. The stone village itself stood on an abrupt rise between the end of the Carthaginian line and the river. It stood there, empty, an obstacle to any advance of the Roman heavy horse.

After the first light, Hannibal had sent his own heavy cavalry, the elite of the Spaniards and Africans, to that side, to move forward at foot pace under the direction of Hanno, son of Bomilcar, who had an instinct for combat.

Hannibal seldom took his eye for long from these horsemen of Hanno now waiting under the slope of Cannae. By then only a group of lesser officers and couriers remained with him on the knoll across from Cannae. All of these watched the advance of the legions, obscured at intervals by dust clouds, almost unbelieving.

One of them, a man named Gisco, shook his head and

said, "It is a most amazing thing to see such a number of men."

Hannibal turned to glance at Gisco and the anxious faces around him. He said quickly, "I'll tell you something more amazing."

They all watched him, expectantly, wondering why he smiled at such a moment.

"In all that number," Hannibal said, "there is no other man named Gisco."

At that they all laughed, Gisco as well, partly because they knew that he did not have too bright a mind but mostly because Hannibal felt like jesting. Their tension was broken. When the couriers sped away to carry their messages, they passed on the jest to horse holders and water carriers. "Ay, the Latins count themselves by tens of thousands, but there's no Gisco among them."

The witness himself then left the rise where Hannibal kept his watch. There the Carthaginian waited patiently while the mile-long mass of the enemy advanced, ordered and armed. The mass pushed through clouds of Carthaginian slingers and darters. From its leading line javelins flashed, a myriad flying needles. Distant trumpets sent their call against the wind. A roar went up as the leading legions struck against the Carthaginians, who awaited their coming silently. It seemed as if the mass of Romans inevitably would break through the thin Carthaginian line, where one man faced three coming against him.

When the lines came together Hannibal gave an order. Servants threw blazing torches into a pyre of brush and dry wood. Dense smoke fanned out into the wind. The smoke was seen two miles away, where Hanno waited with the heavy cavalry beneath Cannae.

Behind this panorama of the battle's opening there were factors not so easily seen. The commanders who had led the Carthaginian army from Spain two years before still held their posts. They carried out the orders of one mind, Hannibal's.

On the Roman side the commanders were strange to each other. Aemilius, experienced but irresolute, led the heavy right wing of cavalry. Two former Consuls, one being Servilius, commanded the massive infantry center.

116

Varro, the least experienced of all, had charge of the weaker allied horsemen at the left of the line. No one man controlled the tens of thousands moving forward.

This rigid Roman line went straight in at the enemy because it was accustomed to no other tactic. It could strike hard, but could not maneuver to do anything else. As the standards went forward the soldiers crowded in to keep place beneath them. It was hard to see ahead of them, with the dust and wind in their faces.

Ahead of them the Carthaginians no longer waited in the national groupings of the earlier years. Hannibal had recast his army into tactical groups. Only the Numidians, now under Maharbal's firm hand, remained together. The heavy cavalry was made up of Spaniards, Africans, and some Gauls drilled as an attack column. It was now the striking force of the army.

The center of the line that should have been the strongest portion was here the weakest—manned by light-armed Gauls, Celtiberians, and Libyans. Yet at either end of this weak center there were solid squares of African heavy infantry in good Roman armor. Each square occupied a slight rise in the plain, so that at the opening of the battle the Africans remained apart and above the clash of the lines.

In that clash the Spaniards and Gauls of the center were driven back and again back by the powerful Roman center. As they retreated the struggling Carthaginians came out on higher ground. For here the plain of Cannae formed a half valley. The crest to which the hard-pressed Carthaginians withdrew made a V, at the tips of which the heavy African squares on the flanks stood firm.

The Roman center, pushing up through swirling dust, found itself pent in by narrowing slopes where their elusive foes struck down at them. It was now entering the V of the flanking slopes. The legions, pressing on, crushed together. Before long only the front-rank men at either side could wield their weapons. Those in the middle could only push against their comrades. By the second hour all the legions had entered the V. It was as if two great doors swung inward before them, from the hinges held fast by the heavy African infantry. The legions on the flanks turned to assault the Africans savagely. They were thirsty by then and tiring in the heat.

"They fought at a double disadvantage; they were hemmed in while their enemies ranged on every side of them; they were tired while they faced those who were fresh and strong."

So at midmorning the center fought to gain the high ground around it, oblivious of what took place elsewhere. There was no commander observing the battle as a whole to warn it of its danger.

At the far left of the Carthaginians, Hanno's heavy cavalry column plunged forward at sight of the smoke signal. It thundered at a gallop straight for the Roman horse at that end. Here, under Aemilius, the Romans had been trotting forward between the infantry and the river. Caught at a slow pace, they could not maneuver on the river side. Nor could they stand the impact of greater numbers on their narrow front.

Under the Carthaginian charge the Roman horse broke back. Aemilius, swept with part of his men against the nearest legion, ordered the survivors with him to dismount, to form a flank with the legion. This added to the disorder when riderless horses plunged into the lines of the legionaries. Aemilius himself fell, wounded by a slingstone, and refused the offer of a mount to carry him out of the action. He did not live long after that.

The tide of Hanno's horsemen swept on. It drove the broken Roman heavy cavalry back, and into the corner where the river flowed into the sea. There the remnants of Aemilius' command disbanded into fugitives.

Hanno had carried out the first of his orders. Now he brought his cavalry wing under control, to carry out his second order. This was to do something almost fantastic—to circle to the other end *behind* the Roman legions.

On that flank, not far from Hannibal's lookout, the Numidians had engaged the allied cavalry wing in their customary fashion of swift attack and withdrawal, throwing iron javelins with either hand, guiding their racing horses with their knees. There, too, Carthalo had created a disturbance with a special unit of 500 horsemen who rode over to Varro's command as if to desert to the Romans.

Once inside Varro's lines, the pretended deserters drew concealed weapons and launched an attack of their own.

While contending in this way with tactics of sheer deception, Varro's wing was struck in the rear by Hanno's victorious Spaniards. The surprise must have unsettled them as much as the shock of the charge of the Carthaginian heavy horse.

Caught between the circling Numidians and the onset of the enemy behind them, the allied cavalry tried to free themselves by gaining open ground. So they were driven farther from the battlefield. The retreat became a race to escape. Varro lost all control over his squadrons. He was carried away by a few who stuck by him.

"At Cannae the Consul who fled was accompanied by no more than fifty men; the other Consul, dying, had almost all the army with him."

By noon there were no Roman horsemen left between the ridge of Cannae and Hannibal's mount. There the Roman legions struggled, packed into a solid mass.

Then for the third time the Carthaginian heavy cavalry came back to the battle. It came like a whirlwind behind the legions of the center and charged into the crowded mass of men on foot. The Numidians were led around by Maharbal to close the escape gap toward the river.

The legionaries, still numbered by the tens of thousands, were encircled. Caught in the depression of the plain between the Carthaginians on the crest and the horsemen sweeping from the river to the sea, they formed their columns to break out. The ground was against them, the speed of the terrible riders against them. Probably by then their own weariness was the greatest enemy.

The columns dwindled to cohorts backed against their standards. They fought on courageously, without hope. By the end of the afternoon most of them were dead on the plain where they had begun their attack. Two thousand climbed to shelter in the ruins of Cannae village. There they were surrounded by Maharbal's horsemen, and they gave up their arms. By then all other fugitives were far from the river, seeking hiding places from the pursuing horsemen.

Toward sunset Hannibal rode over the plain. As he passed, the officers of his people joined him. They exulted as they reported full success. The evidence of it was clear to Hannibal's eye. The huge army of Aemilius and Varro had dissolved into fugitive bands. To his officers the victory seemed all but incredible.

Hannibal ordered the wounded Carthaginians to be searched for and carried to the physicians' tents. When he heard that a Roman Consul had been killed, he ordered the body to be found and buried fittingly with its weapons and insignia.

His men begged him to rest. Hannibal said that a good meal—everything the cooks had at hand—must be prepared, with wine, for men of all ranks.

Maharbal then spoke up. The veteran of Hamilcar's day had a hatred of all things Roman. "Hannibal, in five days you can feast in the city of Rome," he said fiercely. "My riders will go before you, and the Romans will know you have come before they know you are coming."

Hannibal looked at his old lieutenant. "That is easy to say and good to hear. Yet to think about it will take a long time."

Angrily Maharbal exclaimed, "Hannibal, you have many gifts from the gods but not all. You know how to win a victory, not how to use one!"

To this Hannibal made no answer. He repeated his command for all the men to be fed. Then, at the end of his ride of inspection, he returned to his knoll to sleep by the sentries.

The Morrow of Cannae

The son of Hamilcar had drawn that great mobilization of Roman strength to its doom by almost imperceptible steps. He had laid a trail for it to follow, from the Carthaginian outpost deserted in apparent flight, to the visible flight of the highly mobile Moorish riders, toward the Carthaginian encampment that he had moved at the last moment to the battlefield that he had selected, with the seasonal sirocco wind at the backs of the Carthaginians, and the coast at the backs of his enemies. Ironically—as it appears afterward—at Cannae his forces lay between the Romans and their city. As at Trasimeno, his enemies had a barrier of water behind them, and the Adriatic was very much larger than the lake.

The Roman commanders, intent on bringing the Carthaginians to battle, had followed him blindly and had deployed their forces on the last day almost as if Hannibal had directed their movements. It is said that one Consul, Aemilius, had not been willing to cross the Aufidus to the open plain where the Carthaginian cavalry could maneuver at will. Yet he had done so.

Long afterward, when the record of history was rewritten in the days of the early Empire, a scapegoat for the disaster was found in Terentius Varro, "the demagogue and butcher's son." The reason: since the two Consuls gave orders on alternate days, and Varro was in supreme authority that day, he insisted on entering battle against the will of Aemilius. That fable has endured until today, thanks to Livy's eloquence. No one asked, apparently, why eight Roman legions obeyed the orders of such a fool. Actually Varro had common sense enough; he did quite well in command of one legion in the following years. If blame is to be fastened on individuals, it must be shared among the Aemilian leaders; Aemilius Paulus and Servilius and Minucius all had experience in command of armies, while Varro had not. However, all three of them died at Cannae.

They and Varro as well had merely carried out the direct order of the Senate and the Roman People—the order given 200 miles away—to stop Hannibal's depredations and bring him to a battle of decision. But that is not the stuff of which official history is made in an age of military grandeur. Varro joined the other commoner, Flaminius, as the scapegoat for Roman disaster.

The disaster at Cannae was far-reaching. More than 50,000 Romans died there. Captives on the field numbered some 3,000 foot and 1,500 horsemen. Of 33 military tribunes, 29 were lost, with 80 senators, and most of those of praetorian rank. Almost the entire *equites* order perished. (When the Senate convened again at Rome, 177 vacancies had to be filled by impromptu appointments.)

The next morning revealed the extent of the disaster—"a carnage ghastly even to the gaze of our enemies. There lay those thousands and thousands of Romans, mingled without order, as chance had brought them together. Here and there rose up a bleeding figure whose wounds throbbed with the chill of dawn. Some were discovered lying there still alive, with thigh tendons slashed from behind. These bared their throats, bidding their conquerors drain off the last of their blood."

The Carthaginian loss had been 5,710 in killed and wounded.

The news reached Rome only in rumors at first. As usual in such cases the rumors were brought in by civilian spectators or travelers on the road who had all seen or heard something terrifying. The city itself had few officials left in it because most of them had gone with the army. Crowds began to collect at the gates and the temples, and anxious wives thronged from the isolation of their homes into the streets.

Fabius, the ex-Dictator, took immediate charge, appointing two praetors to act for the missing quorums of senators and judges. He sent couriers south and east to reach army officers and find out the truth in the rumors and report to the praetors. The first messengers returned with unbelievable tidings: *there was no encampment to be found; there was no longer an army command; there was no longer an army*.

Probably no one except Quintus Fabius Maximus could have accepted the certainty of disaster and set about remedying it within the hour. His first act was to check the growing panic, and restore some order within the walls. Commands went out to the street guards "to keep married women off the streets—make them stay in their homes; restrain families from lamentation. Maintain silence in the city. Bring bearers of news at once before the praetors. Every citizen must wait in his home for information affecting him."

Almost every family had a member or relative in the vanished army. No one was allowed to pass out of the city, and guards appeared at all gates to stop the flight of panic-stricken families. Fabius withheld the casualty lists that came in to the praetors, while he created a thin illusion of security within the walls of Rome. He also invoked the supernatural again to distract the populace; being a member of the college of augurs, he had means to do so. It was announced that prodigies in the past year revealed the anger of the gods. The prodigies, to be sure, were merely the behavior of two Vestal virgins, keepers of the sacred fire, who had been convicted of loss of chastity. Since one of the Vestals had committed suicide and the other had been buried alive at the Collina Gate, there was no more to be done with them. Fabius had the convenient Sibylline Books—the Books of Fate—consulted again. Announcement was made that the Books called for extraordinary sacrifices.

"Among others a Gallic man and woman and a Greek man and woman were buried alive in the Cattle Market in a pit walled with stone defiled in past times by human victims."

Was this ancient barbaric sacrifice a symbolic destruction of the enemies of Rome? In any case, it served to quiet the populace. As soon as the ritual atonement had been carried out, cohorts were summonned in from Ostia at the Tiber's mouth, and 8,000 able-bodied slaves purchased to bear arms, while boys of seventeen and younger were enlisted. Four legions were got together and houses and temples stripped of weapons to arm the recruits.

By then the casualties were known, and mourning filled the city until women clawed their way to the temple doors, to wipe the altar steps with their unbound hair. Fear replaced uncertainty among the plebeian folk. Their dread was of one man, Hannibal. Where would he march? What would he destroy next? For the first time the whisper went from door to door: *Hannibal ad portas.* At the gates of Rome.

Why did not the Carthaginian army march on Rome the day after the overwhelming victory at Cannae? Modern scholars have debated the question. It was raised by Livy, who offers us a picture of a despairing city awaiting the attack that did not come because Hannibal did not seize his chance to gain final victory. His decision, as Livy presents it, saved the city. For in those critical days of August "the Phoenician was sitting still at Cannae haggling over the ransom of his prisoners and the rest of the booty, showing neither the spirit of a conqueror nor the action of a great commander."

The Phoenician, however, understood much better than the historian the situation confronting him on the morrow of Cannae. Outside of Rome there remained strong hostile forces. Some 17,000 survivors of the battle had taken shelter in the adjacent Roman camps; garrisons still held strategic towns; Roman legions held the Po frontier and the base in Sicily, while the army of the Scipios operated in Spain. The fleets that kept the seas had trained soldiers aboard.

As for laying siege to Rome, Hannibal lacked skilled engineers and machines, both of which the Romans possessed. His Gauls would not do siege work; his splendid cavalry could not be used against walls. To invest Rome it would be necessary to close the mouth of the Tiber by a blockading fleet, and this meant that Carthaginian warcraft must first drive the enemy galleys from the coast.

Until now Hannibal's strategy had been to draw enemy armies into the field against his own and to maneuver them into situations where brains alone counted in the result. He had kept from assaulting any Roman fortified position. A movement against the city of Rome would bring the Carthaginians into Latium, the area of hostile concentration, where a siege would immobilize his army against a wall. To rely on speed—as Maharbal had urged—to gain entry to the city by surprise, meant forced marches for 200 miles. And Cannae had not been such a sweep to victory as Trasimeno. Ten hours of close combat with hand weapons had taken its toll of the Carthaginian heavy infantry. How many men were fit to march away the next day? How many horses had regained strength enough to trot? How were the supply animals to be hurried over the trails of the Appennines? What numbers would be left to care for the injured, to guard their prisoners and left to capture the Roman camps with their windfalls of impedimenta?

Only Hannibal knew the answers to those questions. The one thing he could not do was to risk the loss of his army. Quite naturally, then, he remained at the Aufidus

River. But he was getting much more done than Livy pictured him doing.

Carthalo Goes to Rome

The Carthaginian camp overlooked the sun-warmed Adriatic, where great ships seldom appeared. After daylight on the fourth of August two swift galleys put out from a cove on the shore and turned south to speed with oar and sail to carry the news of Cannae to Syracuse and across to Carthage. At the same time couriers started north by the unfrequented coastal road to carry messages to the chieftains of the Boii and Insubres. The messages declared that the last barrier had been broken down, the last army annihilated, and the way was now open for the revolt of the peoples of Italy.

On the Aufidus the Carthaginians spent the morning of August 4 in collecting the valuables from the battlefield—weapons, shields, jewels, amulets of the dead soldiers and seal rings of the *equites*. Hannibal ordered a trench run between the smaller Roman camp and the river, to keep the garrison there from water. In the afternoon the 7,000 Romans who had taken shelter in the camp surrendered on Hannibal's promise that they would be released after payment of ransom. Across the river a brisk skirmish took place around the larger Roman encampment that contained the engines and supply train. After a little 8,000 unwounded legionaries laid down their arms, on terms of ransom. They were hemmed in, exhausted, and they had lost 2,000 of their number. Few officers remained alive among them.

Hannibal addressed these officers without animosity. He said: "You may think I am carrying out a work of extermination. But that is not true. I am fighting for dominion. That dominion has been claimed by the Roman Senate and its dictators everywhere from New Carthage to Sicily. Now I mean to have it. You have fought honorably, and you will be free as soon as your ransom is paid. I want you to be witnesses to what I have said."

In particular, their price was set at 500 *denarii* for a horseman, 300 for a foot soldier, 100 for a slave. Those who had been recruited from allied territory were released as usual without payment. Hannibal's new liberality to the Roman citizens may have had a double purpose. He wanted to see the effect of their return on the Senate and public opinion; and he needed the ransom money. For the first time he had ordered that all silver taken from the battlefield be turned into the army treasury, which was, of course, his own. By now most of the bullion in his chests had been paid out in wages and costs; he had been cut off from the silver supply in Spain.

Hannibal showed courtesy in making arrangements for the ransoming of the legionaries. Ten spokesmen were released to go to Rome to raise the money. They gave him their pledge to return to the Carthaginian camp, and he asked no greater surety than that. But he sent one Carthaginian with them, Carthalo.

To Carthalo he gave specific instructions: if in Rome the officials showed any inclination toward peace, Carthalo was to offer them fair terms.

At this point, then, while Italy became conscious of the stunning blow of Cannae, Hannibal made his first overture to a compromise peace with the Senate and the Roman People. He was to make only one more offer, under very different circumstances. In this case he did not have long to wait. Carthalo returned alone within a few days. He had been met at the Alban Hills by a lictor who informed him that the new Dictator would not allow him or any Carthaginian within the gates of the city. Carthalo was given until sunset to leave Roman territory. After a much longer delay nine of the ten envoys of the legionaries returned. The tenth man had broken his pledge. And the Senate, after due debate, had refused to pay Hannibal for any captives of Cannae.

Perhaps Hannibal had expected no more than that; yet he may have hoped that he could end the remorseless attrition of the battlefields. In all probability he was willing to have peace after Cannae.

By then it was clear that some Roman elements had escaped. A hardheaded officer had persuaded 600 men to break out of the smaller camp that first night. Elsewhere, a youth of society, young Publius Scipio, had found his way at night to a band of officers who were convinced that the war was lost and the best thing to do would be to get out of the country to Sicily. Young Scipio made a dramatic gesture, laying his sword before them and saying that it was for anyone who wanted to escape. They picked up stragglers to follow them.

In the end some 10,000 got together with Varro, the surviving Consul, in the road junction of Venusia, and they reported to Rome that they were ready to take the field again.

When Varro himself returned to Rome for consultation, Fabius met him at the Via Sacra and thanked him in public for not despairing of the Roman state. Varro, as the surviving Consul, publicly named the new Dictator, an elderly ex-Censor (last of the Roman Dictators).

A psychosis of desperation gripped the city itself. Criminals and debtors were released from the prisons to take up arms. Almost all women wore mourning, and spat at those who did not. Buteo, the Dictator, laid a ban on feasting and games. A wealthy merchant who happened to be seen on his balcony wearing a banquet wreath was taken before magistrates, who sentenced him to prison. He stayed there for the duration of the war, fourteen years.

In such an atmosphere of hysteria the ten spokesmen of the prisoners at Cannae had at last gained a hearing before the newly convened Senate. An anxious throng of relatives pressed after them into the Curia. Rumor had it that the ten would be censured for conduct unbecoming Roman soldiers, and that the treasury lacked money to pay their ransom. Once admitted to judgment, however, they were entitled to trail by due process of law.

Those who spoke for the prisoners offered arguments on all the issues in question.

The ransom money, if it could not be spared from the treasury at this critical time, would be paid by the families of the accused.

At this time, when criminals were being taken into the legions, these thousands of trained soldiers would be invaluable to aid the state.

As to precedents for their ransoming—had not

prisoners, Roman citizens, in such case been bought back from the Gauls, and Pyrrhus and even the city of Tarentum in recent times?

Their conduct was in no way unbecoming Romans, because they had been cut off in the camps, without water; they had not surrendered until, exhausted and wounded, they had nothing to gain by further resistance.

In summing up, the defense spokesmen asked the Fathers to think of the honor of these men. They asked only for the privilege of serving under arms again. "Will the conscript Fathers deny them that privilege and cast them off to become Hannibal's slaves?"

When the arguments for the defense ended, there was a demonstration from the crowd in the Curia, and a general appeal for mercy. Many senators, who had relatives among the captives, asked for it.

Torquatus, an old man distinguished in the conquest of the Boii, rose to speak against it.

He argued only one point, the conduct of the accused.

It was the duty of Roman soldiers, Torquatus stated, to follow their officers without taking thought of their lives. Had these men done so? During the night after the battle, a tribune had called on all those in one of the camps to follow him to break out through the Carthaginians. Six hundred had followed the tribune, weapons in hand, to safety and then rejoined the standards of the surviving Consul. The thousands who remained in the camps had chosen to put their lives above their duty. They had done so at a time when fifty thousand brave men lay dead on the battlefield around them. It was not, Torquatus exclaimed, by the cowardice of these accused men but by the courage of the slain fifty thousand that the ancient Roman spirit had been maintained.

The accused had surrendered in the broad light of day, with weapons still in their hands and ramparts still in front of their bodies. They had bargained for their lives against payment of a sum of money to enrich Hannibal.

"No, Conscript Fathers, I would no more vote for the ransoming of these men than I would vote for giving up the six hundred who cut their way out through the midst of their enemies."

The Senate then voted to refuse ransom for the

prisoners. Nine of the ten spokesmen accordingly returned to Cannae to report the refusal to Hannibal. When the Senate learned that one of the pleaders had broken his pledge to go back, he was searched out and sent under guard to the Carthaginian camp.

(As it happened, Hannibal got his payment for the captives before long from the slave dealers of Delos. And the hearing in the Curia gained such notoriety that all survivors of the field of Cannae became marked men. They were formed eventually into two legions to serve without pay as garrisons in Sicily, where they were forbidden to build their winter quarters within a day's walk of any town. Quite soon Varro was given command of one of these legions under stigma! At the same time the Censors sought out and punished all officers who had talked of leaving Italy. So unyielding was the Roman code of warfare.)

All that month of August the city mustered its resources to defend its walls at the coming of Hannibal. He went, instead, to Naples.

"The Loyalty of the Allies Began to Waver."

In contrast to the happenings in Rome, silence covers the plan of Hannibal and the consequent deliberations of the Council of Carthage until the end of this year. The silence is deeper than usual and most difficult to penetrate at this late day. Yet the reported events make up a pattern, and the fragmentary pattern does yield the outline of a far-reaching plan.

Observe what happens in the larger scene of the western Mediterranean during these months after August.

A few days after Cannae two Carthaginian fleets appear off Sicily. One of them skirts the harbor of Syracuse without apparent purpose, and disappears. Disturbed, the Roman naval commander at this island base asks reinforcement from the Senate in Rome and even in that hour of disaster 25 galleys are sent him with a directive to take what action he sees fit "for the good of the state." The

Roman commands, then, are watching the critical, narrow sea between Syracuse and Carthage.

This is just before the death of Hiero II, octogenarian tyrant of Syracuse, who sent the gold statue of Victory to the Senate. Carthaginian agents have been active in Syracuse, and presently Greek officials of the city declare for Carthaginian rule instead of Roman.

More than 500 miles to the north the Boii and Insubres entrap the Roman border army, 25,000 strong, overrunning it and killing its commander. One legion of this army had been made up of freed slaves.

After that—and probably informed of it—Hannibal marches from the shore of the Adriatic that has served him so well. With the Carthaginian army goes the captured supply train of Varro's army, with the Eagles and the fasces of the two Consuls. As if in procession he threads through the Apennine hills. Some cities close their gates, but the peasants of Apulia—the region of Cannae—and hardy Samnites gather to pledge peace with him. Down on the west coast Greek cities hail him. Delegates from proud Capua arrive at his camp to discuss terms. Hannibal grants all they ask—freedom as a city, protection, and no service in the war. ("If you gain a victory, even those who hate you will hold to you.")

But he leads the victorious army down to Naples, the great port of the southern coast.

Reaching the sea he sends his young brother Mago speeding to Carthage. There, at the assembled Council, Mago gives a full report of Cannae, and the allegiance won from Apulia, Samnium, and Calabria—severing the south entirely from central Italy. Mago pours out from a basket 6,000 gold seal rings of Roman nobles, collected at Cannae.

He asks in return a minimum aid to be sent Hannibal, 4,000 Numidian horse, 40 elephants, and a sum of silver talents.

There are objections from antagonists of the Barca family. If Hannibal is indeed victorious, they demand, why has he need of money and men? What else would he ask if he were defeated? If he has indeed vanquished so many of the enemy armies, why does not Rome offer to come to terms? But the Council votes decisively to send the required aid to Hannibal.

It also votes to muster and send larger forces—24,000 foot and horse—to Spain.

Here the pattern takes an odd twist. Why should the greater aid be sent with Mago (who serves as diplomat for the older brothers) to Spain, where the versatile Hasdrubal is doing well enough in fending off the army of the two Scipios? The explanation, however, is simple. With such a reinforcement, Hasdrubal can, if the gods favor him, break through the Roman line of the Ebro, and follow his brother's route over the Alps in the coming summer, into Italy.

From these fragments, Hannibal's plan for all theaters of the Mediterranean war can be conjectured. His peace offer was rejected. After Cannae he had no fear of meeting another Roman major army for a long time. Roman naval power, however, still held the sea barrier between him and Carthage. He was drawing closer to Sicily, won over by a bloodless political revolution. Yet the Roman battle fleets with legionaries aboard them barred the way from his Carthaginians in southern Italy to Sicily and Carthage itself.

Still, reinforcements of small numbers of Numidians and elephants might be slipped across in separate vessels to reach him in the Gulf of Taranto or the Bay of Naples. Hasdurbal could take the land route he had opened, to reach the Gauls who were now in command of the Po. In doing so they would reopen the vital road to Spain.

And by another year another Carthaginian fleet would put to sea carrying an expeditionary force to the great island of Sardinia.

As winter drew near Hannibal must have felt a certain excitement, a sense of vindication. Two years before he had led 26,000 exhausted men down from the Alps into a strange and hostile land. One year more and the dream of the Barcas might be realized, with Carthage again mistress of the western sea, in possession again of the shores of Spain, Sicily, and Sardinia. While Hannibal in southern Italy held Roman land power at bay.

At this point—marching through Campania—he struck

131

his first blow at Roman sea power. The enemy battle fleets, which must in some way be overcome, depended on their fighting forces of legions. Could these still be spared, after Cannae? Hannibal could not tell. But he knew that the fleets also depended on their bases at Syracuse, Naples, Tarentum, Locri, Rhegium and other places. Already Syracuse was lost to them, while his army made haste to Naples. More than that, the crews of the fleets all came from the *socii navales* of those same ports. The Greek and Sicilian crewmen were loyal to their home cities, more than to distant, dominant Rome.

When the son of Hamilcar came in sight of Naples he found that the small city on the bluff had manned its defenses against him. With winter at hand he would not undertake a siege of a port open to supply by sea. At once he turned away to lead his army to Capua, queen city of the southland.

Capua meant more to him than comfortable winter quarters. It could be the capital of a new alliance against the city of Rome.

IV. Struggle of the Two Alliances

"It Is the Most Blessed of All Plains."

When Hannibal entered the gate of Capua under the winter sunset he put aside his role of warrior to become a diplomat. Here he held by a silken thread the wealthiest city of Italy. When he dismounted at the terrace of a palatial home, of the Celeres brothers, he asked if the city council would meet with him, and the throng of Capuan nobles protested. They wanted no intrusion of business in this eventful meeting with the Carthaginian conqueror. They wanted to show Hannibal the sights of the city. Humoring them, he went from terrace to terrace set with figures of Greek gods all looking to the east. Beneath them to the west stretched a plain entirely green, yielding, the Capuans said, the sulphur waters good to the taste and remedial to sickness. "It is the most blessed of all plains," they declared, "for its grapes yield Falernian wine."

After that Hannibal invited the chiefs of the nobles to dine with him after sunset in the house he was to occupy. He spoke with them fluently in Greek, enjoying it after the hard dialects of the midlands. He showed them the courtesy he had learned in Iberian homes while he studied their minds. They had pride, perhaps too much. Capua had been founded by the Eltruscans, the first city of Italy when Rome was merely a town on the Tiber fighting with its neighbors. Capua was still as large as the Tiber city that had subordinated it as a *civitas sine jure*, without law of its own. Had there been, he asked, a leader of the Roman faction here? (He knew that many of these noble families had intermarried with the Roman patricians.) Assured that the leader, a certain Decius, was held in chains in readiness for execution, Hannibal suggested that he be sent instead to Carthage. He promised them that the day would soon come when Capua would enforce laws of its own.

They wondered why he sat to eat on a low stool, instead of reclining with them at the table. He explained that he had grown unaccustomed to lying down. Whatever Hannibal decided as to the minds of the Capuans, he had joy in their hospitality beneath quiet roofs. Around him men talked again of healing by medicine of Galen; they showed him manuscripts copied by skilled hands in the Alexandria Musaeum, or geometric drawings from the hand of aged Archimedes. True, they talked lying down, wine bowls in their fingers; they seemed to be Epicureans rather than Stoics, they lied politely when they swore that his date wine—brought in treasured jars from Carthage—was superior to their Falernian; but they gave him friendship without restraint, taking no thought that he was an African. As if by chance the son of Hamilcar left the captured fasces, symbols of the authority of Flaminius, Varro, and Aemilius, lying on the marble paving of the atrium of the house of the Celeres brothers.

Above Capua toward the sunset stood a bald mount called Tifata. Here Hannibal placed his own pavilion and set his army headquarters guarded by African shield bearers. He chose to appear within Capua as a guest. Although the army actually occupied the city, he ordered men of all units to pay in coin for their feasting and women and souvenirs. They had plenty of silver in their moneybelts, from Roman as well as Spanish mints. From Tifata he had observation over much of the lovely Campanian plain stretching to the sacred promontory of Sorrento (Surrentum) past the ashgray summit of smoking Vesuvius and the small fishing town of Pompeii

(Pompaia), where the old people carved red coral into amulets. That same gray ash of Vesuvius, fertilized by rains, enriched the soil of the shore until it produced the finest wine grapes and figs.

Restless even in this haven of winter warmth, Hannibal took long exploratory rides across the plain. He had a good view of Cuma (Cumae), the oldest of seaports, where warm vapor rising from Plutonian caverns served to heat the public baths. With an escort of hand-picked Numidians, all good pipers in clean white wool cloaks, he rode up into the valley where Fabius had trapped him for a day and the oxen had helped him escape. It amused the conqueror from Carthage to find sluggish peasants sowing winter wheat—the Campanian soil yielded at least two yearly crops—staring at him as if he were a ghost of the battle that had passed by. With more than amusement Hannibal reflected that he had turned the table upon the Delayer since then. Two years before, the astute Fabius had relied upon time as his greatest ally. Now the Carthaginian could afford to delay, and time itself had become a peril to his enemies, who must find grain for their city and men for new armies at once.

Then, too, after the last two punishing winters, his Iberians rejoiced in the warmth of Campania, where good grazing for the horses lay on all sides. This plain resembled their beloved valley of the Betis. His Carthaginians also had a tie with southern Italy; for centuries past—since the Etruscan trading ports had risen at the river mouths—the African merchants had frequented the shores, especially the Gulf of Taranto. In fact, such trade still went on, running the enemy blockade.

Old acquaintances visited Hannibal when he returned to the Tifata post. Delegates of the Bruttian mountain men journeyed from the tip of Italy to offer rude gifts of carved wood and painted pottery they had filched from Greek artisans. Bruttians had served Hamilcar as mercenaries on Mount Eryx, and they knew the name of Hannibal, the lion cub. They were curious to discover how the lion cub had arrived near their fortress at the end of Italy and what he intended to do there.

Before the first winter passed, Hannibal had won the allegiance of some Picentine peasants from the Adriatic shore, of most of the dour Samnites—who chose service to him as overlord rather than pillage by his horsemen— and the Lucanians and Bruttians of the south. There was a deep-seated instinct behind this allegiance. The Apulians, Lucanians, and Bruttians had joined in the last war of independence against the Republic on the Tiber. So had the Greek merchants and artisans of many cities of the littoral. Not a few grandfathers who watched Hannibal pass by remembered when Tarentum had been a free city. The spirit of that time, of the Magna Graecia, still lived. The ways of the countryside, unlike Etruscanland, were still unchanged. The coming of the Roman praetors had benefited the noble class and landowners, not the impoverished peasantry or the common folk of the towns.

In this way, after his rides of inspection, Hannibal realized that the majority of the lower orders favored him, while most of the nobles did not. Then, too, inland, Magna Graecia supported the Carthaginian army of occupation, while the richer coastal cities—in touch with the Roman fleets—held fast to Rome. Of these, Naples was by far the most important. Without the great port of Naples (allied as an equal to Rome) and control of the vast bay, the possession of Capua signified little except as a rest camp for the army. If Naples could not be won over or besieged, it might be isolated from its land communications. Hannibal set about to devise a way to do that.

He understood the questioning raised by his strange presence as overlord without a title. The people around him wondered if he would prove to be another Pyrrhus, dragging the countryside into combat, to be defeated in the end and to sail off alone from their shores. What ultimate purpose did he conceal from them?

Hannibal explained with care that he was no adventuring monarch but the commander of the armed forces of Carthage. He pledged his word that Carthage in Africa sought no territory here in southern Italy, and that he himself would not leave them until their former independence had been established beyond danger of reconquest by the Roman Republic.

Aware that a simple pledge signified little to the troubled peasantry and the Greek-enlightened citizenry, he gave proof of his policy by action. Borderline strategic cities were allowed to make their choice; their people might remain as a member of the new alliance, or, if they held to allegiance to Rome, they might depart unmolested with their belongings for Roman territory. One walled town near Naples chose evacuation. Exasperated, Hannibal loosed his troops to plunder and burn the deserted abodes.

Locri was a small harbor town on the crest of a hill within the southern Gulf of Taranto. Here the inhabitants started to leave in panic. Hannibal ordered Hanno's horsemen not to injure the crowd but to take post between it and the town gate. After debating their fate in such circumstances, the Locrians yielded to Hannibal. They kept the harbor while the Carthaginians occupied the hill. (If he had lost Naples, he had gained a debarkation port, well hidden, in Locri.) Soon afterward Bomilcar—who may have been Hanno's father—brought a small convoy of ships in from Carthage to Locri. The ships landed the reinforcement of Numidians with their horses, and the 40 elephants for Hannibal. How the elephants were put ashore is not explained; probably they waded in from beached vessels.

At last the army of Italy had regained touch with Carthage by sea.

It is well, by now, to call Hannibal's followers the army of Italy. Hanno son of Bomilcar made a recruiting trip through the hills behind Locri and brought in 10,000 hardy Bruttians to serve his master. With their addition Hannibal's forces became a composite of the peoples of the western Mediterranean shores, from Numidia through Liguria to the tip of the peninsula at Bruttium. And as he had done that winter before Cannae, Hannibal set himself to train and arm the newcomers. This time he allowed his veterans of the Alps to rest.

That circumstance created another proverb of the war, to add to "Fabian tactics." This was "a Capuan winter." Their first luxurious winter quarters with baths at hand and slaves to wait upon them had its effect on the veterans from Spain; they were not thereafter the same men who fought swamp sickness to win the triumph of

137

Trasimeno. Livy joined together his three antipathies—his hatred of Hannibal, and of Capua the great city that revolted, and of all common classes—to draw a picture for history to preserve of Carthaginian soldiers emasculated by vices of the treacherous place besotted "by the unbridled liberty of the lower classes." He coined one of his apt phrases: "Capua was Hannibal's Cannae." Yet however the veterans may have been affected by their winter quarters around Capua, they were not the same again in action chiefly for the reason that Hannibal never used them in the same tactics again. After Cannae he was fighting a very different war.

That winter ended with a triumph of another sort. In response to his message after Cannae envoys from Philip V of Macedonia crossed the Adriatic to reach him. Hannibal seems to have feasted them royally in his new city. A treaty was drawn by which Carthage and Macedonia united their forces against Rome and each state pledged itself to aid the other if attacked. In particular, Hannibal agreed that the Dalmatian coast would be freed from Roman occupation and returned to Philip's rule.

Then other Greeks arrived, to send a wave of excitement through Capua. They came from the youthful grandson of the dead Hiero, from Syracuse, "the greatest of cities and most beautiful of the Greek cities." Syracuse (where Carthaginian agents had done their work) desired to become the ally of Hannibal. Again a unilateral treaty for mutual defense was written, and this time it was signed.

Thus Hannibal became the field commander of the alliance of Carthage and Macedonia and Syracuse. His army of Italy, grouped around Tifata, cut off Rome from communication by land with Sicily. Yet the fleets of the Republic were still masters of the sea routes through the Tyrrhenian Sea, the Gulf of Taranto, and the Adriatic, and—most vital of all—the tide-ripped Strait of Messina. However, the matchless harbor and the shipping of Syracuse were lost to those cruising fleets. The two strong bases of Naples (on the Tyrrhenian Sea) and Tarentum (on the Gulf) still served them and their crews. Hannibal now gave thought to Tarentum as well as Naples.

Every month of fair weather more fighting galleys sailed from the inner harbor of Carthage to take the sea.

Behind this struggle of the two alliances, Roman and Carthaginian, lay the ancient cleavage of the Mediterranean itself. The south stood against the north, the somnolent culture of the Hellenistic world against the rule of militant barbarism. And now in final conflict the dying city-states opposed themselves to the force of a single emerging empire.

It is safe to say that Hannibal was aware of this larger aspect of the conflict. It is certain that, in these years, Rome was conscious only of its increasing danger.

"The Sea Was Seen to Be Aflame."

Omens taken at the new year very much disturbed the augurs on the Via Sacra. In a temple of Juno the images dripped blood; a cow gave birth—it was said—to a colt; the outer sea was seen to be aflame.

Oddly enough, as happened after Trasimeno, lesser disasters shocked the city on the Tiber more than the calamity of Cannae. The news of the loss of the legions guarding the Po and the appearance of Hannibal in adjacent Calabria fairly shook the confidence of Roman citizens in their Fortune. The number of their allies had narrowed, almost beyond belief, to the cities of Latium itself, the Sabines of ancient days, the Umbrians and almost forgotten Etruscans.

Upon the loyalty of these remaining allies hung the fate of Rome itself. That year (215) the Senate was forced to levy a double tax on them, and a double conscription of manpower. To rouse the public to the new emergency Fabius called for a twofold dedication of new temples, and funeral games with 22 gladiators—twice the usual number.

He realized, as did many of the leaders of the Senate, that the Roman *imperium* over the allied peoples had a vital weakness as well as strength. Roman rule gave protection and viability; it drew the separate peoples together

139

in a vast whole that could become a united Italy; at the same time it offered to individuals advancement to Roman franchise with superior rights and privileges.

As yet only a minority, Roman citizens, held this franchise among the more numerous outer peoples. A Roman citizen possessed rights of marriage *(connubium)*, transacting business *(commercium)*, and voting *(suffragio)*. By law, he might exercise those rights throughout Italy, while the noncitizen could not do so. So the franchise became a prize, to be offered deserving foreigners, and at the same time it stirred the envy of those not so favored. And they were still the majority. Allied cities conducted their internal affairs as they pleased, subject to drafts of men and material at the yearly demand of the Senate. The Senate alone set the amount of the requisitions in each case. (A proposal, during this crisis, to seat the most deserving leaders of some allied cities among the conscript Fathers of Rome was voted down after indignant orations by the elder members.)

This differentiation between citizen and noncitizen became sharper in the army itself. Recruits from the allies lost all other identity when they entered a Roman training camp; they drew one half the pay of a legionary but furnished their own supplies. Allied troops made up 57 per cent of the armies. They served in the wings, not in the legions, under Roman officers who enforced discipline by scourging. This system had created the great national army of the Republic, and it worked well enough in a successful campaign where requisitions were light and the pittance pay could be eked out with spoils if not by the supreme reward of Roman citizenship. But two years of campaigning against Hannibal had yielded only casualties without spoils; draftees of that year in Roman training centers told each other that their best fate would be to get captured, while still alive, by the Carthaginians, who would feed them well and allow them to walk home again. Then, too, the towns of Etruria and Umbria protested bitterly against the year's requisition of corn, horses, and carts. Hannibal's marches had devastated their harvests, while the fields of Latium, the *ager Romanum*—territory of the Romans—remained untouched.

How could the allied towns furnish the twofold supplies demanded by the Senate and the Roman People?

Faced by defalcation among its allies, the Senate yielded not a particle of its demands. Deserters from the training camps were rounded up by military patrols, to be scourged at the stake before the ranks of their fellows. Some 370 were thrown later from the Tarpeian Rock on the Capitoline height. Punitive expeditions went southeast into the Samnite hills to restore order. Failure of allegiance was treated as treachery and punished as such. One general, Sempronius Gracchus—of the Claudian *gens*—led his troops against a sanctuary on a hill near Cuma, where the inhabitants had gathered in an all-night religious festival. The legionaries surrounded the torchlit shrine and cut down the throng of Campanians.

The impassive rigor of Roman leadership at this time of crisis did not spare citizens. Censors searched out any who complained. This tenacity in the face of disaster may have saved the Roman state; but it lost strategic cities to Hannibal. In the days after Cannae the Capuans had sent their delegates first to Varro, who was then collecting survivors at Venusia. The Capuans had affirmed their allegiance, offering supplies of grain, horses, and weapons to the distraught Consul. Unreasonably, Varro castigated them—demanding that they tell him how he was to use horses when he no longer had men to ride the beasts, and what avail were weapons when no legions remained? That might have been the angry reaction of an exhausted man. Varro, however, then called on the Capuans to equip 30,000 from their city to take the field against Hannibal. That was his reaction as Consul: to recall the defaulting city to its duty. In the end his stupid tirade stirred mistrust in the Capuans, and they left Varro to seek an agreement with Hannibal.

The city of Tarentum had been obliged to keep youths of its leading families in Rome as hostages for the behavior of the once rebellious community. Some time after Cannae the hostages tried to escape to the south. Eighty of them were recaptured and thrown from the Tarpeian Rock. The execution of the youths stirred wild anger in their families, and the Tarentines sent spokesmen to seek Hannibal at Tifata.

141

Tidings of the loss of Syracuse to the Carthaginians fairly shocked the leaders of the Senate. Syracuse was hallowed by legend and vast resources. The token statue of Victory, the gift of Syracuse, seemed to mock them with its gleaming gold. Were the immortal gods venting their anger against the city that served them? The island of Sardinia was in revolt. On his far coast the king of the Macedonians had made a treaty—senators had seen it in writing—with their archfoe the Carthaginian Barca.

Torquatus, preserver of the ancient spirit, was sent with a hastily assembled fleet to Sardinia.

Yet the fears of the superstitious did not equal the anxiety of the leaders who had less superstition than trust in the ancient order. That order had rested upon the solid base of an army superior to all enemies. Always, even in the black days of Gallic invasion and the battlefield triumphs of Pyrrhus, the final mobilization of Roman manpower had brought victory to the sacred Eagles and so to the city itself. The Roman leaders could imagine no other way of preserving the city. But would their last mobilization, now beginning, lead to anything other than a second Cannae? What means could they find to counteract the almost miraculous magistery of Hannibal on the battlefield?

Hitherto Rome had relied upon previous experience to achieve success. This custom, due to a lack of imagination, had gained almost the force of a law carved upon stone. But the Romans had had no previous experience with a mind like Hannibal's.

Already under the ceaseless questioning, some changes began to appear in the traditional Roman order. Fabius became Censor, and not a second dictator. "Misfortune prevented the Romans from delaying further." The Aemilian-Scipionic leaders—being for the most part, in any case, dead—lost their command of the Senate. They had favored plebeian consuls as well as conquest beyond the seas. "The gods did not will that plebeian consuls be elected." Even the election of patrician consuls came under question. What could be accomplished by such political commanders, serving for only one year, against Hannibal? (Fabius and the augurs worked the omens of thunder and behavior of the divine images to prevent one elec-

142

Miles 0 50 100 200 *palacios*

tion.) The popular assemblies ceased to put forward their candidates to win the war. "In the critical state of the nation" the Senate began to heed the warnings of experienced officers in the field. Two of them, Gracchus and Marcellus—a Claudian and a veteran commander—were given authority as proconsuls not limited to one year. Marcellus was to be known as "the sword of Rome."

Out of this soul-searching came the rudiment of an idea that was hardly a plan. It was to send men of proved ability to hold back Hannibal at every city wall, at every river, and especially in Sicily. Fabius took the field again.

Marcellus hastened to Nola, the outer defense of Naples. Hannibal had begun the siege of Nola.

The Gate of Tarentum Opens

Hannibal's new allies presented him with a complexity of problems. These had to be met by ingenuity as well as diplomacy. The Capuans, who had been pledged immunity from the war, greatly distrusted the presence of Samnites and Gauls, their ancient enemies, in the camps around them. The Gauls, although now resembling legionaries in their equipment, still had their old craving for plunder. Bruttian mountaineers expected to pillage the aristocratic Greeks of the seaports which were Hannibal's primary objective.

In fact after Locri fell to the Carthaginians, the Bruttii sent delegates to protest to Hannibal. They had enlisted, they said, to capture the ports, not to safeguard Greek merchants heavy with gold. Hannibal merely referred them to Hanno who directed operations on the southern shore. Dissatisfied, the Bruttians gathered together and assaulted Croton. This happened to be a strong little harbor, with the usual walled town on a hill, beside the promontory where stood an unusual sanctuary—that of the Lacinian Juno, where pilgrims left costly gifts behind and herders claimed that their animals were protected by the goddess from wild beasts. The Carthaginians desired neither the port nor the wealthy shrine to be gutted by the

144

irate mountaineers. Hanno arrived on the scene to post guards around the temple, and to remove the upper-class merchants from Croton to safety to Locri. The Bruttians were allowed to pillage the waterfront and deserted estates, while Carthaginian officers took over the harbor.

In this ceaseless marching through the network of southern towns to meet Roman columns landing from the sea, Hannibal had to rely on his lieutenants, Hanno and Maharbal especially, to command separate divisions. They served him well. The overlord of a Magna Graecia-to-be fairly lived on horseback—passing the stormy months of the second winter beyond Cannae on the Adriatic—while he kept the newer recruits and elephants with him. The veterans of the old army seem to have been spared heavy duty. He had not been able to keep his promise to them, to allow contingents of the Spaniards and Africans to return home, because the route over the Alps remained closed; nor could he allot them land in Italy as yet.

Hannibal still avoided assaulting a town defended by walls and engines; if he could not win over the inhabitants, he encircled the place, cutting off its food. Casilinum yielded from hunger despite the attempts of headstrong Gracchus to relieve it. But always Hannibal returned to Nola, the last town holding out on the roads into Naples; there the lower classes, favoring him, almost succeeded in throwing open the gates. ("One malady, so to speak, had entered all the city-states of Italy. The common people, at odds with the upper class, drew the state to the side of the Carthaginians.")

Deputies from the Samnites complained that Roman expeditions from Nola devastated their lands. For once Hannibal showed exasperation. "You complain to me," he assured them, "of everything that happens to you." But he led his division, largely of Bruttians, to besiege the wall of Nola. There he met a new tactic of vigorous defense at the hand of Marcellus. That seasoned commander executed 70 leaders of the populace, and guarded the gates closely while he sallied out unexpectedly with trumpets blowing and heavy cavalry at the gallop. The Carthaginian recruits hugged their trenches, dispirited by constant rain and the savage attacks of the legionaries. Hannibal stormed at them. "Do you claim to be an army of Carthaginians? Then act like one. Take Nola for me and I will lead you wherever you want to go."

For the first time his forces suffered heavier casualties than the Romans. More than that, 272 Numidians and Spaniards deserted to join Marcellus—on a promise of land to be given them. Marcellus had turned Hannibal's weapon of subversion against him. Then abruptly one night the Carthaginians disappeared from their trenches. The Roman general moved out very cautiously to discover what route they had taken. But Hannibal was far distant, hurrying through the hills toward Tarentum with two men of that city who had offered to let him into a gate.

Having failed at Naples and Nola, the Carthaginian would not let slip the chance to steal into the second largest port of the south. He prepared for the attempt with patient study of its details.

The young Tarentines seemed to be genuine. Both had lost relatives among the hostages at Rome. Philemenus, the more eager of the two, had set up a routine by which he could pass the guards of a postern gate at night; he had accustomed them to let him in from hunting, and to be handed some of his game when they did so. So far so good, but any slight mishap might stop such an entry at a single gate. Could the other youth, Nico, remain within the city, to lead sympathizers to another entry, and force it open at a signal from Hannibal? Nico could do that.

There was painstaking discussion of terms: the Carthaginians agreed not to garrison Tarentum or to demand any tribute. There was a minute study of the city streets leading to the market place, and on to the citadel on a height thrusting into the harbor. The Roman garrison withdrew into this citadel at night, except for the guards of the outer circuit wall. Hannibal verified the account of Philemenus and Nico by other agents, and agreed on a night and an hour of that night for the approach.

During the talks he had kept much to his sleeping couch and spread the rumor that he was ill to account for the delay in one camp. Numidians were sent out, as well, to raid the countryside as if for provisions. The night before the attempt he made a fast march with several thousand light-armed Gauls and Spaniards—accustomed to movement in darkness. The same 80 Numidian horsemen spread out in a screen around them, holding or killing any passers-by along the road. The picked force hid out for the day, behind the grazing cavalry (who had become a familiar sight by then in the region). During the evening, Hannibal let his swordsmen sleep. Before midnight he roused them to move out.

The detail of the approach is given in Roman annals.

"Hannibal's guide was Philemenus with the usual shoulder load of game. Soon they parted—Philemenus to lead armed men to his usual postern, Hannibal to approach the Temenitis Gate [main entry on the land side]. The Temenitis quarter has many tombs inside the walls. As he neared this gate Hannibal gave his signal by fire. Nico, seeing it, gave the same signal. Then both fires were put out. Hannibal led his men silently to the gate. Within it, Nico's band sprang on the sentries and killed many sleeping in their beds, and opened the gate. Hannibal ordered the horsemen with him to wait outside, to meet any enemy in the open. He entered with his infantry.

"And on the other side of the city Philemenus was approaching the postern by which he had been accustomed to come and go. His whistle and well-known voice aroused a sentry, who opened the little gate as Philemenus was saying they had a boar so large that two of them could hardly lift it. He himself followed it in with a huntsman who had his arms free. As the sentry tried to see the animal of such marvelous size he faced the men carrying it and Philemenus ran him through with a hunting spear. Then about thirty armed men rushed in, to kill the other sentries, and break open the adjacent gate. Through this rushed the column of Carthaginians. The Tarentine youths led them silently to the market place where Hannibal joined them. At once he sent Gauls through the city, in two companies with Tarentines to guide them. He ordered them to occupy the principal streets and, when the uproar began, to cut down any Romans but to spare Tarentine citizens. To aid in this, he told the guides to warn any of their own people they met to be quiet and fear nothing.

"Already an uproar had begun, but what it was about

no one in the city knew for certain. The Tarentines believed the Roman soldiers must be plundering the city; the Romans thought it was some kind of uprising treacherously started by the townspeople. Their commander, roused early in the confusion, escaped to a skiff in the harbor and was rowed around to the citadel. The confusion grew worse at a trumpet call from the theatre. For this was a Roman trumpet purloined by the traitors, and being sounded off unskillfully by a Greek, no one could tell who was giving the signal and to whom.

"When day broke, sight of the Punic and Gallic weapons ended the uncertainty of the Romans who had survived in the citadel. At the same time the Greeks who saw dead Romans everywhere realized that the city had been captured by Hannibal. He ordered all the citizens, except those who had followed the Romans into the citadel, to assemble without arms. Then he spoke to them with kind words, reminding them of how he had released their fellow citizens captured at Trasumennus and Cannae. He castigated the haughty rule of the Romans. At the end he bade each one go back to his home and write *Tarentine* on the door. After all doors were marked, he released his followers to plunder the houses of the Romans, and the booty was considerable."

This Robin Hood entry into Tarentum had been carried out with the forethought of a campaign. But it had not managed to win the citadel at the harbor's mouth, and from that stronghold the Romans were not to be dislodged. Hannibal had his major port at last without the ability to use it.

The Claws of Archimedes

On another night at another harbor a very different attack took place. In the hours of deepest sleep before dawn 60 penteconters moved with slow-swinging oars in to the Achradina or inner harbor wall of Syracuse. The leading vessels presented a strange appearance, being roped together in pairs, with only the outer oar banks rowing, moving thus like men in a three-legged race. The upper decks and rowing platforms of the great ships were packed with legionaries carrying heavy iron shields. In front of the bare masts, suspended there by ropes and pulleys, reared strange contrivances—heavy ladders rising from the foredeck with platforms projecting from the upper ends. When the ships so equipped touched against the sea wall of the city, these ladders would be swung against the summit of the wall and the heavily armed infantrymen would run up the ladders to gain footing on the wall. The legionaries would then cut their way to right and left and link up with others ascending from other assault craft. No Greeks of Syracuse would be able—past experience had shown—to hold their ground against legionaries armed with iron.

Between the pairs of ladder-bearing penteconters advanced vessels manned by bowmen, slingers, and the crews of the scorpions, or light stone projectors. Missiles from these escort vessels would cover the attack of the cohorts climbing the ladders. Behind the leading line followed penteconters with reinforcements to hold the wall and fan out along the harbor front.

This night attack from shipboard could not, of course, gain all of Syracuse, which consisted of three separate cities within an eleven-mile circuit of walls that often topped sheer cliffs. In fact, Syracuse had never been taken before by assault, and the Romans had heard rumors of its defensive engines invented by Archimedes, an eccentric stargazer, which might overpower the machines on their ships. But once entry into the harbor had been gained, the full force of the besieging army might be brought around by water and thrust into the city like a spear point pushing through an opening in armor.

The attack flotilla was commanded in person by Marcellus, who had led the army across the Straight of Messina. Marcellus had been ordered to capture Syracuse by any means and at any cost. He had been given this command "because he had not been defeated by Hannibal" at Nola. His second-in-command waited ashore at the besieging camp.

The sea was calm. The slight outer swell ceased as the fleet passed Naso Point and entered the protection of the

149

harbor. All Greek shipping seemed to be laid up elsewhere in the shelter of the small commercial harbor. Oars swung more slowly with a muffled creaking that merged with the lap-lap of water against the hulls. The ladder craft passed from starlight into the loom of the sea wall and the heights beyond it. The officers drew long breaths of relief, because they had passed within the range of the giant stone casters that had kept the Roman vessels at a distance by day.

Then the blackness of the wall in front of them changed slightly here and there. Openings seemed to appear in it. From the openings shot short heavy spears. The spears on a level with the decks crashed into the close-packed armed men, causing flurries in the ranks. Trumpets and distant calls sounded along the wall.

As the ladder craft moved steadily in, long arms swung over them from the parapet. The arms were derricks, because chains rattled beneath them and something indistinguishable swung at the ends of the chains. Metal of great weight dropped on the prows of some of the ships, causing no noticeable loss of life but rending the framework of wood. The chains rattled overhead, and the bows of the ships began to rise as if Neptune, god of the sea depths, had thrust them away.

The giant claws fastened on the bows hauled them higher until the masses of men slid down the decks and the sterns of the ships began to take water. Then the claws loosened suddenly as their chains were let run; the injured vessels surged down into the water; the swinging ladders crashed overside. Sometimes the fantastic machines overhead dropped lead balls the size of a calf that tore through the hulls, letting in the water. Other balls of flaming pitch set fire to the woodwork. Ordinary missiles also rained down from the wall.

Perhaps all this damage would not have stopped the advance of the legions by daylight on firm land. The effect on the dark water, however, was devastating; the ladders could no longer be used. Marcellus had his trumpeters sound a withdrawal.

"So the genius of one man, Archimedes, defeated the efforts of innumerable hands."

The tenacious Romans turned to the land wall of Syracuse, advancing siege works under cover of machines of their own. But the land wall also had been immunized by the inventions of Archimedes who understood much more about ballistics than the engineers of Marcellus. The land assault failed.

Hannibal had sent two Greek officers to the garrison of Syracuse, which consisted of some mercenaries and Roman deserters, the small Sicilian army, and a multitude of civilians. "Slaves were called to wear the wreath of freedom," Livy relates, "and criminals were released from their prison chains. All this assorted multitude elected Hippocrates and Epicydes [the officers of Hannibal] to be their generals."

The Roman generals settled down to a siege of exhaustion. In the end they won entry to the great port by treachery within the walls on the night of a feast. Once masters of a quarter, the legions cut their way systematically down to the harbor where the ships had failed. With them entered the pestilence of the camps. It was a bloody business, with rich reward in valuable works of art of Greek masters. Legend relates that the seventy-five-year-old Archimedes was engrossed in tracing mathematical equations upon a sand table when the soldiers entered his chamber. Apparently he called out angrily to know who was disturbing him, and Marcellus' men speared him and went on with their ransacking. So died the old man who had been the supreme astronomer and mathematician of the Hellenistic age.

Word of the agony of Syracuse went swiftly through the island and stirred resistance in the western half. There an army from Carthage faced Marcellus, and Hannibal sent a commander of his Numidians to direct it.

Hannibal himself was barred by the Straight of Messina from crossing into Sicily. Nor could he be spared from his post on Mount Tifata. Yet with increasing anxiety he followed the course of the conflict across the wider theater of the Mediterranean.

After Cannae his brother Hasdrubal had attempted to obey the order to break through the army of the two Scipios and to march into Italy. Attacking too rashly,

151

Hasdrubal's army had been broken on the line of the Ebro. The Carthaginians had been driven into the south of Spain by the capable and cautious brothers Scipio.

Bomilcar's expedition to Sardinia had evaded the Roman guard fleets but not a storm that drove it to shelter in the Balearics, always friendly to the Carthaginian cause. By the time it landed on the rocky Sardinian coast, Torquatus had crushed the revolt of the islanders, and his legions made short work of the ill-found Carthaginian expedition. Ironically, in doing so Torquatus, the champion of ancient tradition, armed the men of his *socii navales* (crews of his ships) against all tradition.

It is often alleged that the city of Carthage failed to send aid to Hannibal in Italy. Surely the single convoy of 4,000 men and 40 elephants landed at Locri was a pitiful support for the great general who withstood the massed power of Rome. By way of explanation—and to fit the Roman legend of the oath-bound Hannibal who dragged his city into the war—it is said that Carthage, the abode of merchants, had no heart in the conflict and so granted only token aid to her headstrong son. That is not the truth. To the extent of her resources, Carthage sent forces to carry on the war elsewhere. The conquest of the sea routes would have been a guarantee of victory for Hannibal.

Urgently he had requested reinforcement for Syracuse. Carthage sent a convoy with an armed force of 13,000. It landed near Syracuse, to be decimated by pestilence in the camp. Its remnants, under Hannibal's officer, were scattered eventually by the inflexible advance of Marcellus. Carthage had no means of training recruits to become an army of Italy, nor were her commanders equal to the Barca brothers.

Bomilcar, her most resourceful admiral, took his fleet once fairly into the port of Syracuse, but withdrew at the approach of a Roman battle fleet. More than 100 galleys now took the sea of Carthage, without a competent commander. It is true that the city of the Byrsa, shielded from the impact of the conflict, did not make the ultimate effort or produce the man for the emergency that was necessary to Hannibal at Tifata.

A reinforcement of some 20,000 was mobilized, to be

152

convoyed across to the Gulf of Taranto. After Hasdrubal's defeat on the Ebro this army was diverted to Spain. Probably it was done with Hannibal's consent because Mago—his *alter ego* at Carthage—went in command of it.

Then, too, the unceasing efforts of Carthage were made to appear weaker than in reality by one circumstance. The Roman blockading fleets kept their stations, at Ostia, off Sardinia, off the Aegates islands, in the Straight of Messina and at Brindisi (Brundisium) at the entrance of the Adriatic. Some 200 galleys escorted Roman convoys and searched the coasts to intercept the Carthaginian. Not long after Cannae the Romans added 60 warcraft to the fleets, to replace old or damaged vessels, and funds were borrowed from rich citizens to hire new crews when Hannibal's erosion of the coastal ports thinned down the ranks of the crews.

These galleys of Italy did more than carry Marcellus' forces in that night attack on Syracuse. They provided the lifeline of the Scipionic army in Spain. They saved Sardinia. One scout vessel of the blockade intercepted the envoys of Philip of Macedonia on their way back from Tifata. (The chief envoy, a Greek named Xenophon, had got through a Roman control point on land by convincing his interrogators that he was en route to the Senate, not to the Carthaginians! His masterly storytelling did not go down with the naval officers on his journey back.) This made it possible to send the full text of the unilateral treaty of Carthage and Macedonia to the Senate while Philip waited a critical year before new emissaries could bring him a duplicate of the treaty from Hannibal. Then when the Macedonians at last appeared on the Dalmatian coast, a Roman fleet cruising offshore scattered their warcraft, and kept Philip's army from crossing to the Italian coast. That year's delay on the part of his allies was to cost Hannibal dear.

So little did historians esteem their naval service that the name of only one Roman commander at sea is preserved. Yet Otacilius was kept at his hard duty for almost the duration of the war.

By 211, the seventh year of the conflict, the fleet of

Carthage had grown to 130 galleys. That year brought unlooked-for news of victory in Spain.

Election of a Proconsul for Spain

A Cannae in Spain! Both commanders of proconsular rank, Publius and the bald Gnaeus Scipio, slain! Their armies all but annihilated, the remnants fleeing to the Ebro without leaders.

These tidings shocked the throngs in the Forum of Rome. And further details added to the stupefaction. Over in the heart of Spain sworn allies, Celtiberians, had deserted the Scipios; a youthful Numidian, Masinissa, had appeared there to delude the Roman legions with encircling horsemen; worst of all, the two armies of the valiant Scipios had been caught separately by the swiftly moving columns of the Barca brothers, Hasdrubal and Mago, and a third general, a Carthaginian. Here enemy leadership had triumphed. The route to the Ebro, if not to the Alps, lay open to the Carthaginians.

And in Italy itself Hannibal prevailed. His frontier encampments east and west of the Apennines, at Luceria and Casilinum were now within 150 and 110 miles of the city on the Tiber. The most daring of cavalry leaders, Sempronius Gracchus, had blundered into an ambush while hunting or bathing in a river. His body had been delivered under truce to the nearest army post by a Carthaginian civilian, one Carthalo.

The shade of Gracchus had joined the wraiths of Flaminius, of Aemilius, of that other consul-elect in Cisalpine Gaul, with those of the Scipios in the underworld beneath the sunset. Only Marcellus seemed to be able to beat back the elusive African who appeared at the head of no proper army but a pack of rebellious Gauls, Greeks, Capuans, and Bruttians. And Marcellus could not be spared from Italy to hold the line of the Pyrenees in Spain.

By election time in 211, the Fathers in the Senate faced the eighth year of the war with profound misgivings. No grain shipments could be expected from devastated Sardinia or plague-ridden Sicily. Marcellus' blood purge of the rebel Sicilians had been a proper measure in restoring order but it had taken many hands from farm work. At the same time discipline had fallen off in the Roman commands owing to outbreaks of insubordination. The legions made up from slaves after Cannae had been disbanded as useless except for looting the countryside. A centurion named Poenula had marched off two legions vowing that he would find and kill Hannibal, and Poenula had returned without the legions.

The Censor showed the Senate leaders some hard figures. By now they had 23 legions in service in Italy. This mobilization took away an eight part more than one half of the year's enrollment of 270,000 men fit for service. In the year of Hannibal's appearance from the Alps that enrollment had numbered 770,000. How many were left to harvest the remaining valley lands and to man the vital shipping?

A young magistrate wearing a spotless toga listened to the arguments outside the vestibule of the temple of Jupiter, and made an odd remark. "You talk of nothing but Hannibal; you think of nothing but Hannibal. Yet the city of Carthage is your enemy."

Those who heard him gave heed because he was Publius Cornelius Scipio, twenty-five-year-old son of the late commander in Spain. Moreover this younger Scipio had been present at Trebia and Cannae, where he had drawn his sword to check the flight of unworthy officers. Yet Scipio had never held military command, instead he amused himself with politics at the portals on the Forum.

They pointed out to him the truth, plain as the signet ring on his finger. "Hannibal is within a week's march of the Collina Gate. Carthage is in Africa."

Scipio answered with odd intensity: "Even so, if you destroy Carthage, what is left of Hannibal?"

He was one of the young eccentrics. Often he persuaded the keepers of Jupiter's temple on the Capitoline to open a door for him at night so that he could meditate there alone until daybreak. "One is never less alone," he said in explanation, "than when one is most alone."

The superstitious found an explanation of his solitary

séances in the rumor that Scipio had been fathered by the god himself, incarnate with his mother. Certainly he had been heard in murmured talk within the otherwise deserted temple. Who was with him at such a time? Then, too, the youthful Scipio, handsome as a Greek ephebe, made no attempt to remain alone when an attractive girl, or even a slave woman, looked his way.

The question of Scipio's strangeness might have remained merely a topic of bathroom gossip if it had not been for popular demands coming from the assemblies of the Thirty-five Tribes. The hungry populace of the *Civitas Romana* was in one of its refractory moods, influenced by the drift of uprooted peasantry into the city and the casting of deserters off the Tarpeian Rock. The assemblies inveighed against the farming off of new taxes to speculators, and against the magnates who operated the new shipping. They had evidence that some of the magnates deliberately sank vessels with only token landing, collected payment from the public treasury for the loss of valuable loads. But, more than such rational anger, irrational uneasiness prevailed. ("The populace felt forsaken by its gods, and gave up many ancient rites to seek after new divinities.")

Manifestly the throngs in the Forum believed that Scipio, one of the few heroes of Cannae, held communion with unseen deities.

All this the Fathers perforce took under consideration in the pre-election deliberations. The mystical Scipio was effeminate-looking, with his hair curled in Greek fashion; he was under age to hold even praetorian rank; yet he was a youth of the Cornelian *gens,* and in the shrine chamber of his palatial home hung the death masks with the memorial tablets of some thirty ancestors of consular rank. Moreover he believed without question in his own ability, whether god-inspired or not. The Fathers decided that no other candidates should oppose Publius Cornelius Scipio when he took his stand on a tribunal of the Forum to announce that he was a candidate for the Spanish command as proconsul. An elderly statesman possessing all the required dignities could accompany him as a figurehead.

So it befell that the younger Scipio was elected unani-

156

mously to be proconsul. Some critics remarked that only idiots would send him to Spain, where the graves of his father and uncle awaited him.

In many characteristics Scipio resembled that other eccentric, Julius Caesar. He was consumed by ambition, cynical of the human beings around him; he was coldly intelligent, while capable of unsuspected audacity. He could be charming if persuasion served his purpose. Probably after Cannae he became disillusioned with the chain of command at Rome, and wanted to be far from senatorial direction. Almost from the first Fabius distrusted him. Yet he had waited patiently at the threshold of the Senate, the seat of authority, to gain a high post at a moment of political upheaval. While doing so he had created a legend about himself. When the crowds longed for supernatural aid, Scipio appeared as a medium, so to speak, of the unseen gods.

His instinct had hit upon the crux of the great conflict—that Hannibal served Carthage, not himself.

In a different way that was as true of Scipio and Rome. The elegant politician of the streets resolved to carry out his father's plan, to seek victory through the conquest of Spain as a bridge to Africa.

Neptune at New Carthage

Scipio landed with his figurehead and two legions at Emporiae, safely north of the Ebro. There the remnants of the defeated forces had been reassembled with reinforcements hurried from Rome. To them the young commander displayed a dual personality—that of a kindly friend and an inflexible disciplinarian.

Searching out the officer who had taken charge after the disaster, Scipio found him in a centurion, Lucius Marcius, no older than himself. He kept Marcius at his side, confessing frankly that he was ignorant of all circumstance on the Spanish front. He wanted to learn what towns were friendly and why, what hostages were held and why, what had happened for good or ill during the last eight years and why. While he talked with Marcius he rode out on wide inspections of the uplands between the Ebro and the lofty Pyrenees. That, said the surviving veterans of his father's command, was the line to be held and only that was safe. Scipio smiled and praised them for their professional acumen. He had a skilled professional in Laelius his legate (lieutenant). To the general surprise he named the centurion Marcius his chief of staff.

Scipio made a habit of dropping by to talk at the standards of the different cohorts. He told the assembled men that the defeat by the Carthaginians had come about through no lack of courage but because the Roman army had been divided into two. He promised them that would not happen under his command, and he let the men feel that he possessed some inner certainty of what *would* happen.

And through an autumn and winter he drilled his new legions; they marched until they dropped under heavy equipment—and the stragglers went rationless or tasted the scourge at the stake; they raced into squares to face unseen cavalry; they hauled engines up mountainsides; they faced iron javelins thrown in the Spanish manner; and they marched again.

Scipio was warned not to move far from the coast. The three Carthaginian armies held the hinterland, and the midland people were treacherous. Scipio fully agreed. He would not venture far from the sea, where serviceable galleys waited. To make certain of this, he cross-examined informants until he could be sure that Mago's command wintered near the Pillar of Hercules (Gibraltar) while Hasdrubal waited in Cantabrian land, and the other Carthaginian near the Atlantic. All, therefore, were more than ten days' march from their base at New Carthage.

Scipio's new interest in the coast led him to question naval captains about any tide pull in the almost tideless Mediterranean, and the effect of offshore winds. The fleet off the Ebro was kept in readiness to put to sea.

Then before winter had fairly ended, Scipio in person took the legions on a long march south. They did not turn back. At dawn they marched again, south. Scipio explained to the cohorts that their impedimenta were following with the machines. And he said they would not stop until they were in New Carthage. After that the legions quickened their pace. The fleet kept them company, in sight of the shore.

Scipio's audacity in surprising and capturing the stronghold of the Carthaginians in Spain has called forth the admiration of military experts. There were probably no more than 1,000 troops in garrison and 2,000 reserves at the city of Hasdrubal the Splendid. But Scipio might not have succeeded in this first venture if he had not invoked the aid of the god Neptune. Before they sighted New Carthage on its promontory between the sea harbor and the lagoon, he promised his followers a crown of gold for the one who first scaled the wall, and he pledged them that Neptune would aid them in a way that would be clear to all of them at the propitious moment. He, Scipio, had seen as much in a dream.

In the event, the hurrying legions had hard work to beat back a sally of the Carthaginians, and they failed to rush the eastern land wall after that. By the end of the afternoon Scipio still drove them to the attack. Then he went himself with 500 legionaries and engineers carrying ladders around the north side of the wall, into the lagoon. The Romans waded in, up to their knees and to their thighs. There was no one else in the water beside them. The fleet, perforce, waited outside the harbor entrance. The small Carthaginian forces were engaged closely elsewhere on the land wall.

Scipio kept on, wading through water that did not submerge him. It may have been the slight ebb tide at that hour, or the pull of the offshore wind; the men following Scipio, however, believed that only Neptune could have held back the water. Eagerly they scaled the lagoon defense and broke through into half-deserted streets.

Thus in seven hours Scipio's army stormed the Carthaginian citadel, where it was least expected to appear. Scipio gave new force to the legend that he had foreknowledge if not aid from the gods.

He also gained in one day the single large port that sheltered the convoys from Africa, with the stores and treasury of silver of Hasdrubal and 18 serviceable ships. He gained a fortified base for his army, and opened it to fleets from Rome.

Hasdrubal could not set out overland for Italy while Scipio held New Carthage.

That circumstance heartened the throngs on the Via Sacra. News of the capture of Hasdrubal's city stirred general enthusiasm because it was entirely unexpected. At the same time trophies from Marcellus were hung in the temple of Virtus (Bravery) outside the walls. They were the statues of Greek gods brought in from plundered Syracuse. With them arrived an orb of gold, delicate in its tracery as lacework, a globe of the earth designed by Archimedes.

It was said in the streets that up to now the Roman People possessed everything needed for victory except a Hannibal. Now young Scipio supplied that want. Was he not favored of the gods, as Marcellus was bravest of the brave?

Message of the Dead Hand

"At no other time were Carthaginians and Romans alike equally involved in changing fortune, in a more uncertain state of hope and fear."

And at this time, in the critical years from 212 to 210, all traces of Hannibal himself become very faint on the palimpsest of the histories. It is next to impossible to make out what he hoped for or feared. It is only clear that he managed to escape observation by his enemies except when he appeared at the head of an army. Otherwise he seemed to wander at will through the now familiar valleys of his domain, from the towers of Casilinum to the White Cliff at the Apennines' end.

He had not lost his impish humor. A Roman command receives a prophecy of disaster written in good Latin, with the place and date specified. Going its way regardless of such intimidation, the column fulfills the prophecy of its overthrow. Another command post receives another missive, an order from a proconsul sealed properly with his signet ring. The order is about to be executed when someone remembers that the proconsul has been killed and the Carthaginians must be in possession of his ring. Did Hannibal sense the gigantic jest of his role as ruler of southern Italy, leader of the finest army of Italy?

His Carthaginians bedevil their methodical enemies. Messages flash from hill to hill with the speed of sight— by fire telegraph, still unknown to Romans. The Iberians are observed dancing around fires at night; when a cohort's line approaches a Spanish line, casting javelins at the proper moment, the Spaniards squat to earth to let the volley pass and rise to cast their own iron shafts. Marching Carthaginians cross a river in flood dry-shod, on a bridge of small boats, and carry the bridge away with them. Phantom ships are sighted coming up the Tiber, and are not seen again. What were they?

The Carthaginians have a way with ships. Hannibal shows the Tarentines how to move their galleys from the blocked inner harbor of their city—where the Roman garrison still bars the entrance by the chain at the citadel. He has the Tarentines warp their small vessels on rollers over a city street to the beach on the open sea. Tarentum, the one port that can be used by his Macedonian allies, is never far from his thoughts. He watches details unheeded by his enemies—aware that the unhappy legions of Cannae have become disheartened in Sicily, and that Etruscan peasants have found their way for the first time into his borders. His sources of information can seldom be traced. Many Numidians, ostensibly deserters to the gratification of the Roman command, make their way back to him with eyewitness accounts of the enemy. A visitor from Alexandria appears at Tifata, rather surprisingly because Ptolemaic Egypt is antagonistic to Hannibal's ally, Macedonia. Yet Hannibal learns from him that the hard-pressed Senate is bargaining with Ptolemy for shipments of grain. A Roman officer, although captive at Tifata, remains close to Hannibal's side. They are seen much in talk, but about what?

Tifata is now fortified, and other towns are garrisoned by the Carthaginians. For Hannibal has lost Capua.

Inevitably the Romans had concentrated their efforts against Capua. Nothing in the rebellion of Magna Graecia had stirred their anger as much as the defection of its mistress city. Moreover, the legend of Hannibal's invincibility had been broken by his repulse at the siege of Nola. And siege works around Capua could be supplied from the coast, up the river Volturno. By then various officers had devised tactical improvements; light-armed contingents were strengthened, to oppose the dangerous Carthaginian light troops, Spaniards and Balearians; in the cavalry—principal weakness of the Roman armies—javelin throwers were trained to mount behind the horsemen, and to dismount to throw their missiles at the dreaded Carthaginian heavy horsemen.

So the southern commands of the Republic were all set in motion toward Capua. The alarmed citizens of that city sent an appeal for aid to Hannibal who was then engaged at the citadel of Tarentum. And Hannibal had released Hanno with the heavy cavalry to do something about the situation of the Capuans. There ensued the rapid maneuvering aided by the fire telegraph that resulted in the death of Gracchus, the scattering of one Roman column (according to prophecy) and the discomfiture of the boastful Poenula. The two forces that managed to reach Capua retired hastily to hills and dug in.

Thus the siege of the rebellious city was broken off but not abandonned. Tenaciously, the armies of two proconsuls closed in again, to fortify a circuit around the walls of Capua. Again an appeal went to Hannibal. This time he came himself to the scene by forced marches with his veteran infantry and 32 elephants. A message smuggled into the city urged the Capuans to be prepared to sally out with all their strength at the hour and the place where they should see him attacking the Roman siege lines. By so doing they would force the entrenched enemy to resist at front and rear at one point of their extended siege works.

Obediently the citizens assembled upon one wall with boys and women who hoped to watch and encourage their warriors with noise. They accomplished that much only too well; it is said that the racket from the wall prevented Romans and Carthaginians alike from hearing the commands of their officers. But the fighters of Capua did not

162

succeed in entering the inner staked rampart of the besiegers.

It is clear that Hannibal, on his side, made a swift attack with heavy infantry backed by elephants clad for conflict in leather. The Carthaginian attack broke through the outer entrenchment. The head of the assault penetrated the Roman camp, and was supported by Spanish infantry. Three elephants got in and raised havoc among the tents and lines of horses and baggage animals. The elephants were finally driven off by fire. The combat here was savage, because a proconsul was wounded, a legion routed and only rallied by a tribune who called it back to its standard. Some Spanish detachments cut their way through to the Capuans and gained the city with them. The Roman siege works held, in the main, and Hannibal had to withdraw his attack forces.

His strength was less than that of the two hostile armies in the siege works. And his position at the end of the day was critical, being between the Roman lines and the swift-flowing Volturno. At this point he made one of his rapid changes of plan. By means of one of the useful Numidian "deserters" he got a message through to his Spanish officers and the city garrison. It urged them to hold out for a few days; after that the enemy armies would retire from the siege.

Hannibal himself took the road to Rome.

"He Has Not Come to Besiege Rome."

It was a delicate operation to disengage a small army by making a river crossing. The Carthaginian—who must have anticipated as much—was helped by the inaction of the unwounded proconsul, who held his forces within their lines that night. Hannibal had taken the precaution of fortifying a camp as a bridgehead on the river bank. That evening his men collected all available boats and crossed unnoticed in the darkness with the surviving elephants. On the far bank they joined the horsemen of

163

Hanno and Mago who screened their march north. By daylight all Carthaginians were out of sight of Capua.

Did Hannibal hope to surprise the great city on the Tiber, still intact after seven years of campaigning in Italy? It is sometimes said that he did. His departure had all of the appearance of a swift march against Rome itself. The Carthaginians took the inland road, the Latin Way; the easier coast route, the Appian Way, was studded with enemy towns, and often under observation from passing warships.

Soon, however, Hannibal gave his hard-marching column a day of rest in camp. After that, entering enemy territory, the horsemen fanned out through the valleys to trample growing crops, to burn ripe grain and to spread terror with torch and sword. The news of his march, accordingly, was carried by riders back to the proconsular armies outside Capua, and on to the gates of Rome. Yet in the valley under the gray rock height of Casinum (the Mount Cassino that held back the Allied armies so long on their way to Rome in the last World War) Hannibal allowed his column to rest, ruin, and forage for two days.

Quite clearly he was not making a forced march to surprise the city. He was looking back, not forward. He allowed his enemy time to observe his line of march and even to exchange communications between the Senate and the Capua lines. He had one hope—that the two proconsuls would abandon their siege works to follow him, to defend their capital. He now had all his cavalry with him, and in such open valley plains as that beneath Casinum he might outmaneuver and destroy the armies hurrying in pursuit as Flaminius had hastened after him.

This hope was almost realized. News of his approach touched off a memorable panic in the streets of Rome. As it happened after Cannae the first comers spread wild reports, of the countryside in flames and Numidians galloping after them. *Hannibal ad portas!* Women broke out of their home confinement to rush to the temples. The Senate went into day-and-night session out of doors in the Forum where it could see and be seen. All senators who had held high rank were ordered to assume authority as of their former ranks.

The eldest of the Cornelian family—very unlike young

164

Scipio—demanded that the field armies be recalled from Capua to save the city.

Fabius Maximus spoke for the wiser heads. Fabius had had a long experience with Carthaginian maneuvering. This time he made only a brief reference to Jupiter as the protector of the city. How, he demanded, could Hannibal, who had failed to break the siege lines at Capua, expect to storm the walls of Rome? "He has not come to besiege Rome but to break the siege of Capua."

And the Senate's message to the proconsuls in the field instructed them to send north only the legions that could be spared from the siege without weakening it.

In obedience a column some 15,000 strong took the Appian Way from the Volturno to the city. It was delayed some time at the river crossing because Hannibal had burned the boats he had used. Still the relief column, making forced marches through the coast towns where stocks of food had been assembled, reached the southern gates of the city before the Carthaginians appeared on the skyline.

Hannibal, in fact, came down the Tiber from the Anio crossing, and burning villages marked his way. Sight of the Carthaginian horsemen stirred new dread in the countryside. At night the wild war cry of the Africans sent refugees crowding into the gates. Hannibal camped within three miles. With an escort of horsemen he appeared on a rise outside the Collina Gate and made a leisurely inspection of the adjacent walls.

They were manned by defenders, with engines. Three legions garrisoned the city. The legions from Capua took station on the plain under protection of the walls. Although the strength of the defenders seems to have been 35,000 men, no effort was made to sally out against the invaders, and the Carthaginians went about their business of despoiling the suburban temples and carrying off portable wealth.

Perhaps in defiance, a sale was made in the Forum shops of the land occupied by the Carthaginian camp, at no less than the market price of ordinary times. A report of this sale went through the city streets.

A day later a single envoy appeared with a trumpeter from the Carthaginian camp. He proved to be a civilian with a brief message: "Hannibal offers for sale all the shops of the Forum. What price shall I tell him is bid?"

In some way Hannibal had heard of the bravado sale of the ground on which he camped, and had sent back a jest of his own. Fabius was not amused. For the first time the Carthaginians were ravaging Latium itself, the core of the *imperium Romanum*. They rode through the sacred Alban Hills; they tore apart the shrine of the goddess of Mount Soracte, 30 miles to the north. North and east and south rose the smoke of burning towns, while five legions waited within the walls of Rome.

Then Hannibal was gone, with his elephants and captured Eagles. This time he left no indication of his line of march.

The effect of his raid, however, was soon felt. He had replenished his stock of gold, silver, and valuables, while the treasury of Rome had lost that much. The next year Latium could not pay its allotment of taxes and supplies; twelve colonial and allied centers reported that they could give nothing because they had nothing left. Again the plebeians complained; they were bearing the intolerable burden of the war, while the magnates who had started it suffered no hardship. Rebellion was in the air. (For the first time, in these years of exhaustion, the Senate drew on the private funds of the wealthy in loans to be repaid at the end of the war.) A general cry went up: *why was nothing being done to end the war?*

Rome itself was bleeding to death.

"Not less than the Carthaginians and the Campanians," cried an orator in the street, "are our consuls ruining the Roman People. Our houses are burned by the enemy, our slaves—who tilled the fileds—are now taken away by the state. For a pittance paid to us, our slaves must go to row the galleys. Who of us has any gold or silver left? Let him beware, for the state will take it away. We have nothing left but our land. Tell me, citizens: what authority can compel us to give what we no longer possess?"

In the confiscation of precious metals, wives were allowed to keep one ring, and the head of a family might retain one ounce of gold for each member of the family. Mysterious fires broke out in the principal streets. Authorities blamed the conflagrations on Capuan spies.

Despite all the arguments of the Fabian faction, the appearance of Hannibal and his horsemen at the Collina Gate had revived the legend of his invincibility. There was a new outbreak of religious hysteria. Prophets appeared in the streets to predict the anger of the gods and the doom of the city. It was said that a statue of Victory had been struck by lightning. The battle trophies from Spain and the captured gods of Syracuse no longer appeared to be omens of triumph.

These years, 211-210, brought the Roman economy to exhaustion, and, as after Cannae, it was no longer possible to allow Hannibal to carry on such operations in his own manner and time. The now aged Fabius took the field again, and before long Marcellus was summoned to Italy to stop the devastating marches of the Carthaginians. "Fate was sweeping Marcellus toward Hannibal."

End of a City

When Hannibal disappeared from the suburbs of Rome, the Senate expected him to return to Campania. Instead of doing so, he swung his small army wide through the Samnite hills, across Apulia, down to the very toe of Italy. There, under the White Cliff he struck swiftly at Rhegium, the Roman port of embarkation for Sicily, opposite Messina. Rhegium was the last seaport on the extreme southern coast to hold out against him.

By this unexpected move Hannibal seemed to try to aid the all-important Carthaginian fleets. (These were still off the western end of Sicily, raiding Sardinia, and attempting to transport the Macedonians across the Adriatic. They still failed to challenge the mastery of the Roman fleets, 215 vessels strong. But a Tarentine fleet, combined with Carthaginian, thoroughly shattered the hostile squadrons guarding the Strait of Messina. Here seamanship prevailed over armed fighting force on the decks. Hannibal had wrested the harbors of Locri, Croton, Metapontum, and Tarentum from his enemies.)

Rhegium, however, was strongly held. When surprise

failed to gain it, Hannibal turned away as he had done at Naples.

Then Capua surrendered.

The capital city of Magna Graecia was cut off and without means of withstanding the steady approach of the Roman siege works. There was bitter debate in its senate on the last day, before envoys went out to ask for terms of surrender. Some of the nobles hoped for leniency from the other Senate on the Tiber; most of them had no such hope. One of these, Vibius Virrius, declared that only one liberty was left them—to prepare their bodies in a fitting way for burning before the entrance of a Roman legion.

"About twenty-seven senators followed Virrius home. After they had feasted with him, to deaden their minds as far as possible with wine, they gave each other their right hands and took poison. They wept for their own fate and that of their city. Some remained, to be cremated on the same pyre with him; others went off to their different homes. Being filled with food and wine, they made the poison in their veins less effectual in hastening death. Most of them were in the throes that night and part of the following day. All of them, however, died before the gates were opened to the enemy."

The first legion marched into the gate of the Appian Way. Sentries were posted, and all weapons collected, with the detachments of Carthaginians in the garrison. Capuans of senatorial rank were taken out to the quarters of the proconsuls, who sentenced 53 to execution, the others to be sold as slaves. The quaestors of the Roman camps collected together 2,070 pounds of gold and 33,200 pounds of silver from the homes of the captives. The balance of the citizens were sent into exile, and the city itself condemned to lose self-rule and magistrates.

Since the countryside was fertile, under excellent cultivation, and the handicraft workers highly skilled, the region was turned into a production center for the benefit of Rome. It became "a dwelling place of aliens and freedmen, tradesmen and petty artisans."

So Capua, like Syracuse, paid the penalty for taking arms against the Senate and the Roman People—although the Capuans had, in reality, given no effectual aid in money or men to Hannibal's forces. "The enemy," Livy relates, "was forced to acknowledge what power the Romans possessed to exact punishment from faithless allies." And something more of ancient culture, another city center of the weakening Hellenistic world, disappeared from the pages of history.

The fall of Capua released the besieging armies for the most part. Marcellus came up from Rhegium to lead an advance against the elusive Carthaginian host of Hannibal.

Claudius Marcellus had had an ovation at Rome after his capture of Syracuse. He was middle-aged, a saturnine veteran, capable of rapid and competent action; he had gained victories by pressing an enemy to a final stand at swords' points. And he believed himself to be a match for Hannibal. "He acts," Hannibal once said of Marcellus, "without resting at all. If successful, he pursues, and if worsted he strikes back."

In truth Marcellus was a man who exulted in combat. He had a habit of challenging enemies to single combat and killing them with his sword. When he entered Rome in one official triumph, he appeared in a chariot beside the body armor of a slain Celtish chieftain, hung in lifelike manner on a wooden frame. He longed to come to grips with Hannibal.

By now (209-208) the army of Italy had become little more than a moving skeleton of itself. Nine years had taken toll of the veterans who crossed the Alps, and some of them were followed by children strong enough to carry their shields. Perhaps it numbered somewhat more than the original force; Roman deserters, Etruscans, and exiled Campanians filled up its ranks. The squadrons of Numidians seemed to perpetuate themselves—as perhaps they did by recruits slipped across from Africa. But Hanno and his heavy cavalry had disappeared from the records, with Maharbal. Only Hannibal knew the strength of his marching host at this point and he did not choose to reveal it. Moreover he needed to garrison the vital remaining ports of the Gulf of Taranto, his only access to the seas. Left undefended, these would be seized and held by the enemy. Once, when Locri was besieged by a Roman column, Hannibal threw himself into the town, to lead a sally timed to meet a charge of swift-moving Numidians from outside. This maneuver, that failed at Capua, succeeded here, and the siege of Locri was broken. Again in Salabria 500 Numidians fought to the death in the streets to defend it when they might have broken out to safety.

The year 209 was drawing to its end. The Romans feel their way behind Marcellus into the fastness of the far south. The object of Hannibal's rapid movements becomes obscure. Seemingly he protects the seaports, yet withdraws before Marcellus from the rugged heights of Bruttium toward the rolling plains of Apulia. Marcellus presses hotly, striving to bring his camp close to the enemy camp and to fight it out, standards ranged against standards. At the end of one day he closes with the Carthaginians as they are making camp and drives them. On another day his legions are charged by elephants, and the experienced soldiers mass together to cast volleys of javelins at the great beasts. Once, at least, a legion is put to flight with its allied wings, losing four standards.

That night Marcellus gave the wing men only barley to eat, and ordered the legionaries to attention in ranks with drawn swords but without their scabbards. He gave them a tongue-lashing that the men said was harder to bear than the battle:

"Am I speaking to soldiers? I do not recognize any in these cohorts and maniples. Where did you leave your standards? Hitherto Roman legions have at times been defeated by the enemy. You have gained the unique distinction of showing your backs to the enemy."

After his castigation Marcellus, a Consul, led the disgraced men into action himself. He seemed to be nearer to closing with the elusive Carthaginians each day, and his eagerness and exasperation increased accordingly. He had been warned of Hannibal's tricks—to beware of messages with forged signatures, of Carthaginians appearing fully clad and armed like Romans, of cavalry in hiding behind retreating infantry. But he noticed only the hill in between because it angered him.

Hannibal had a way of settling his lines for the night close behind a small hill. This prevented the Roman lines from drawing near, and it also gave the Carthaginian

170

command excellent observation over the surrounding ground.

Since he had retreated into wooded country, it became difficult to get sight of the Carthaginian's encampment. One afternoon it was screened by tree growth in front of which stood a small hill, brush-grown but without visible occupants. Marcellus, studying it, ordered the height to be occupied before the Carthaginians could dig in upon it. He led out two squadrons of horse, one being Etruscan, taking his fellow Consul with five lictors and staff officers along to observe the surroundings from the summit. A trail led to it, crossing a depression beneath the hill.

These 200-odd Romans were trotting through the depression when the attack came. Numidian horsemen charged down from the crest of the hill, and other squadrons swept out from the sides to close in upon the Roman commanders crossing the hollow way.

The Etruscan wing men fled back, and they were the chief survivors. Marcellus was pierced by a thrown spear and dropped from his horse, dying. The other Consul, wounded, was brought away by his officers to die later. Besides the two Consuls, the Romans lost another 5 fasces to Hannibal in the ambush of the advantageous hill.

That evening Hannibal moved his lines forward and placed his tent on the height. There he ordered the burial of Marcellus' body. Not knowing Roman funeral ritual, some of his Spaniards did a ceremonial dance with torches at the grave. As for the Roman army, virtually stripped of commanding officers, it withdrew rapidly to the nearest mountain and dug in there. After that, pursuit of Hannibal's army was given up. And a general warning went out to all commands to disregard any order signed with the seal of Marcellus because the seal ring of the late Consul was now in enemy possession.

In Rome the tidings of the loss of the two Consuls increased the general despondency. For nine years every action against Hannibal had brought disaster of one kind or another. No commanders able to cope with him survived, and the drain of life on the commoners could no longer be endured.

Then the news of the capture of New Carthage by the

proconsul Scipio heartened the people. By way of proof, Laelius, Scipio's legate, arrived with a whole wagon train of silver bars and strings of captive Carthaginians. Laelius also brought a trophy, a shield embossed with silver bearing the likeness—so it was said—of the head of Hasdrubal Barca. This shield was hung for all to see in the temple of Jupiter on the Capitoline, where Scipio had kept his night vigils. This head seemed to be an omen of victory.

The Senate dispatched word of the fall of New Carthage across the other sea, to Philip of Macedonia (then locked in conflict with the Aetolians, barbaric northerners brought into the conflict by Roman diplomacy). Over the Mediterranean the balance of power was changing at last, that of the Roman alliance rising, that of Carthage and the independent cities sinking.

The Warning of the Sacred Chickens

Tarentum's citadel still held out after three years of siege. At long last a strong Carthaginian fleet arrived to blockade the fortress by sea. It sailed away at the approach of Roman squadrons. (The weakness of the Carthaginian admiral, Bonilcar, after the fall of Syracuse remains a riddle without solution. Perhaps Carthaginian manpower did not suffice to send reinforcing armies to Spain and man a powerful fleet at the same time; perhaps the Carthaginian sea captains simply did not have the spirit to fight it out with the superior Latin fleets.)

Then the city of Tarentum fell.

For all his swift maneuvering Hannibal could not be in two places at the same time. It was more than 200 miles by land from Rhegium at one end of his curtailed dominion to Salapia at the other end; and he could not cross the Gulf of Taranto by ship as his enemies were able to do. He was far down in Bruttium when Fabius Maximus struck at Tarentum by land and sea.

The Delayer approached with his usual caution, hoping to win through the city wall to the courageous garrison on

172

the citadel point, and so to bring his war galleys into the harbor. Chance aided him. An officer of the Bruttians who garrisoned the city, involved with a woman, offered to admit Fabius and a detachment of soldiers into the gate by the harbor. The Romans in the citadel were alerted to the attempt. Fabius arranged a noisy diversion by his troops on the other side. By entrance under cover of darkness he secured the harbor front and his cohorts began to pour in behind him.

Philemenus, who had admitted Hannibal to the wall in much the same fashion, mounted a horse and rode off to an unknown fate. Carthalo, in command of the Carthaginian garrison, was made captive by the legionaries. Persuasive even under those circumstances, Hannibal's chief of intelligence convinced his captors that he was related by guest-friendship to the Consul (Fabius was serving as Consul for the fourth time). The careful Roman record of the assault tells what followed.

"Carthalo had laid down his arms and was on his way to the consul when he was slain by a soldier who met him. Other soldiers slew men everywhere, whether armed or unarmed, Carthaginians and Tarentines alike. Everywhere Bruttians also were slain either by mistake or out of old inbred hatred of them—or to make it seem that Tarentum was captured by force of arms rather than treachery. Slaves to the number of thirty thousand are said to have been made. With them was taken an immense amount of silver, both coined and wrought, with three thousand and eighty pounds of gold, and so many statues and paintings that they rivaled the ornaments of Syracuse. Fabius left to the Tarentines the colossal statues of their angry gods." [These were too heavy to be moved by his engineers.] "Then the wall was torn down and completely destroyed."

Hannibal had just managed to raise the siege of the port of Caulonia, more than 150 miles distant when he heard of Fabius' move against Tarentum. Immediately he started along the coast by forced marches, only to learn of the fate of the city and the Carthaginian garrison. "So the Romans have found themselves a Hannibal," he said, "to take Tarentum."

He was not willing to let Fabius escape so easily. Nearing the port of Metapontum, he arranged to offer the aged Fabius a second prize to be snatched at. His army went into one of its hidden encampments around Metapontum, while several citizens of the town hurried to the Consul with an offer to admit him to its walls. The Carthaginian garrison, the pseudo-traitors explained, could easily be overpowered.

The astute Delayer, however, was not a Marcellus. Tempting as the offer seemed to be—and his officers longed to gain the spoils of Metapontum—Fabius hesitated. Something had aroused his suspicions. To convince his soldiers that the expedition would not be propitious, he took the augury of the sacred chickens that served to foretell fate for a Consul. As usual in such cases the augury went as Fabius wished. The chickens refused to eat the grain scattered before them. And Fabius' army was preserved from Hannibal's trap.

After it was all over Hannibal said a very strange thing to his officers. "We have lost the war in Italy unless we can gain new strength."

He said that in his quarters on the quiet gulf. The army surrounding him had been undefeated for ten years in Italy. His enemies, in fact, avoided meeting it. Why should he believe the war to be lost?

Did his clairvoyant mind sense the happenings to come? Tarentum had gone, and with it the great port where Macedonian allies might debark. New Carthage, his own city, was lost. In Italy itself he had failed to win over the majority of the peoples. No bridge of ships could now be extended from Sicily to Africa. This picture of the western Mediterranean had always been first in his thoughts, and now it was darkening.

There remained one possibility. If he could add power to his veteran survivors of the army, he might vanquish the assembled Romans in a last battle.

He sent a messenger to Carthage to urge his brother Hasdrubal to come with all his force over the Alps into Italy.

174

V. Scipio Against Hannibal

The Woman Question

Genius is more than a capacity for taking infinite pains; it is an ability to see clearly the realities around it and to be guided by them. Few men have ever possessed that ability for long. Napoleon Bonaparte had it in his earlier years; by the time he led his *grande armée* to Moscow he believed that he was following his own peculiar destiny. That, of course, proved to be true, but the destiny was not what Napoleon imagined it to be.

Young Publius Scipio almost alone among the Roman leaders understood the reality that their enemy was Carthage, a city, and not Hannibal, a man. In Spain he perceived the realities that had escaped commanders preceding him. Long after him, Henry IV of France remarked that "Spain is a country where large armies starve and small armies get beaten." (Napoleon also was to find that out by hard experience.)

Scipio found himself in a huge peninsular tableland, half desert, where towns were remote and supplies scanty, where the great distances called for horsemen rather than the hard-hiking infantry that did so well in the small Italian valleys. He understood very quickly why the Carthaginians kept, unreasonably, in three separate commands—

to feed themselves. They camped separately, and fought united. If he went after one, the two others might come after him as they had done in disposing of his father and uncle. So Scipio kept his one army close to its base at New Carthage, at the terminal of the sea route to Rome, near to the all-important mines of the Silver Mountains. Those mines began to yield silver worth 20,000 drachmae a day, vital to exhausted Rome.

He knew that he could not allow himself the luxury of time. Behind him Rome was caught in the vicious circle of economic exhaustion, spending the last temple treasures of gold to man more legions, to suppress more rebellion—even in Etruria—and to lose more lives in battle, which required more legions to be replaced, while Hannibal waited, like a wizard, apart from the circle he had conjured into being. (And Scipio hurried off Laelius with the tons of precious silver and the trophy for the temple of Jupiter, his reputed father.)

Across all eastern Spain lay the gigantic shadow of Hannibal. Blue-blooded Iberians remembered his courtesy; his wife had given birth to his son up in a tower of Castulo, above the mines; the fiercely combative Celtiberians and Ilergetes waited for word from him; almost all these silent introspective peoples had kinsmen with his army of Italy. Scipio understood that it was useless to carry on a campaign in Spain unless he won the support of at least part of its inhabitants.

Probably it was the influence of his surroundings that gave Scipio another simple idea. The best way to contend with Hannibal was to imitate him.

Now Scipio had been near to the mysterious African in the hailstorm on the river Trebia; he had felt his power exerted in that hot afternoon at Cannae. Those hours had scarred his spirit; he had brooded over them during the darkness at the deserted shrine of Jupiter. He felt a growing contempt for his fellow officers who cried out at the degenerate African, the monster of cruelty, the magician of innumerable tricks, the treacherous Phoenician. Scipio's supreme accomplishment was to understand the reality of Hannibal.

It was incredibly difficult for the Roman, brought up

among the death masks and the honor records of his ancestors, to obliterate all such tradition from his mind and get outside himself. The European could not fully understand the oriental Semite, but he could follow out the other's thought. Scipio prepared to use Hannibal's weapons against him.

After the first hours of bloodletting and spoiling at New Carthage—traditional with Roman troops after assaulting a hostile town—Scipio had ordered his legionaries to keep their swords sheathed. More than that, he ordered that native Spaniards were not to be treated as subjected tribes. He set captured artisans to work in the shipyards and promised them liberty at the end of the war. It was vital to him that these Spaniards should expect benefits to come from Roman rule, and his plan envisaged a Roman Iberia producing a yearly treasure in silver. In evidence of his good will he released all Iberian and Celtiberian hostages he found quartered in New Carthage. They were relatives of reigning chieftains. To them he said in effect: "The Senate and the Roman People will free you from your demanding Phoenician masters. Henceforth you will have law and order, and the protection of the Roman People, ever victorious over their enemies."

Scipio could be charming; he fully understood the instinct of barbaric chieftains to be on the winning side. He also estimated correctly the influence of noble Iberian women on their husbands. Spirited matrons and girls had influenced his earlier years; he believed women to have personalities as well as the functions of childbearing and obedience in the home required of Latin wives. His legionaries had touched on this in one of their rude marching chants:

> Says Publius Cornelius,
> All the gold's for centuri-ons;
> All the silver's for triari-i,
>   And all the warm wenches are for—
> Publius Cornel-i-us.

Among the hostages there happened to be an Iberian matron who had taken the girls and children under her

177

wing; she was also the sister-in-law of one Indibilis, an influential chieftain. Scipio arranged quite a scene at his reception of this Iberian dowager. Through his interpreters, he greeted her with deference; he gave toys with his own hand to the small children. The matron, it seemed, had something else on her mind. She hinted as much to the striking-looking Roman commander who wore his snowy toga like a robe of honor. Puzzled for a moment, Scipio understood her anxiety. She feared for the nubile girls grouped behind her. Thereupon he called in some young officers from the antechamber; while the matron watched he gave orders that these noble Iberian maidens were to be held in deference as Scipio's sisters, under any circumstances.

This scene of chivalry, however, was disturbed by an amusing contretemps. Several junior officers brought in a Spanish girl of their own careful selection. She was a dark-eyed beauty of unknown family, picked out by the zealous juniors for the enjoyment of the proconsul. After an instant's stupefaction, Scipio met the misadventure deftly. This girl, he declared, was indeed most fair and attractive; accordingly her family should be sought out, that she might be returned to the care of her father by order of the proconsul.

Whatever effect the treatment of the women may have had, Scipio won the friendship of Indibilis and some important chieftains of the eastern coast, up which he gravitated, from New Carthage to Tarraco beyond the Ebro. There in the north, the Ilergetes, were at least quiet, but the strong Celtiberians of the middle plains held to their alliance with the Carthaginians. Scipio was creating something of a legend about himself, a legend of personal benevolence in command of Roman power. This legend would vanish at any defeat by Carthaginian arms.

Meanwhile he gave unsparing attention to details. To offset his weakness in horsemen, he moved to get into touch with the Moors and Numidians on the adjacent African coast. He also drilled his dependable legions in new mobility; if they could not maneuver with the speed of the Carthaginian horse, they could at least be shifted from place to place at a rapid pace. In this tactic he scrapped

178

entire the traditional rigid frontal advance of the massed three ranked legions. (Hannibal had defeated that by simply occupying it in front while he encircled it from the sides and the rear with his striking forces; Scipio had watched that happen at Cannae.) He also quickly adapted for Roman use the longer, two-edged Spanish sword and the dangerous iron throwing spear. (These became the service weapons of the later armies of the Caesars; the names, *gladius* and *pilum*, both derive from the Spanish Celtic.)

It surprised Scipio to discover how few citizens of Carthage were in the field. His enemies, then, relied on alliances with other, physically hardier peoples. Such alliances, as Scipio had observed in Italy itself, could be broken down by fear or the prospect of greater rewards elsewhere. At the same time the young Roman commander felt acutely the strangeness of the quarters vacated by Hannibal and Hasdrubal in the palace above the harbor at New Carthage. The chambers of the Barca brothers had no military aspect, or trophies. They had shrine niches in corners, and Greek papyri for reading in wall niches. The only mask visible appeared to be not a death mask but a thing for an actor to wear in a theater. There was also a map of the Iberian peninsula, deftly traced on a sheet of silver. It revealed roads and mountain chains and rivers as if in a picture. In Rome Scipio had been given only a list of the distances by road from place to place in Italy. Carefully he memorized this picture of Spain while he prepared to move out against his enemies.

In the summer of 208 Hasdrubal made it necessary for the Romans to move against him. Hannibal's brother had wintered in the midlands among the Carpetani; now he marched southeast to the Carthaginian end of the Silver Mountains, near Castulo. By so doing he threatened the Roman-held mines. Scipio then left the coast to advance southwest into the mountains. In so doing he never for a moment forgot that while he approached one Carthaginian army, he did not know where the other two might be.

Hasdrubal at Baecula

"Hasdrubal was always a brave man," Polybius tells us. "He bore defeat with a spirit worthy of his Barca father. Most generals do not envisage the consequences of mishaps ... but Hasdrubal neglected nothing in his preparation for a struggle. He seems to me to have been worthy of our respect and emulation."

Unmistakably Scipio respected his antagonist. Not long before, the quick-witted Hasdrubal had made a monkey of a very able Roman commander, Claudius Nero. Nero had managed to pen the Carthaginian's forces in one of the blind valleys of Spain, very much as Fabius had done with Hannibal in Italy. Then Hasdrubal had opened negotiations with Nero, discussing terms all of a week at the valley's end, while his army climbed out of the trap behind him. At the end of the week Hasdrubal broke off the parley to depart himself—and Scipio arrived, to replace Nero. Hasdrubal and Nero were to meet again, but not in Spain.

Probably Scipio was not aware that Hannibal had urged his brother to break out of Spain that summer, but he had been warned by the Senate not to allow Hasdrubal to pass the Pyrenees.

Scipio found the Carthaginians in a long valley beneath the town of Baecula. Hasdrubal was encamped on a low plateau backed against the hills with a small river flowing beneath, and the numbers of his forces impossible to discover. (Actually Hasdrubal commanded 25,000 Africans and Spaniards, while the Romans numbered 30,000 with unknown contingents of Spanish allies.)

The position was most difficult to attack, yet Scipio must attack. He did so warily, forcing the crossing of the stream. After long hesitation beneath the plateau, Scipio went in, and up, swiftly. He shifted his forces, to leave the weaker light-armed elements in the center, while his heavy legions under command of Laelius and himself went up on the flanks through dry arroyos at the ends of

180

the plateau. In this way he moved to encircle the Carthaginian encampment, with his real strength coming in at the flanks.

Scipio succeeded in this maneuver after heavy fighting on the plateau's slopes. His pincers closed in on the Carthaginian camp, crushing through Hasdrubal's lighter forces, counting some 8,000 enemy dead or captive. His legionaries despoiled the camp.

But the Carthaginian heavy forces were gone, with 32 elephants and all the horsemen. Hasdrubal was away to the Pyrenees.

Scipio could not pursue him. The other two Carthaginian armies waited, watching him, and New Carthage must be defended. Scipio sent reinforcements north to the mouth of the Ebro, where Hannibal had crossed ten years before.

Hasdrubal, however, struck north along the headwaters of the Tagus with his small mobile army. Somewhere on his march he conferred with Mago. They agreed that Mago would start for the Balearics to raise a new levy of slingers and cross later by sea to northern Italy, where the three sons of Hamilcar would meet. Then Hasdrubal went on to the Pyrenees, to a western pass held by friendly Basques (that of Roncesvalles, of Charlemagne's storied march). In the far land of the Celts he was also among friendly folk and he recruited many of them as he pushed on to the Rhone—too late in the autumn to attempt the crossing of the Alps.

Word of Hasdrubal's coming sped to Rome from Marseille. The city still mourned the deaths of two Consuls at Hannibal's hand. It seemed as if the angered gods had struck down all Roman leaders who went out against the Carthaginian wizard. There remained no single man of proved ability. Old age incapacitated Fabius. As for the young Scipio, he had gained some success, but he had let Hasdrubal slip by him, and in any case he would not leave his command in Spain. Again, after ten years, Rome felt her danger. In the north Etruria was forsaking the federation; Liguria was adding its strength to Cisalpine Gaul.

"All these misfortunes befell us," it was said, "when

181

one enemy army and one Hannibal faced us. Now there will be two mighty armies and two Hannibals in Italy."

The new Carthaginian would appear precisely in the most dangerous spot, on the river Po. And after that, what might not Hannibal himself accomplish?

In the election, two Consuls were named for the year of crisis—two men of ability without fame. Claudius Nero, who had campaigned against Hasdrubal in Spain, became patrician Consul; he would have the task of holding Hannibal in check. A certain Livius, who did not desire to serve, became plebeian Consul, to command the army of the north. The election, the ritual of sacrifice, and the military planning were carried out as in all the past years by Roman tradition. No one had real expectation that Nero and Livius would prove to be equal to the two sons of Hamilcar Barca.

Message from the Po

After the melting of the snows (207) Hasdrubal crossed the Alps more swiftly than Hannibal, and apparently by the same pass. As before the Roman command had hoped to intercept the Carthaginians in the mountains. But the invaders swept down the Po, joined by bands of dour Ligurians and raising the spirits of the volatile Gauls. They locked the Roman frontier force into Placentia, as Hannibal had done, and swept on, south and east around the great spine of the Apennines. Hasdrubal still had a dozen elephants alive and he moved fast.

Then happened an incident that affected the whole of the Mediterranean. On leaving the Po Hasdrubal dispatched a message to his brother. It named a rendezvous for their armies in Umbria, on the Adriatic coast. Six riders, four Gauls and two Numidians, carried the written message. Some of them may have been told it. Probably a Gaul led the way south, avoiding enemy encampments, toward Hannibal's lines far down in Lucania.

Hannibal had been there, but he had broken through the Roman lines to gain the Adriatic coast. At that time, he was circling back to pick up all his detached forces, and to thrust north through dogged resistance to the plain of the Aufidus not far from the field of Cannae.

The messengers from the Po tried to follow him. They were caught by Roman foragers near Tarentum. Hasdrubal's letter was carried to Claudius Nero at the Aufidus lines, not to Hannibal.

With the message in his hand the anxious Nero had one of those flashes of foresight that lead routine-bound men to attempt extraordinary things. He put it in conventional words that he "judged the situation of the state to be no longer such that they should carry on the war by routine methods." He abandoned his army confronting Hannibal to start out of his area of authority in the south with one selected legion and 1,000 picked horsemen to join Livius in the north with the news of Hasdrubal's rendezvous. The letter itself he sent to the Senate with an explanation; yet he did not wait for permission to leave his command. Instead, he dispatched riders ahead to warn villages along his line of march to bring supplies to the road, with horses, mules, carts—anything that could carry leg-weary men a stage further on their way. He set a pace that only a legion could maintain.

(It is often said but it is not true that Nero stripped his army of its strength and left the usual number of camp-fires burning at night to hoodwink Hannibal. He took only 7,000 with him and left more than 30,000 in forti-fied lines on the river, while other forces held Tarentum in the rear of Hannibal. Nero simply realized that the few days were priceless in which one Carthaginian brother did not know what the other was doing, while the Romans could know what both were doing.)

Hannibal waited on the Aufidus for the message that never reached him, unable to move to the north until he learned by what road Hasdrubal would come south. The departure of one legion with mounted escort did not en-lighten him. For once, his cavalry scouts failed him.

Hasdrubal was past Rimini, coming down the Adriatic coast. Like trained hounds gathering at the approach of a bear, the Roman forces drew together east of the Apennines. They assembled under Livius south of the Metaurus (Metauro) River. The Carthaginians crossed it by Fanum Fortunae (Fano) only to find the Roman lines before them. The country was strange to Hasdrubal, although he had Gauls with him who knew the roads. For a little he delayed to study what lay ahead, perhaps hoping for directions from Hannibal.

Nero came in to the Roman lines near Sena Gallica at night. He had sent ahead a warning to conceal all evidence of his arrival. Under cover of the darkness his nearly exhausted men were crowded into the tents of Livius' command so that no new tents were raised. Livius and his staff argued that the legion from the south must have in interval of rest before action. But Nero, who had had experience with Hannibal, insisted that delay would be disastrous. The army of the Roman People must attack at once. It was so agreed.

Even then, discipline almost defeated the purpose of the two Consuls. A Carthaginian scouting partol noticed the presence of men who showed signs of hard marching in the enemy camp. And the trumpeter who gave the call to battle stations before Livius' tent sounded the call twice as duty ordained. The astute Hasdrubal guessed that two Roman Consuls faced him instead of one, and that the enemy strength had been increased. He drew back his own forces and that night attempted to slip away up the valley of the Metaurus to gain the Flaminian Way to the south. His move out to the west began well but the guides could not find their way to the road in the dark. By daylight the Romans had cut him off from the road. Perhaps he might have retreated to Po; instead he drew up his forces for battle.

This battle of the Metaurus is known as one that changed the course of history. It is also the last time the peoples of Italy arrayed themselves against the Roman legions, forerunners of the empire of the Caesars. For Hasdrubal aligned his army in its national groups—Ligurian, Gallic, and Spanish-African. He gave his elephants to the Ligurians. For a while the great beasts crushed their way into the advancing Romans. Reinforcements of Ligurians and Gauls were streaming in to the river. They did not reach Hasdrubal in time.

For hours the conflict hung in the balance. Then Claudius Nero upset the balance. He was on the far right end of the Roman line, with his 7,000 occupying a knoll protected by a shallow ravine. The enemy in front of him happened to be Gauls who did everything except cross the ravine to get at him. After watching the Gauls in front and listening to the trumpet calls and piercing war cries at the other end of the long line, Nero understood that Livius' legions at that point were at death-grip with Hasdrubal's Spanish-Africans. After listening long enough, he deserted his post again. He left some cavalry to act fiercely on the crest of his knoll to amuse the Gauls.

Then he led his leg-weary legion around the battle.

Nero passed behind the Roman line, along the highroad, to come in on the flank and rear of Hasdrubal's heavily engaged forces. His legion was still intact. It added the final impact that broke through the hand-to-hand fighting of exhausted men.

As his ranks gave way, Hasdrubal rode into them to rally them and was killed. After that the disciplined Romans thrust deep into the leaderless allied groups. The Gauls, little harmed, marched off, and the reinforcements turned back with the fugitives. There were few survivors among the Spanish-Africans, and no one to take Hasdrubal's place. His army ceased to exist. In the Carthaginian camp the legions of Livius released 4,500 Roman captives. The Roman army had suffered severely but it was still effective and heartened by its unexpected victory.

That night Claudius Nero started his legion on the road to the south. In six days of extraordinary marching—for 210 miles—he was back in his encampment on the Aufidus. He went at such a pace that the villages along his road had no news of the battle until he reached them.

In Rome the Senate had kept in session in the Forum from sunrise to sunset. The citizens came and went, hanging about the rostra and the temples to catch any word arriving from the battle fronts.

185

"A vague rumor came that two horsemen of Narnia had reached the Umbrian gateway, to report from the battlefield that the enemy had been cut to pieces. At first men heard this without believing it. Then came a letter from Lucius Manlius at the gateway, regarding the news of the Narnia horsemen. This letter was carried through the Forum to the tribunal. With such rivalry and disorder did people rush up, that the messenger could not get near the doors of the Curia. Then word went around that the riders themselves were approaching the city. People of all ages rushed out, eager to take in with eyes and ears so great a joy. The mass of them reached all the way to the Mulvian bridge. . . . The Senate decreed that since the Consuls Marcus Livius and Gaius Claudius [Nero] were safe with their army and had slain the leaders and legions of the enemy, there should be a thanksgiving for three days."

As soon as he regained his encampment on the Aufidus, Nero gave order that "the head of Hasdrubal, which he had brought with him and kept with care, should be thrown in front of the enemy's outposts. And that African prisoners in chains be displayed to the enemy. Furthermore that two of them, released from chains, should be sent to Hannibal to tell him what had happened."

This was done as ordered.

A triumph was decreed for the two Consuls on their return thereafter to Rome. Then the Senate commanded that Etruria and Umbria be purged of all those who had given aid or any kind of assistance to Hasdrubal.

The rejoicing at Rome kept up for many months. The people heard that Hannibal, the son of Hamilcar, had received his brother's head and at once left his lines on the Aufidus. Taking many Lucanians with him, he evacuated the Gulf of Taranto as far as Metapontum and withdrew into the hills of the Bruttii. There, at the end of Italy, he waited. No one suggested attacking him.

"Nor did the Romans provoke him so long as he remained inactive—such power did they believe to be within this one commander, although everything around him crashed."

186

For the first time since he had left New Carthage twelve years before, Hannibal had lost the initiative in the great war. It must have seemed ironical to him that his enemies with their vast forces in Italy made no move against him. True, he did not allow them to realize how weak his own force had become. Only the skeleton of his army of Italy survived, with the addition of a few Lucanian farmers, Greek seamen, Roman deserters, and the uncouth Bruttii mountaineers. Probably his real safeguard was the unreal legend of his name.

In this tip of Italy he still held a larger domain than Carthage itself. He had seaports, although very small ones, at Locri and Croton near the lovely Lacinian temple. He had food enough for his remaining men and even a store of silver for their needs. Inevitably Hannibal must have pondered whether he should take ship to try to cross to Africa and Spain, where his thoughts centered now. Perhaps a sense of fatality, after Hasdrubal's death, kept him waiting in the battleground of his hills. Perhaps hard reasoning made it clear that if he departed from Bruttium his army would disintegrate; while in Spain or Mago and other Carthaginian commanders were being reinforced by men and ships from Carthage. And almost certainly he expected the Roman Consuls to close in with all their strength on his last domain. As a Carthaginian he longed to avenge the contemptous casting down of Hasdrubal's head.

All the next year the news that reached him in driblets from incoming ships deepened his anxiety. After the harvest, convoys of grain ships from Sicily put an end to hunger along the Tiber. The fields of Latium were under cultivation again. Crews released from the fleets went back to farms elsewhere.

Across the Adriatic the king of Macedonia sensed the change of fortune and made his peace with the Aetolians, the satellites of Rome. This ended the brief alliance of Carthage with Syracuse and Macedonia. ("If you are defeated even your friends will leave you.")

And then came the disastrous defeat in Spain. At Ilipa, Mago and the Carthaginian commanders—with Masinissa, the Numidian—engaged all their great forces in ranged battle with the young Roman proconsul. Scipio shifted his lines during the conflict to crush in the Carthaginian wings and drive the remnants headlong toward the shore of the Ocean. Only Gades remained as a rallying point, and Hannibal knew that the Gaditans, like the Macedonians, would not support Carthage in her need. If he could have been at Ilipa before the battle!

Then Gades was making overtures to Scipio, and the Romans marching in. Ancient Gades was following the way of Tarentum, opening her gates to the masters who would never depart.

Resistance began, too late, on the part of the Iberians and Celtiberians. Indibilis wrenched himself free from the Romans, to be pursued swiftly; remote in the mountains, the fortress of Ilurgi resisted the Roman engines, and its men and women died in the streets under the swords of the legionaries. Astapa burned, with its people. Hannibal knew them well. Castulo, stronghold of his wife's family, yielded. In the far north the Ilergetes and Edetani raided Roman stores; Scipio's legions herded them into a valley and cut them to pieces.

Scipio gained submission through fear. Spanish war bands joined him against their feudal foes. Scipio rewarded them all. He could be as merciless toward his own men. Beyond the Ebro a legion turned against its officers. Scipio summoned 35 of its leaders to come before him at New Carthage to draw their pay. There the 35 were surrounded by his legionaries and scourged at stakes before they were put to death.

At the new year the Romans held funeral games at New Carthage. They had gladiators—swordsmen—enter the arena in mimic combat as sacrifice to the War-god. After the pantomine ended, the blood was washed into the dirt of the arena and incensed burned upon it.

Hannibal brooded over the youth Scipio, so like Fabius in certain ways, yet so unlike him. By whatever means, Scipio had gained complete mastery over Spain. The dominion of the Barca family had ended, after a little more than thirty years.

Mago remained. He carried off and executed some of the magistrates of Gades; with a few ships and 2,000 followers, he entered the strait and attempted to surprise New Carthage from the sea. Failing, he sailed off to the Pine Islands and Minorca to recruit men there as he had planned with Hasdrubal. From Croton Hannibal sent a message to Carthage, to urge that Mago land at the Ligurian gulf to head the resistance there and hold the line of the Po against the legions.

Landing at a harbor called Genua, Mago disappeared into the foothills. The two brothers were far apart, Mago beneath the Alps and Hannibal at the tip of Italy.

As the thirteenth year began, a lethargy seemed to fall on the Romans in Italy. They were weary; they had much to repair and more to subdue. In the relief of the last years, they were content to rest. Against that lethargy Publius Cornelius Scipio set his determination and his astute mind.

The Banquet of the Genial Syphax

The great battle of Zama, in which Scipio opposed Hannibal, did not begin on a hot spring day of the year 202. It began several years before that in the mind of Publius Scipio, and what he accomplished in the interval had much to do with what happened on the plain of Zama.

As early as May of 206—soon after Ilipa—Scipio risked his first crossing to Africa. What befell him there is quite unbelievable, and it would make a cloak-and-dagger romance but it is all true.

After Ilipa, as usual, the youthful proconsul sent stunning spoils and trophies back to the Forum, the seat of the political power he craved. He counted on mastering the rest of Spain with his now veteran army and gifted lieutenants, Marcius and Laelius. That done, he expected to cross the strait to carry the war into Africa and force

Hannibal to leave the other land bridge of the Mediterranean, at the juncture of Sicily—to abandon Italy and return to defend Carthage. It was quite simple, as brilliant strategy always is. His father had had the idea before him and had started diplomatic parleys with Syphax, monarch of the Numidians, who had supplied Hannibal with horsemen until now. The elder Publius Scipio had planned to turn Spain into a base for the African expedition as Hannibal had done before the march to Rome. What Hannibal did was the best possible example to follow.

Perhaps when he embarked on a high-floating pentecounter at the port of Tarraco and put out to sea the younger Scipio had no realization that he was changing the nature of his Republic: that it would presently cease to be an Italian state and would become an empire expanding across the sea to new horizons. That was of course a dream of the Aemilian and Scipionic heads of families. Scipio himself, however, was merely a commander of one army to whom, in a dire emergency, consular power had been loaned; moreover his area of authority ended at the Pyrenees. (Nero had risked disgrace to himself and the Claudian *gens* when he gambled on marching from southern Italy, and won fame by the gamble.) Scipio's authority would end virtually with the subjection of Spain—except for the customary parade when he returned to Rome and the adoration of his wife. Instead of that Scipio craved with every cell of his body to become the victor in the war itself, over Hannibal. The circumstance that this appeared to be as impossible as piling Mount Pelion on Mount Ossa did not deter him.

The brief sea crossing was pleasant. It was, of course, risky. Scipio had only the protection of a safe-conduct from Syphax, chieftain of a barbaric and slippery people, who had insisted on meeting him in person on the African shore. Another pentecounter escorted the proconsul's vessel, more to add prestige to it than to afford protection. The two vessels rounded the point of Siga, the rendezvous. In the scanty harbor seven Carthaginian galleys rode at anchor in a buffeting breeze. At sight of the Roman ships, the galleys swarmed with seamen preparing for action.

With remarkable audacity Scipio kept his pentecounters
190

headed in, without calling to battle stations. A gust of wind carried them through the galleys to the quay where, as guests, they could claim safeguard from the African king. The Carthaginian captains realized as much and broke off action.

Then in the hall of his host, Scipio came face to face with another guest, a Carthaginian. He was Hasdrubal by name, son of Gisgo, a middle-aged and astute noble who had been co-commander with Mago, son of Hannilcar, at Ilipa! Scipio must have had a moment's soul-searching.

Syphax suggested a festive dinner to honor their reunion. He was delighted to have under his roof the great adversaries of the war in Spain—bound by the truce of his home. Elderly and expert in dark negotiations, Syphax was proud of his mastery of the warlike Numidians. His capital at Cirta stood on the edge of Carthaginian authority, and Syphax had all a tribeman's respect for the six-story dwellings and the vast temple of El, the god of the east that made Carthage unique. He also felt a growing respect for Roman victories in Iberia, across the way from Siga, and for the eagle-faced commander who could walk casually into his door. On his own account, Syphax could summon up skilled horsemen by the tens of thousands; but he seemed aware that he should not offend the Romans, while he could not turn against the Carthaginians. Scipio, while eating, described the advantages of Roman rule in glowing terms (through interpreters).

Syphax, who desired no personal part in the war, suggested that Scipio use the opportunity to become friends with the lord Hasdrubal. Scipio declared he would be glad to do so; he had no animosity toward his enemy—in fact found him delightful company.

The Numidian said: then why not agree on terms of peace?

Scipio said that was a different matter; he was only an officer who carried out the orders of the Senate and the Roman People, who in turn decided when a war might end in a peace.

"That man," Hasdrubal observed to his host after Scipio's departure, "is even more dangerous in talk than in battle."

The Roman carried away Syphax's promise that he

191

would become an ally; the Carthaginian took away Syphax's pledge that he would never cease to be friend to Carthage.

Scipio, however, had another string to his bow. Above everything he needed good horsemen in Africa. To get them he won over the brilliant cavalry leader who had helped destroy his father and had stood against Scipio himself at Ilipa. Masinissa, prince of the Massyles, had been educated in Carthage; he had been loyal to Carthage until he saw the remnant of Carthaginian strength driven west to the island of Gades, where horsemen could not operate. Then, too, Scipio had laid Masinissa under obligation by releasing a young nephew of the tribal prince from captivity. And Scipio was not afraid to meet with Masinissa alone at night. The African guerilla leader fell under the spell of the Roman's charm and of his own ambition. For he was at the moment disinherited. Masinissa gave his pledge that when the proconsul landed an army on the African coast, he would join him with a great strength of Numidian horse.

Now Masinissa—it is apparent now—meant to keep his word while Syphax had no such intention. Yet Masinissa was out of power, little more than a refugee in Spain, while Syphax had both prestige and power. It did not seem to disturb Scipio that Masinissa hated the very name of Syphax.

Something, nonetheless, disturbed him very much because he scrapped entire his plan of invading Africa across the strait. Did he believe, after visiting Siga, that the long march by the coast to Carthage was not practical? Did he fear for his base in Spain? In those weeks resistance flamed through the interior; Ilurgi held out until death; the women and children of Astapa crowded into walls to be burned by their men rather than submit to the Romans. The shadow of Hannibal still lay on the land.

Scipio planted a colony in the lovely Betis Valley— seed for Romanization in a future day. Leaving his army but taking the invaluable Laelius with him he embarked on a ship for Rome. It was then, by no coincidence, the eve of the new year's election.

Immediately on his arrival the conqueror of Spain encountered opposition from the older elements of the Senate. Since he had left his area of command without an order to do so, ancient law barred him from entering the city itself. His persuasion brought the Senate body out of the walls, to hear him at the temple of Bellona, sister of Mars. And there his persuasion failed to win him the triumphal entry he demanded with audacity. A triumph could be granted only to a victor of consular rank, which Publius Cornelius Scipio did not possess.

That was precisely what the young soldier meant to have. Owing to his popularity the Senate could not refuse him permission to enter a gate as a simple citizen. Thereupon Scipio made quite a show of his entry, with veterans and captives from Spain following and cartloads of silver bars going before him. The populace always delighted in a spectacle, particularly one with trumpets and treasure. After that Scipio staged a procession to the temple of Jupiter, his devine patron, to sacrifice no less then 30 oxen, and he drew another great audience. Legend clothed him almost as tangibly as his spotless toga. Would-be clients waited at his door for his morning appearance. His sayings penetrated the Sacred Way. Each day there was a new saying, always crisp and startling. "I have not come to wage the war—I am here to finish it." And then: "Until now Carthage has been carrying on the war against Rome; now Rome will carry it against Carthage."

The popular assemblies agreed with every word, and Scipio was swept into consulship for the coming year. With him the Aemillian-Scipionic party gained ascendancy; Claudius Nero, victor at the Metaurus, was passed over in the fall of the Claudian party; Licinius Crassus, an average personality, who held the ancient post of Pontifex Maximus became the second Consul. Since tradition forbade a Pontifex Maximus to leave Italy, Licinius was given command of the battle front against Hannibal at Bruttium, and the Sicilian front fell to Scipio, as he had desired. Sicily was a bridge to Africa.

As Consul Scipio held the rank he needed, but he did not have the authority to depart from Sicily. His first suggestions that he lead the army from there to Carthage met with a hard opposition.

Behind that opposition lay the rigid concepts of the past: the agrarian policy of the landowning group—Agriculture and Italy—that sought only the recapture and colonization of Cisalpine Gaul (where the Carthaginian Mago headed the Ligurians and Gauls). Much more formidable, age-old tradition conceived of the Republic as expanding only across land frontiers by the force of the massed national army of legions and allies. Hannibal had frustrated this traditional way of defense for thirteen years.

The eccentric Scipio embodied the entirely new concept of a single man in power, a virtual *imperator* or emperor, leading the Romans out to sea into the wealth, the trade, and the dangers of the outer Hellenistic world.

Perhaps only Scipio visualized clearly whither the policy of the elders was leading the Roman state. Content with the victories in Spain and at the Metaurus, they were allowing Hannibal to hold his ground in Italy. Subconsciously they conceded that he could not be dislodged. They thought only of how they might defend themselves against him. And Carthage remained intact. Another year or two or five and they would come inevitably to a negotiated peace, after which their great antagonist would sail back with an undefeated army to a city unharmed except in a portion of its treasure by nearly twenty years of conflict.

On the steps of Jupiter's temple Scipio repeated a rumor he had heard. "Hannibal occupies his leisure at the temple of Juno Lacinia on the southern shore. He is making a bronze tablet on which will be inscribed his triumphs." And Scipio named them. "At the Ticinus, on the Trebia, by Lake Trasumennus, at Cannae. I wonder if he will not put at the end: Victory over the Roman People?"

194

To enforce the consent of the Senate to his project of an expedition from Sicily, Scipio threatened to carry it before the popular assemblies (which favored him in any attempt to end the conflict). This amounted to rebellion against the will of the Fathers, and it aligned the leaders of the Senate against the soldier from Spain. It brought on a full debate. Fabius Maximus rose to speak against the project of the African expedition, which meant against Scipio.

The Delayer spoke with the wiles of a seasoned orator and the repressed hositility of a very old man toward a youth coming into a fame as great as his own. Why, he asked the Senators, should he set himself against one who was younger than his own son?

He paid tribute to Scipio, to the "daily increasing fame of our very brave Consul." He deprecated his own fame, and appealed to the younger Senators. "I have kept Hannibal from conquering so that you men of steadily increasing strength may conquer him." And suddenly he cast stubborn fact at them. Why, when Hannibal was here, next to their doors, should they go to Africa in the hope that he would follow? Let them gain peace first in Italy before carrying the war to Africa.

"Tell me—may the gods avert the omens—if a victorious Hannibal should advance upon our city—for what has happened can happen again—are we to summon our Consul out of Africa as we summoned Fulvius from Capua?"

He let his listeners sense the danger of the African coast, and recall the fate of the other Consul, Regulus, who had invaded it. Savagely, he belittled Scipio's achievements in Spain. What had Publius Cornelius undertaken there, except to voyage safely from Italy along a friendly coast, to take command of an army already there, trained by his dead father? True, he had taken New Carthage—when all three Carthaginian armies were absent from it. Upon what, then, did Scipio count in risking the fortune of Rome by crossing to Africa, where no port and no friendly army awaited him? Upon the alliance with the Numidian, Syphax? In Spain his Celtiberian allies had turned against him and his own soldiers had mutinied. On the other hand at the Metaurus two Consuls had united their forces to prove that an invader could be defeated in Italy. And—"where Hannibal is, there is the center of this war."

Fabius asked the Senate to consider whether Scipio was acting for the good of the state or for his own ambition. Already he had risked the fortune of Rome by crossing in two vessels to the far African shore, without authorization, although he was then a commanding general of the Roman People.

"My opinion," he summed up, "is that Publius Cornelius was elected Consul for the Republic, not for himself. Our armies were enlisted for the defense of the city and Italy, not to be transported by consuls in the manner of tyrants to whatever lands they choose."

It was a strong speech, delivered by a man of Fabius' prestige. At the moment Scipio stood in defiance of the Senate. Apparently he made no attempt to answer it as an accusation. He replied that he was content to have them form their own opinion of his life and achievements, and he would abide by the opinion they expressed. As to his plan, could they have a more effective example than Hannibal himself? Hannibal was not disturbed by imagined fears in entering Italy, although he faced the Roman citizen army. Nothing like that existed in Africa.

Ironically, the debate in the Senate turned into a debate about Hannibal himself and the action to be taken against him. Although Scipio lost the debate he won what he wanted, permission to act as he pleased. The Senate granted him leave to cross from Sicily to Africa "if he thought it to be to the advantage of the state." Yet, almost unbelievably, it denied Scipio the right to take legions from Italy or more than 30 ships, except for the few needed to service Sicily. For the rest he might enlist whom he pleased and build vessels—all at his own cost.

What followed was due entirely to the initiative of one man, Scipio, driven by personal ambition. It was carried out at first at his own cost and risk.

The two regular legions that awaited him in Sicily were those of the forgotten men of Cannae, serving out their exile.

These legions, the Fifth and Sixth, were "weary of growing old in exile." To them Scipio appeared like a god out of a machine. He restored them to active service, and such service! Embarkation for Africa to seek the loot of Carthage and final victory! Thereafter these lost legions of Cannae, now overage, became Scipio's devoted dogs.

The young Counsul had also brought with him from Italy some 7,000 volunteers who much preferred service with him in the unravaged fields of Africa to the battlefields facing Hannibal, where an epidemic was raging in the regular army encampments. These volunteers had all seen service and had learned to be choosy about commanders. Then, too, Scipio had doubled their pay. Despite his affability, the general from Spain was choosy about whom he enlisted. When enthusiastic nobles of Syracuse—his base of operations—banded together in a volunteer squadron with glittering house trappings and armor, he lectured them politely on the actual hardships of warfare, and generously offered to release the Syracusans if they would donate their equipment to be used by trained soldiers.

At the same time Scipio cultivated the good will of Syracuse, still licking the wounds of Marcellus' blood purge. Most of the Greek householders had claims for damages suffered at the hands of Roman soldiers. The young champion of a new order heard their pleas and granted their indemnities.

His quaestor (finance officer) from Rome happened to be a gawky redheaded plebeian from the farms, Marcus Porcius Cato. This Cato (who would gain everlasting fame from three spoken words, *Delenda est Carthago*) had a farmer's narrow puritanism and a keen nose for the political wind; he was, besides, a protégé of the aged Fabius. When he protested against his commander's heedlessness with money, Scipio answered that he was responsible for the safety of the state, not for so many coins

197

counted out of a box. The feud between the would-be censor and the dynamic leader endured for a long time.

While Scipio put his embryo army—more than 12,000, less than 20,000—through rugged field training, he sought for every means of aiding it. He sent out a call for ex-officers with engineering experience; he collected transport shipping with the avidity of a miser. Experience in Spain had taught him that the Romans had two advantages over the Carthaginians, their skill in siege operations and their navy. Those two advantages he must possess over Hannibal. With stronger fleets his base of Sicily would become a deadly danger to Carthage; with weaker fleets it would become a embarkation point for disaster.

Now there is a fable of the Latin annalists that at this juncture all the allied cities of Italy, notably the Etruscan community, poured out stores of shipbuilding materials upon Scipio despite the opposition of the Senate. And that in 45 days 30 vessels were thrown together from fresh-hewed timber and launched to a general whoop and applause. Those 30 galleys belong with the rowing machines by which Romans learned seamanship in an earlier day; they make a first-rate story but they never existed. In 204 the Etruscan cities were being flagellated for their recent rebellion, and with the arrival of Mago they would rebel again. Elsewhere the allied cities were protesting bitterly that they could not meet their year's quotas "despite the anger of the Roman People." The Senate refused to hear their magistrates until the quotas were met. In reality, Scipio brought 30 galleys from Italy and managed to find as many more in Sicilian waters. With no stronger battle fleet than that he had the resolution to prepare his expedition to go.

This fable in turn has led some modern historians to picture Scipio as preparing his expedition without any aid from a thankless Rome. That also is not true. And the actuality is much more creditable to Scipio, to the Roman Senate and, incidentally, to Hannibal. The difference between Scipio and his government was still that of their debate, of ideas. The Senate majority was right in believing that Scipio with the larger army of the other Consul could wear Hannibal down by years of attrition in his Bataan-

like end of Italy. Scipio realized that perfectly. But he had
the imagination to understand what must follow it: that
an exhausted Italy, once free of Hannibal, would never
take up the conflict anew to invade Africa. (And Scipio's
fame would be, accordingly, less.) The Senate gave him
little aid at first because it had none to give. The danger
of a breakout by Hannibal toward Rome was real, unless
superior military forces penned him in. It was a great feat,
seldom recognized, on the part of the one-eyed Carthaginian to hold the major Roman strength pinned, as it
were, against his hills for three years. It was a plan requiring cold nerve on the part of Scipio to take to the sea
with his small force and the odds all against him.

To hearten his recuits and gain information, Scipio
launched his lieutenant, Laelius, first to sea. With a strong
enough squadron Laelius got across to a port called
Hippo Regius (Bône) by the Romans, far to the west of
Carthage. There he landed to ravage the countryside and
meet with Masinissa, who arrived on the scene with only
a few horsemen—although Hippo lay within his ancestral
domain. What Masinissa had to report was not encouraging. Syphax was going over to the Carthaginian cause.

"Why does Scipio the Consul delay?" Masinissa demanded. "Tell him to come quickly."

The young Numidian warned Laelius that a Carthaginian fleet had put to sea to search for him. And the
Roman raiders withdrew promptly, to regain Sicily safely.

Scipio made much of the spoils they brought back, but
the prospect of the sea darkened swiftly for him. Carthage, aroused by Laelius' raid, mustered her forces to
resist. Along the African coast watch posts and beacons
dotted the headlands. Within the city the land wall was
manned, a levy of men and money carried out, while the
shipyards of the inner harbor went feverishly to work.

The results appeared swiftly. The fleet that had missed
Laelius took to sea again with a treasure chest and rein-
forcements of 6,000 men, 800 Numidians and their horses
and 7 elephants. It evaded the Roman watch at sea—as
Mago's fleet had done—and brought in its convoy to
Genua, with orders for Mago to put himself at the head
of the Ligurians and Gauls, to attempt to join Hannibal.
To aid Hannibal himself a convoy of 100 vessels, unes-

corted but laden with men, grain, and silver, sailed direct for Locri in Bruttium. Accident defeated it. A storm scattered the convoy, and 20 transports were sunk by Roman galleys; some survivors regained Carthage safely but not a single vessel reached Hannibal's coast.

The truth became apparent that lethargy gripped the half-disbanded Roman navy; the vigilant squadrons of Otacilius' day no longer barred the sea lanes. In growing uneasiness, Scipio heard that Hannibal had left his inland frontier and was on his way to Locri.

On the nearest available galleys, Scipio gathered what force he had at hand, with ladders and engines, and started for Locri. It was only a short distance from the Sicilian coast, but it lay outside his area of authority. Scipio ignored that circumstance in his anxiety to forestall the wizard of Cannae. Even in his haste he was careful to take ships and machines with him.

Locri was the larger of the two ports still remaining to Hannibal in Bruttium. Already a small Roman force had gained entry into it by the usual treachery—a group of Locrian artisans had been released from captivity in Sicily to return home on a pledge that they would let the Roman column into the wall. The town itself lay between two heights defended by citadels, and the Roman attack force had gained only the southern citadel. A certain Pleminius, an officer of Scipio's, held command here. The Carthaginian garrison had withdrawn to the opposite height.

Hannibal, approaching swiftly from the north, sent word to his garrison to sally out on the night when he came in to attack the Roman-held citadel. The townspeople, who had hailed the Roman soldiers as liberators, now fell silent and withdrew into their homes.

That day Scipio's galleys rowed into the harbor and his cohorts entered the streets between the heights. His scouts went out on the northern road and sighted Carthaginian horsemen approaching. In the evening Hannibal's advance drew in to the wall. Scipio's cohorts hurried out the gates, to draw up in combat line. Hannibal arrived to find an enemy fleet in the harbor and a strong force in the town. His column had brought neither scaling ladders nor catapults. After taking off his garrison from the citadel, Hannibal withdrew.

It was hardly an incident, this bloodless brush of the armed forces. In all probability Hannibal learned only afterward of Scipio's presence. However, it heartened Scipio's legionaries, who had faced the invincible Carthaginian and had seen him retreat.

Embarkation for Africa

Locri had consequences that all but ruined Scipio's undertaking. His legate, Pleminius, proved to be an unqualified brute when placed in command of the captured port. In his sadistic revelry Pleminius executed the Locrian leaders who had co-operated with the Carthaginians, commandeered young women for the brothels, carried off the treasure of the town's sanctuary, and ended up by scourging two tribunes of the Roman army. The Locrians, repenting their change of masters, sent envoys to complain to Rome.

Scipio could use cruelty to gain an end, as when he had condemned the leaders of the mutiny in Spain to public torment—and his legionaries had clashed swords against shields to show their approval—yet he did not have Marcellus' brutal nature. For reasons best known to himself, Scipio upheld Pleminius. The Senate reviewed the case, and Scipio. The scourging of the tribunes, immune by Roman law, was an offense, and the profaning of the temple was an offense against the gods. Moreover their Consul in Sicily had risked his life again outside his legal area. To these considerations they added a confidential report on Scipio's conduct in Syracuse, from the hand of the quaestor, Cato. It accused the Consul of un-Roman behavior.

Scipio, it seemed, relaxed at evening with Greeks in talk over wine bowls; a commanding officer, he went around in sandals and flimsy Greek chiton, and entered athletic games in the gymnasium. Ironically, the new debate over Scipio ended in the sending of a senatorial committee of investigation to Sicily, with power to remove him. Characteristically, Scipio made ready to receive the investigators with a full-dress rehearsal of the invasion. Off the coast the Senators beheld galleys stripped for action; in the harbor several hundred (confiscated) transports lay moored rail to rail. Within the arsenal doors grain and weapons piled high. At the quays waited catapults and ballista and scorpions (mostly taken from Syracuse). Best show of all, on the drill plain marched and counter-marched the new legions, rhythmically all moving machines.

The Senators had experience enough to know efficiency when they saw it. Delighted at this apparition of a new army at almost no cost to the public treasury, they returned to Rome to praise Publius Cornelius Scipio as a true son of his father, a worthy soldier in the ancient tradition.

That was the beginning of Scipio's favor with the Senate, and thereafter all available support went to him.

On the heels of this invasion pageant, Scipio ordered the real invasion to start. As his forces took ship, he received a stunning blow that he was quick to conceal. Envoys arrived from Syphax to announce that the Numidian chief felt himself to be bound to Carthage. A personal letter warned Scipio against the campaign in which Syphax was to have aided him. "Do not invade Africa."

Scipio did not give out the message or the warning. To explain the appearance of Numidians at his quarters, he said that their king, like Masinissa, had sent to him to make haste. Then he ordered all commands to embark.

At dawn Scipio went on board the flagship waiting with one wing of the fighting galleys to escort the convoy of 400 assorted vessels, and some 30,000 men including the warship crews. On the deck he killed the sacrificial lamb with his own hand and threw the entrails into the sea. Those watching him said he invoked the power of Neptune to aid the ships of the Roman People.

Scipio prayed: "Grant me the power to visit fate upon the state of the Carthaginians."

The trumpets sounded, and Scipio called to the pilots to steer toward the shore of the Syrtes, well to the east of Carthage. When the last ships of the convoy were out of hearing by the crowd on the shore, he changed the order. The pilots were to head directly for Carthage.

A fortnight passed before a courier galley arrived from Africa with the first report of the expedition. Public announcement was made to the expectant throngs in Syracuse: "A victorious landing, and a town captured at once with eight thousand captives, and great spoil." The galley had prisoners aboard and chests of valuables to exhibit in proof.

Matters, however, had not gone as well as all that.

Scipio's Darkest Hour

Africa roused from her peacetime inertia to resist the invader. Africa had always been symbolized by the poets as a woman. Legendry reveals the queen of Carthage as *Dido,* won and then abandoned by Aeneas, a supposed ancestor of the Romans. Tradition relates that Carthage itself was founded by a refugee princess of Tyre. This womanly eponym may have derived from the worship of Tanit, the Great Mother, whose temple crowned the Byrsa. It expresses in varying terms of sex conflict the struggle of Africa against Europe, of stratagems and invention against force and mechanism, of an ancient culture against barbarism. Regulus, the invader, had believed himself to be conqueror of the African coast, only to find himself cast back into the sea.

Intangible forces gathered unexpectedly to oppose Scipio, also a Roman Consul, after his daring and completely successful crossing in the midsummer of 204. He had made his landing on the shore near Utica. That City of the Sea, older than Carthage—called Utica by the Romans—had shared Marseille's jealousy of the maritime imperium of Carthage and was, besides, strategically placed near the mouth of the Bagradas River, not 20 miles from her younger sister of the Byrsa. He had counted on winning over or swiftly storming Utica. By so doing he would have gained a fortified base open to the sea within a day's march of the great land wall of Carthage.

Unaccountably the Phoenician-Greek city chose to resist, and it beat off his attack. He was forced to begin siege operations in a hostile country.

The coast itself proved to be hostile. He had counted on setting the hinterland—the tens of thousands of Numidians under Syphax—against the Carthaginians. Yet Syphax, as he had warned Scipio, mobilized his manpower to aid Hasdrubal, son of Gisgo, who had little enough manpower. And a woman was in some measure responsible for this. She was Sophonisba, the daughter of the astute Hasdrubal. Sophonisba, a youthful beauty, had been tutored by Greeks in music and beguilements; she was also devoted to her father and to Carthage. Hasdrubal had sealed his compact with the old Numidian by giving him Sophonisba in marriage—to report his doings and to influence him. She showed herself to be more than capable of doing both.

Masinissa related as much when he appeared in the siege lines. Scipio had counted on obtaining some strength in Numidian horse from the exiled chieftain; only 200 showed up. Except for his hand weapons, Masinissa had no visible resources but an unquenchable spirit. He laughed when he explained that he would have been hunted down and killed if he had not escaped by spreading the rumor of his death.

A woman, an enigmatic old chieftain, a fly-by-night bandit, and a silent hostile coast almost without harbors—these joined together to confront Publius Cornelius with problems that could not easily be solved by the swords of his legionaries. Winter came on with Utica still withstanding him, while a Carthaginian-Numidian army mobilized in the southern plain. Scipio got in some supplies by raiding the fertile Bagradas basin, and ships brought some grain from Sardinia. He then withdrew his encampment to a rocky promontory just east of Utica. There he beached his galleys, set the crews to work in the siege lines, which had to be maintained. He christened the camp Castra Cornelia. While he prepared to hold it against Syphax and Hasdrubal son of Gisgo, he sent highly optimistic reports to the Senate—with an eye on the skeptical Cato—aware that he might be recalled at the first news of defeat.

Winter storms cut him off from active communication with the northern coasts; they also gave him a respite from attack by sea from the growing Carthaginian fleet. Of all the dangers on the African coast, this was the greatest.

Fantastically, that winter of 204—203 found the two masters of warfare, Hannibal and Scipio, penned in a promontory and a peninsula, both on an enemy coast. For those few months both were almost out of touch with events elsewhere. Yet Hannibal—because Scipio could send only guarded communications to his Senate—probably had the clearer outlook over the sea as a whole.

Over it stretched the *mainmise* of exhausted, tenacious Rome, held fast by 20 legions and 160 war vessels, not counting the African expedition. From Gades on the outer Ocean to the Dalmatian coast the legions encamped, and within their ring of iron lay the islands, from the Balearics to Sicily, now the vortex of the war.

Beyond the Ebro the last resistance was dying out in Spain. Beyond the Po Mago had not been able to advance. For the first time Rome held fast to a bridgehead on the African shore. The city of Carthage was still secure on its fortified promontory. But the Romans had become masters of the sea empire that the Barcas had sought. Hannibal's anxiety was now for Carthage itself.

He had given ground grudgingly to the pressure of two Roman armies, defending ravines and valley trails, to gain precious time. Now his enemy threatened Consentia, largest market town of Bruttium, while Hannibal held firmly to Croton, his last evacuation port.

The irony of his situation did not fail to strike him. On the headland by Croton perched the temple of Lacinia, the ancient Greek shrine that Hannibal had been at some pains to protect. The temple served him as observation post and a quiet spot for meditation—a Tifata on the sea. There at the entrance to the shrine chamber he placed his valedictory tablet of bronze. By now the Carthaginian leader had seen—and read—innumerable Latin tablets giving honors, titles, and designations of victory of dead patrician Romans. He had studied their laws carved into stone. Now he set up his own memorial, the roll call of his victories for fifteen years in Italy.

It was the parting jest of a man who had never cared for warfare. Hannibal had not lost his sense of humor.

Decision at the Great Plains

When spring came Scipio broke out of his bridgehead at Castra Cornelia. He did so before the stormy season ended and before the Carthaginian fleet could put to sea.

During the winter months his small force of cavalry had tricked and scattered a large force of mounted volunteers from Carthage—when Masinissa's desert riders lured the eager Carthaginians to the trained Roman horse waiting in ambush. After this prestige success Scipio's mounted arm began to build up.

Scipio himself engaged in an odd winter pastime—peace negotiations with both Syphax and Hasdrubal, whose encampments hemmed in his promontory. He had remembered Syphax's anxiety to end the war, at the Siga conference. Lengthy discussions between emissaries debated the question: could not all armies withdraw and all matters be restored to a *status quo?* Scipio said neither yes nor nay—while his officers, disguised as servants of his spokesmen, painstakingly observed the situation, readiness and strength of the two hostile camps. For Hasdrubal's Carthaginians had built their winter huts apart from the tents of the Numidians. Finally Scipio admitted with obvious reluctance that he had no authority to grant what Syphax desired.

But while the old Numidian pondered the Roman's apparent reluctance and the informal truce prevailed, fires broke out in both encampments one night, and when Carthaginians and Numidians roused to put out the flames they ran into the swords of Scipio's legions. The horsemen of Masinissa burst into the disordered camps, and Hasdrubal and Syphax awoke only in time to flee. The Romans saved a plenitude of spoil, stores, and horses from the conflagration.

By violating the truce Scipio and Laelius had driven the Africans from their siege lines at Castra Cornelia.

Thereupon Scipio exploited his advantages of an experienced command and disciplined troops without pity or a day's delay. The burning of the camps had sent Carthaginians in retreat to their city and the Numidians in flight toward Cirta, Syphax's reign center in the west. Three weeks passed before the leaders strengthened and regrouped their followers in the common ground, called the Great Plains, to the south. Syphax was urged to greater effort by his Carthaginian bride, Sophonisba. He was aided by an unexpected arrival. From the western coast 4,000 Celtiberians marched in to join him. These were veterans of long experience. How and why they came to Carthage has never been made clear. Apparently they crossed to Africa to rejoin the fighting that had ended in Spain.

It began for the Celtiberians swiftly enough in Africa. With unlooked-for audacity, Scipio let out his two best legions with his growing strength in horsemen, Numidian and Roman, from the siege lines. In five days of forced marches almost without baggage he reached the mobilization center of the allies in the Great Plains.

The battle that followed—in which some 16,000 Romans moved against 20,000 allies—was a disaster for Carthage. Laelius and Masinissa crushed in the Carthaginian wings; Scipio's advancing legions changed front as they came on, the front line and *triarii* shifted to the sides. The Carthaginian center with its core of Celtiberians was enveloped—as the Roman legions had been encircled at Cannae—by speeding horsemen and converging lines of heavy infantry. The Celtiberians made no effort to escape. Being Spaniards from the new Roman province of Spain, they knew their lives were forfeit and they chose to die sword in hand. It is said that it took the entire force of the legionaries to put an end to them.

Scipio possessed one other advantage over his enemies. He had two superb lieutenants in Laelius and Masinissa. He loosed Masinissa in headlong pursuit of fugitives toward Numidia in the west and dispatched Laelius with hard-marching cohorts to follow, to support him and to watch him. Leaving his siege lines at Utica to care for themselves, Scipio struck at Tunis (Tynes) on the great lagoon south of Carthage. Tunis had little in it except quarries and tradesmen, but its lagoon gave a safe haven to the Carthaginian fleet.

Then at Tunis Scipio sighted what he most feared to see, the enemy fleet putting out from its harbors. Without losing an hour he set off on horseback with a small escort—the legions following—for Castra Cornelia. There the Roman galleys had been fitted with siege engines and pressed into the bombardment of Utica, while the transport vessels lay at anchor without protection. Scipio won the race to his encampment. There, at the run, he turned himself, his crews, and available soldiers into engineers. Since his few fighting galleys were in no condition to put to sea, he barricaded them in. Probably no one except a Roman would have thought of building a wall of defense out of sailing transports, and only soldiers of the Seven Hills could have contrived the mechanics of doing so. They lined up the heavy transports, bow to stern in several layers seaward of the galleys; they unshipped masts and spars, to bind the vessels together, and shifted boarding platforms from the galleys to bridge the outer vessels. Then the legionaries armed themselves and set up engines to defend their unique wall of ships.

The Carthaginian admiral made the mistake of waiting offshore for his enemies to sally out, which, naturally, they failed to do. When the Carthaginian galleys moved into the Utica shore the next day, they found the wall of transports manned by soldiers, and there was further delay while they puzzled over this new tactic. The Carthaginians, however, were as skilled seamen as the Romans were artificers. The conflict off Utica ended with the galleys of Carthage towing off in triumph some 60 Roman sailing craft. And for a while Scipio had to remain to watch Castra Cornelia.

Meanwhile Masinissa swept through his ancestral Massyleland with whirlwind speed, to break up the resistance forming around his feudal enemy, Syphax, to overthrow Syphax himself and put the wounded chieftain in chains to exhibit him to the countryside. Wherever opposition stiffened, Laelius caught up with his heavy infantry and broke through it. But this land had been ruled by Masinissa's ancestors; the townsfolk had no leader once Syphax was enchained, and the Bedouin desired only to follow the victor.

Cirta fell, and at the palace door Masinissa found Sophonisba awaiting him. Legend has it that she begged the young Numidian not to allow her, a Carthaginian, to fall into the hands of the Romans. The poets say that Masinissa conceived a mad passion for her. She was desirable, and probably Masinissa sealed his triumph over the wounded Syphax by taking his young wife. Laelius, arriving to bring law and order into this disordered conquest, protested that the woman Sophonisba had been a Carthaginian agent, and was now the captive of the Senate and Roman People. Masinissa, feeling power restored to him, would not listen. However, Laelius persuaded him to allow Scipio to judge the matter.

Presently the three men returned to the Utica lines, where Scipio decided that the wounded Syphax was to go as a captive chieftain to Rome. Both must have recalled their meeting at Siga, where Syphax's hospitality had protected the young proconsul. In the legend that grew up around Sophonisba, it is said that Syphax blamed her for beguiling him from his friendship for Scipio, and that he warned the Roman commander that she would do no less to Masinissa. It is highly unlikely that a Numidian who had reigned for a lifetime would blame his downfall on a woman; it is extremely likely that the careful Scipio did not want Masinissa to keep a Carthaginian wife at his side and such a wife as Sophonisba. Scipio had urgent need of the Numidian horsemen.

The two talked it over, and Masinissa flung out of the Roman's tent to meditate for a night on his own. He also had need of his ally, for without the Roman legions Masinissa could not stand against the power of Carthage.

And the legend ends the woman's story with a scene of Greek tragedy, which Livy relished. Masinissa, it seems, sent one of his Numidians back to the palace at Cirta with poison to put in a cup, and a demand that Sophonisba make her choice whether to die or to go as a captive with Syphax to Rome. Whereupon she told the messenger, "I did not expect such a wedding gift from my husband." And she drank the poison.

However it was brought about, the Carthaginian woman

was killed. The old Numidian went with his chains to be exhibited with other evidences of Scipio's triumph in the Forum. The hostile coast had been subdued. In reward, Masinissa received royal gifts from Scipio, who addressed him as king henceforth. A gold crown was presented him with an embroidered robe and a curial chair of state. He was enthroned before the paraded legions. So he became the first of the oriental monarchs to be known as the client kings of Rome.

Yet the story of Sophonisba's death has outlived Masinissa's fame.

Carthage Calls Her Sons Home

After the disaster on the Great Plains Carthage felt her danger. Until then the Council on the Byrsa had been divided—as so often happened—by conflicting opinions. The strong peace party cried the failure of the Barca faction and demanded terms with the Romans; another group called for Hannibal's return; a third party urged a greater effort to oust Scipio from his bridgehead (where he was then carrying on his deceptive *pourparlers* of the winter). In the crowded streets beneath the Byrsa the trade guilds, artisans, and simple citizens called loudly for Hannibal. The Shofet could not decide the varying counsels.

Then between mid-March and the end of June the Roman legions surged into the roads of the hinterland, the one field army of Carthage vanished at the Great Plains. From the Syrtes to the end of Numidia the city was cut off from access to the continent; refugees swarmed in with their belongings but without food; the harvests of the vital Bagradas basin lay open to enemy reaping; hunger was felt in the crowded streets. All prospects had changed.

Three walls now protected the city at the end of the promontory, ample garrison troops manned the walls; the fleet served to safeguard the harbor entrance. But the city could not endure for many months without food from the hinterland. The garrison lacked the training to oppose an

210

army like Scipio's in the field; deprived of the Numidian levies, the city lacked manpower to form a new army and had, besides, no one to lead it against Scipio. Hasdrubal, father of Sophonisba, had committed suicide.

The Council put Hanno, a veteran of Hannibal's campaigns—who had led the heavy cavalry at Cannae—in command of all defense. And the Council sent it's messengers to Mago beneath the Alps and to Hannibal, to order them back with their armies to Africa. Then the Council replaced its admiral, the overcautious Bomilcar, with a better seaman, who also bore the name of Hasdrubal. Under the new admiral the fleet had made its sortie against Utica, to return with the unusual captures of 60 Roman transports. These sailing vessels, when refitted, made a valuable addition to the great convoy needed to bring Hannibal home across the sea infested with enemy fleets.

Up on the Ligurian coast, the faithful Mago had shipping of his own, and was himself quite adept at maneuvering over the seas. In his pocket harbor of Croton, Hannibal had few vessels. Moreover he had not set foot on the deck of a ship for a generation. And it was Hannibal Carthage wanted. The hungering crowds at the three gates of the Byrsa never ceased to shout his name.

It was July (203) by then and good sailing weather.

At this crisis we are confronted by a hiatus in the historical record. It is an abrupt as the stopping of a motion picture film, to resume in another later scene. In July Hannibal waits in the Bruttian mountains; in early autumn, or October, he is across the sea in Africa with his army, fully equipped. A Dunkirk has taken place during the time lapse, and nothing said about it. At least the Latin historians chose never to explain how he got out of Italy.

Modern commentators have taken note of the puzzle. One points out that ships at sea are hard to find. That is true; even a Nelson failed to sight the convoy of Napoleon on its way across the Mediterranean to the Nile. That, however, does not explain how Hannibal got to sea unobserved. He was facing two Roman armies in close-locked lines; these were capable of cutting his forces to pieces during the embarkation, to gain their first victory

211

over him. And once afloat, of course, his army, packed into transports, was at the mercy of a battle fleet that could have ended his career once and for all.

Another historian puts forward the ingenious explanation that because the Roman Senate was then negotiating under truce (as will presently be manifest) with Carthaginian envoys, and because it was contrary to Roman law to negotiate while enemy armed forces stood on Italian soil, the Senate desired to have both Hannibal and Mago off the shores in order to carry out its negotiations legally. That is hardly possible. The truce with Carthage did not extend to the Carthaginian armies in Italy. Hannibal had not been granted a day's truce since he emerged from the snow pass of the Alps. In the event, a Roman fleet did intercept and capture part of Mago's convoy.

In this case the simplest explanation of the riddle may well be the only possible one. Hannibal got away unseen as he had managed to disengage his army once before, across the Volturno at Capua.

Croton stands in full view, with its shallow half-moon bay, on a shore as level as a table top. But behind the little port rear the rugged La Sila heights as far as the eye can see. The Carthaginians held those heights, while the Romans, having occupied Consentia, were on the far slopes.

As the day of departure drew near—when Hasdrubal the Admiral arrived with his sizable convoy—Hannibal gave all the men still serving him their choice, whether to accompany him or to stay in Italy. Most of them chose to go with him. In addition he left behind some of the weaker elements, with the innumerable women and their children who had become part of his army of Italy. (The tale that he massacred all those who refused to embark at the temple of Juno Lacinia is merely a purple patch of the Latin fable.) Hannibal did order all the cherished horses to be killed since they could not be taken on the vessels. He also had the detachments which were to stay in Italy occupy the Carthaginian posts on the heights until the Africa-bound contingents were embarked and under sail. The Roman commands had no evidence of his departure, and in all probability a good deal of time passed before they were convinced that Hannibal had actually vanished to sea.

It is one of the most fantastic facts of Hannibal's career that he arrived in Italy with forces of Spaniards and Africans, and departed with Bruttians and Gauls, for the most part, with many Roman deserters. If any elephants survived, they were left behind. Hannibal himself never spoke of the hour when he watched the mountains of Italy and the white speck of the Lacinian temple fade into the horizon. (The picture of him gnashing his teeth in anger at being summoned away by a Carthage that had failed to sustain his war is a storyteller's embellishment of the old fable that Hannibal himself had planned the war. Carthage had no means of bringing him to Africa against his will. He had prepared for the evacuation with his usual care; after the Great Plains the vortex of the conflict had shifted to the African coast, and Hannibal abandoned Italy as Hamilcar had left Mount Eryx, without protest.)

The manner of his evacuation proves that his Africa-bound army could not have been large. Its number is estimated of late as 12,000 to 15,000. It may well have been less than 12,000. Only sailing craft could have made up the convoy; galleys with small deck space and large complement of rowers could take on a few passengers. Then, too, after the September equinox freshening winds and storms made it dangerous for the slender galleys to venture on a long voyage. And Hannibal and his admiral made a long voyage from Croton.

Now it is fairly clear what the Roman fleets were doing at this point, and where. Between 160 and 140 fighting galleys had been based on Ostia, Sardinia, and Sicily. The greater part of them served to escort new convoys to Africa, for supplies and reinforcements to Scipio had top priority in those months. ("All eyes were turned to Africa.") One squadron intercepted vessels that strayed from Mago's convoy.

Mago himself had been wounded in a last battle on the Po, when he tried to disengage his forces, or to make a final attempt to get through to Hannibal. Mago died on the voyage, or was shipwrecked in a storm. Most of his ships, laden with his Balearians, Ligurians, and Gauls reached Carthage eventually.

The Roman fleets off Sicily were between Croton and Carthage. They watched for the coming of Hannibal's convoy and watched in vain.

Hannibal and his admiral circled wide around Sicily. Perhaps they were seen by the outpost on Malta. But it would have been too late by then for the Sicilian fleet to intercept them. Their course did not take them in to Carthage; they came in from the east, landing on the eastern coast of what is not Tunisia, more than 80 miles south of the Sacred Mountain of Carthage. Once ashore at this unlooked-for spot, Hannibal moved his army quickly north to Hadrumetum (Sousse) a harbor and sizable town outside the zone of Roman patrols.

After 34 years Hannibal stood on African soil again. Both his brothers were dead. And on him centered the anxiety of Rome, dismayed by his crossing safely from one continent to the other. "Hope and anxiety increased daily," Livy relates. "Men could not make up their minds whether to rejoice because after sixteen years Hannibal had left Italy, or to worry because he had crossed over to Africa with his army intact. Quintus Fabius [the Delayer], who died a little before, often predicted that Hannibal would be a more terrible opponent in his own land than in a foreign country. And Scipio would have to deal neither with Syphax—king in a land of untrained barbarians—nor with Hasdrubal, a general very quick to flee, nor with irregular armies hurriedly raised from a mob of countrymen. For Hannibal had been born, one might say, at the headquarters of his father, the bravest of generals. He had left evidence of his mighty deeds in Spain and the Gallic land, and in Italy from the Alps to the Straits [of Messina]. His army had endured hardships that no one believed human beings could endure. Many of its men, who would encounter Scipio in battle, had slain Roman praetors with their own hands, and had wandered through captured cities and camps of the Romans. All the magistrates of the Roman People at that time did not have as many fasces as Hannibal might have had carried before him, and all taken from our slain commanders."

In its anxiety the Senate decreed four days of games in

the Circus to propitiate the gods, while a banquet was served for Jupiter in his Capitoline temple.

The Shape of Things to Come

If the Senate worried, Scipio must have been stunned. He had expected—indeed had worked for—the arrival of Hannibal in Africa. Yet he could not have anticipated that the wizard of Cannae would slip away from the major Roman armies and make his way through the blockading fleets "with his army intact." Nor that the other veteran army of Cathage would transfer itself or most of itself abruptly from the river Po to the Bagradas.

That autumn in Scipio's enlarged bridgehead Utica still defied him; he had failed also to take Bizerta (Hippo Diarrytus) on its western bay. He was still dependent on Castra Cornelia as a supply port. Carthage, impregnable to attack, mustered its full resources. Laelius, his right hand, was held in Rome after escorting Syphax there. The intractable Masinissa was off in the west to raise more desperately needed horsemen, and to recover all Massyleland for himself.

It seemed as if all, or almost all, that the dead Fabius had prophesied of evil in Africa, was coming to pass. Could, or would, Masinissa rejoin Scipio in time? Could enough of the armed forces now released in Italy be shipped south to Africa to compensate for Hannibal's arrival? *Would* they be sent in time?

Before anything could happen, winter set in, putting an end to major transport by sea. As at Castra Cornelia a year before Scipio was isolated in a corner of the African coast, with the difference that now he had Hannibal in the corner with him.

Confronted by this crisis Publius Cornelius Scipio ceased to be merely a brilliant regional commander of Rome and became one of the inspired men of history. In so doing he forfeited the political career that he had sought until now, and drew upon himself the envious hatred of the man named Cato. Faced by such great opportunity and danger at once, Scipio no longer took thought of that.

By good luck, or by the foresight that brings good luck, Scipio had effected an armistice with the Council of Carthage. At the end of the last summer he had wanted time to reorganize his forces, while the men of the Byrsa had wanted time to get Hannibal home, after the Great Plains disaster. Therefore it was not at all strange that they had agreed on the truce in Africa—it did not obtain in Italy—but the manner of agreement was rather remarkable. Scipio had met with the bearded envoys of the Council and, after studying them, had given them his conditions for a peace. Nothing was unusual in that, and both parties used subterfuge, as Scipio had done before the burning of the Carthaginian camps, to gain a respite. By a stroke of genius, however, Scipio had offered as his fraudulent conditions the real terms by which he hoped to end the war.

They were:

Return of all captives, fugitives, and deserters to Rome.

Withdrawal of the Carthaginian armies from Italy.

Cession by Carthage of Sardina and Corsica with Sicily, and an end to interference in Spain (Scipio's former province). Surrender of war galleys, except for 20. Payment of 5,000 talents of silver as indemnity (about $4,000,000 in money or bars, of a much greater purchasing power then than at the present day).

There was also a clause about provisioning the Roman forces in Africa during the armistice, and something about the recognition of Masinissa as king in his own country.

Now in laying down his conditions (without consulting the Senate) Scipio seems to have thought through all the complex of conflict for so many years; he isolated the realities of the years to come—that Carthage should not be destroyed, and Rome should possess the empire of the sea. Futhermore he understood that it would take generations to bring Spain into any sort of order, and upon this he was determined. Perhaps he envisioned his own return to Spain; certainly he made no demand for the surrender of Hannibal, who might prove to be harmless in Africa without a battle fleet and without Spain. Then the two continents, divided, might keep the peace.

216

Knowing the penchant of the Carthaginian statesmen for argument, Scipio gave them only three days to confirm the truce and submit the terms to Rome, or not. The Council accepted the conditions, influenced by the anti-Barca faction yet hoping to gain time through negotiation. The arrival of Scipio's terms and the Carthaginian envoys at Rome somewhat naturally puzzled the conscript of Fathers who could not understand what had come over their commander in chief in the midst of a successful campaign. Like senators everywhere and at all times the Fathers resented terms that had not first been debated by themselves. Party orators made speeches on behalf of the shipping interests, the landowners, the Claudian against the Scipionic. This debate was complicated further by the unexpected arrival of the robed Carthaginian envoys. Some of these, it is true, admitted that Hannibal had been guilty of acting without their approval. The Romans fully agreed with that. But most of them—in fact they united in doing so—tried to resurrect the old treaty that had bound Carthage to Rome before the outbreak of the war. As if that could come into question now! The Roman senators, disagreeing profoundly among themselves, agreed entirely on the question of the old treaty. That could no longer be discussed. They also agreed that they should be paid more indemnity. Some of them may have suspected that the terms were a subterfuge, but on whose part and for what purpose? As Fabius had told them, when they voted to begin the hostilities, matters appeared different in the Senate chamber than on the battlefield.

Then came the news from the battlefields, that Hannibal and Mago had disappeared from Italy with their forces.

This aroused instant suspicion, and started the debate anew. More, the Senate peremptorily recalled Laelius, who was on his way back to his commander. Questions were put to him: what did Publius Cornelius mean by this negotiation; did he *want* Hannibal in Africa, and if so why?

The adept Laelius made a brilliant answer: "Publius Cornelius did not anticipate the departure of Hannibal before peace had been signed." And he probably urged the bewildered Senators to trust their commander, and send

217

reinforcements at once. Whether the Senate signed the peace terms or not remains a controversial point, and it hardly matters. In the end the Senators agreed with Laelius because they referred the issue to the popular assembly, which demanded full support for Scipio, by every available ship, sack of grain, and armed man in Italy.

But Scipio had made new enemies in the Forum; the Claudian party got the key officers in the new election, after the naming of a temporary dictator to appoint new counsuls. Winter storms swept the seas. At length a convoy of 120 transports and 20 escorts put out from Sardinia under a praetor, Lentulus, and got through to Castra Cornelia. Another was preparing under Claudius Nero, who had made the march to the Metaurus. But the largest convoy of 200 vessels and 30 galleys was caught off Sicily in a storm, and most of the cargo craft were driven ashore within sight of Carthage. Roman galleys managed to take off their crews, but the ships laden with foodstuffs and war gear remained swaying in the surf under the twin peaks of the Sacred Mountain.

The sight of them was too much for the hungering populace of Carthage, who besieged the Council doors until the shipping of the harbors put across the bay with the war galleys, to seize the enemy provisions brought to their hands as if by the will of the unseen Melcart. The truth is that a new spirit inflamed all Carthaginians once they knew that Hannibal had landed.

At Castra Cornelia Scipio tried hard to make the armistice hold for a few days more. (Nero's convoy would soon be on the way.) He acted with restraint, sending envoys over to Carthage to protest the seizure of the ships and demand the return of the provisions, of which he had need. His envoys ran into a tumultuous demonstration, with Hannibal's name cried out at them. Anxious councilors smuggled the Romans back to their penteconter, and Carthaginian war craft escorted it out of the harbor. After the escorts turned back, fate intervened again. Three cruising triremes of Hasdrubal's squadron sighted the Roman vessel and—regardless of the truce—attacked it. The big vessel fought them off and saved itself by beaching near a Roman post.

Still, Scipio acted as if the truce held—sending urgent

advice to Rome to guard the Carthaginians there against harm from the crowds. With the advent of spring, good sailing weather was at hand and Nero might come in with a new legion. Masinissa was still far to the west, occupied in taking over more towns in the territory of Syphax. Couriers from Cirta brought in an ominous rumor that the sons of Syphax were mobilizing horsemen to join Hannibal. Somewhere in the hinterland, Scipio knew, the Carthaginian armies had united—the remains of Mago's army with the recruits of Hanno from Carthage and the veterans of Hannibal.

Unquestionably, Scipio reasoned, Hannibal would waste no time in forming these contingents into a new army.

At a day early in summer—the date is not known—Scipio decided to wait no longer. He had struck early the year before at the Carthaginian mobilization on the Great Plains, and he seems to have feared to give Hannibal more time to organize an army. Whatever his reason, he took all dependable troops out from the Utica lines and marched up the Bagradas River, away from his base, and support from the sea. He went without the best of his cavalry, the Numidians. Every day he dispatched riders to the west with orders for Masinissa to come in. He marched southwest, following the river as long as he could, burning villages, trampling crops, and roping the inhabitants of the once fertile area of Carthage into slave trains.

This devastration caused the villagers along the river to speed messengers to Hannibal's winter encampment at Hadrumetum, to urge their champion to make haste to protect them.

The Council of Carthage also urged him to advance against Scipio.

Hannibal told the messengers: "That is something I can judge better than you."

But they left him with the knowledge of Scipio's line of march, and the fact that the Romans had no Numidian horsemen with them as yet. To all appearances Hannibal was not ready to move out. Yet he did so at once.

The great encampment broke up. The armed men filed from the huts on the shore, Ligurians, Gauls, Balearians, Bruttians, and Carthaginians taking their place in the long column advancing swiftly west, out of the shelter of the coast ranges into the plains. The aging Hanno led out his recruit cavalry; a band of 2,000 Numidians followed a prince who had been loyal to Syphax. Eighty elephants swayed along the track.

There was little baggage because Hannibal was moving at speed to intercept and surprise Scipio before Masinissa joined him. With him went some 37,000 humans, not yet welded into an army.

Ironically, Hannibal was advancing into country he had never seen, unless as a nine-year-old boy, while the Romans marched through territory already familiar to them.

The Day of Zama

Consider for a moment the two adversaries because history does not tell of another such pair in opposition to each other. Hannibal is a master of strategy, most dangerous on any ground he had selected himself, being quick to draw advantage from the terrain. He manages, as no one else had been able to do, to bring in his strongest attacking force on the blind spot of his enemy. There is no way of anticipating where it will come—if Hannibal has been able to choose the site of the battle. Until now this annihilating blow has come usually from his Spanish-African horsemen, and they are no longer with him.

Scipio also is cautious in preparation, although audacious in a action. Then he relies upon one tactic, the converging attack of his legion line, which he has the unique ability to shift during the opening of a battle. He has complete confidence in his disciplined legionaries, and they in him. He may or may not have a greater strength of horsemen than his enemy.

Both Hannibal and Scipio understand, as few other leaders have understood, that war has only one purpose—to gain a truer peace.

The southern plain was still green after the last winter's rains. Perhaps Scipio had his first warning of Hannibal's approach from the Carthaginian's spies. They were caught within the Roman's encampment near a village called Naraggara. It is said that after questioning the disguised Carthaginians, Scipio ordered them taken through the camp to see all they wished to see—or that he wished them to see. Then, unexpectedly, he released them to return to the Carthaginian camp near a village called Zama.

Once he learned that Hannibal was cutting across his line of march, Scipio wheeled his columns to the east, toward his enemy, until he had crossed a small river not yet dried up by summer heat. (The exact site has never been determined.) There to his surprise he received a Carthaginian envoy who said that Hannibal wished to talk with him in a personal truce between the lines.

Now Scipio did not know where the Carthaginian army waited. He judged by the overture that the wizard of Cannae no longer hoped to strike unexpectedly into his march column as at Trasimeno. His Romans, however, were six days' march from their base. No protecting hills appeared within sight. Being without strong cavalry support, his legions might fare badly on the plains to which he had led them.

Then, while Scipio debated, he beheld a thrilling sight. From the west Masinissa rode in, clad in his glittering new insignia, with a cloud of horsemen covering the plain behind him. They numbered 6,000, and another 4,000 followed on foot somewhere behind them, but these did not matter much. Scipio had barely won his gamble of meeting with Masinissa before encountering Hannibal, but he had won. Now he had greater strength in horsemen than his enemy.

Thereupon he released the messenger of the Carthaginian with the answer that he would meet with Hannibal. The encampment could be left safely to Laelius and Masinissa.

The story of their meeting is told by Polybius, who served Scipio's family two generations later. From the Carthaginian encampment on the low rise at the other side of the valley Hannibal rode out with a mounted escort, which her presently left behind to advance on foot with an interpreter. On his side, Scipio did the same, also taking an interpreter. Although both spoke Greek fluently and Hannibal understood Latin, they gained advantage by having time to reflect while the linguists repeated their words, and they also had witnesses at need.

When they met, both kept silence. Hannibal was the elder and taller man, his lined, sunburned face shadowed by his headcloth that concealed his grizzled hair, his head turned slightly to favor his good eye. Scipio stood bareheaded, helmet on his arm, in restrained tensity, handsome and expressionless. Except for the crest on his helmet and the gold inlay of his breastplate he wore no evidence of rank, and no lictors waited with his escort.

After a long interval, Hannibal spoke and waited for the interpreter.

"You have been successful, Roman Consul. You have been fortunate, too."

Scipio waited.

"Did you ever think," Hannibal went on, "if there is anything to be gained for Rome by going on with the war? More, that is, than you possess at this moment? Did you think if you are defeated here, your army will be lost?" He thought for a moment. "I would not propose peace if I did not think it would benefit both of us."

Scipio waited. Evidently Hannibal had heard the terms of the armistice offer. When Scipio spoke he asked what Hannibal proposed to offer, other than the Roman terms.

All the islands of the sea, Hannibal said, including the smaller islands between Italy and Africa (such as the Malta group) and Spain to be abandoned by Carthage. He did not mention giving up war vessels, but he would not yield fugitives or deserters now in the Carthaginian ranks. (By Roman law, these would include most of his veterans from Italy.)

In answer Scipio explained that he could not concede to Carthage more than his government had agreed on in the terms already signed at Rome. (They had been Scipio's terms, whether signed or not.)

At that the two men made a gesture of salute and parted. There had been no possibility of agreement between them unless Hannibal had offered to concede more than the capitulation already laid down by Scipio. Instead, he had offered less. There was left to them, in equal

222

measure, only the duty of attempting to destroy the other's armed force.

That night Scipio showed himself in a gay mood. At the last-hour officer's conference he had little to do except to caution the overeager Masinissa as to the mission of the Numidian cavalry, which would operate as a unit on one flank. Yet that of itself made Scipio's task simpler, because all other horsemen would now be given to Laelius at the opposite end of the Roman line. Scipio took some thought for the number of elephants observed in the Carthaginian encampment. In all other respects his plans had been made beforehand; his legion commanders knew them. Scipio told the officers: "Tell the men their hardships will soon be over. After tomorrow they'll collect the spoil of Africa. After that they can go home, each man to his own town."

In the Carthaginian camp it is said that Hannibal went from unit to unit, talking with the men he had known in Italy and with the newcomers from Carthage. Quietly he gave the commanding officers their instructions, and perhaps only Hanno, the veteran of the Alps, understood clearly what those instructions meant. The others were content to obey carefully, trusting in Hannibal's greater understanding. He told them that for sixteen years his Carthaginians had prevailed over the armed Romans, and that there was no obstacle, nothing hidden from view, in this valley of Zama that they could not make their way through.

"Those people over there haven't had time to build walls, and they couldn't bring along their engines. Has anyone seen a catapult standing among their silver eagles?"

Because he seemed to be amused, his officers felt hopeful.

Hannibal did not sleep that night because the first element of his attack was stirring and moving out in the last hours of starlight. There was almost no water in the camp, because the nearest river threaded the plain behind the Roman lines. If this had been his old army of Italy, Hannibal might have slipped it away under cover of darkness. He could not retreat over open gound with his mixed command confronted by Numidians in strength,

223

nor could he attempt to hold his position without a constant supply of water.

It took time to get such a number of elephants moving in the hour of the first horizon light. The elephants were not willing to stir in darkness. From his post on a knoll Hannibal watched them depart. Behind them followed the men of Mago, the silent Ligurians, and muttering Gauls, with additions of wild Moors and a few Spaniards. Hannibal had armed these lighter forces heavily and drilled them to move as they advanced now, shoulder to shoulder. They were battle-wise.

Only the messengers on the knoll with Hannibal saw what was happening in that gray light. His forces were not forming the usual long battle line; the three elements, Mago's forces, the Carthaginian recruits, and Hannibal's veterans were advancing separately in three waves. In this way the three small armies, as it were, would fight separate actions under their own officers. And ahead of all went the powerful elephants. The last formation, his army of Bruttiun, Hannibal held back. Presently he went to join it himself, to keep it apart under his personal command. He relied on these veterans. He planned to keep them intact, to be led in late in the battle, when all other formations were broken up. The Romans could not observe them at first—not in the treacherous early light.

Hannibal had that one hope.

So it befell on the field of Zama that three separate battles took place instead of one.

Early as Hannibal had moved, the Roman alignment was already in motion toward him, slow-paced, taut as a mechanism in which every part fits into the whole. The standards might have been so many stakes rising from a fence. And at the ends the massed horsemen kept to the slow pace. The line of the infantry advanced in the usual three ranks, the front, the spearmen, and the supporting *triarii*. But all the maniples had most unusual open lanes between them—openings screened only by light-footed javelin throwers.

The armed masses came together in mid-plain, where Hannibal and Scipio had met in talk.

Suddenly all the Roman trumpets and horns sounded in

a single blast. It startled the line of elephants in advance of the Carthaginian array.

And then appeared the reason for the strange openings in the center of the Roman lines; the elephants, frantic in action, turned into them, to be met by showers of missiles. The great beasts turned back or raced forward through the lanes. Those near the ends tended to swerve toward the Carthaginian horsemen. In a few moments they were out of hand and virtually out of the action except for the confusion they left behind them. At that point Scipio ordered forward his mounted wings.

The Carthaginian horse were too few to check the charges of Laelius' and Masinissa's trained squadrons. On both sides the Roman charge crushed forward, and very soon the Carthaginian horsemen broke apart, and the combat of the riders swept away over the plain, and pursuers and pursued vanished from sight.

Already the Ligurians and Gauls were locked in conflict with the leading Roman line "in a trial of strength, man against man" as Hannibal had foretold. So strongly did the men of Mago hold their ground that the Roman advance was stopped. The *triarii* came through the intervals to merge into the swaying masses, and the Romans moved forward again. But the Carthaginians of the second wave did not advance to aid the tiring Ligurians and Gauls. Hannibal had ordered his formations to keep apart. When the survivors of the first wave did give back, they found the men of Carthage with weapons poised against them, and maddened groups of Ligurians and Gauls turned savagely on the Carthaginians, who beat them off.

Inexorably the Roman line advanced on this second army of Hannibal, the massed Carthaginians. These recruits from the city itself, led by the aged Hanno, were shaken by the retreat of Mago's men. The Roman front rank had cast away all its javelins; the legionaries came on with shields braced and swords slashing down over them. Their pressure intensified as the second-rank spearmen joined the combat. The Carthaginians fought with a desperation that checked and held the trained legions. It was late in the morning when the Carthaginians gave back, breaking to the sides. They left the ground obstructed by knots of wounded and dead.

Behind the dead stood Hannibal's last array, the veterans of Italy.

Their dark ranks were intact, waiting. Hannibal had held his great striking force apart during the early hours. The tiring legionaries faced the veterans, who had prevailed over them until now.

Scipio could not retreat. Trumpet calls sounded from end to end of the legions; legates rode headlong to the tribunes and the shouts of the centurions rang over the deep groaning of the wounded men. Orders reached the men in the ranks: rest, recover weapons, pass back the Roman wounded, clear the ground. *Do not leave the standards.* Scipio never ceased his watch of the army of Italy, three hundred paces distant. On either flank of that army the fugitives from the earlier combats were rallying to hold the ground vacated by the Carthaginian horsemen. In this swift regrouping Scipio sensed Hannibal at work. There was still no sign of the Roman cavalry returning to the field.

Scipio waited until his legionaries had regained breath and weapons, and had been given water. Then he gave swift orders anew. The three lines of the legions changed; the spearmen who had been in support of the suffering front line marched off to one flank, the *triarii* to the other. The Roman line lengthened, extending beyond Hannibal's array. Then it advanced again.

With sheer audacity Scipio attacked Hannibal's fresh army with an equal force of wearied fighters in a long thin line that closed in on the weak enemy flanks. In so doing he gambled on the stamina of his men, and on the acumen of Laelius and Masinissa.

So began the last of the battle. What might have happened then in the meeting of Hannibal's Bruttians with the legions will never be known.

For the Roman horsemen came back. Forming as they came under Laelius and Masinissa, they charged full into the rear of Hannibal's veterans. The Bruttians had been facing out to the flanks to meet the converging attack of the Roman infantry. Now their rear ranks faced about to meet the thundering horsemen. They fought on silently,

226

unbroken. There was no longer any hope. No Carthaginian horsemen remained to check the charge of the Romans. Scipio had triumphed in another Cannae.

The encircled veterans could not escape from horsemen. They fought where they stood until most of them died.

When an opening appeared Hannibal and a few riders got away. They did not rein in at the almost deserted Carthaginian camp. No effective force remained there to hold it, because Hannibal had thrown all his strength into the battle in the valley. (Scipio said afterward that Hannibal had done everything possible for one man at the battle of Zama.)

Hannibal rode on without stopping to the east, to Hadrumetum, ninety miles away. There transports waited with stores and a garrison of sorts. By his flight he saved his city the indignity of surrendering him. He had no illusions about attempting to carry on the war. In those hours until sunset of the day of Zama he had lost the army that he had led for sixteen years. An attempt to defend the city itself without an army would merely bring on a siege that would end in starvation.

From Hadrumetum he sent a warning to the people within the walls: "We have lost more than a battle; we have lost the war. Accept the terms of peace offered you."

While he waited he heard how the last resistance ended in Africa. Too late to be of any aid, the Numidian horsemen of the far west appeared under the sons of Syphax. They seemed to be numerous and threatening but were soon broken up and driven off by the veteran Roman forces. If they had joined Hannibal before Zama, the battle might have been very different. Scipio had struck his blow with ice-cold calculation immediately on the arrival of Masinissa, before the coming of the western Africans; by his devastation of the Bagradas Valley, he had forced Hannibal to move against him in that interval of time. And now the long-awaited convoys from Italy were coming in with fresh legions and new consuls at their head.

There was no question, however, as to Scipio's authority. He had won the final victory as commander in chief, and Rome looked to him alone to end the war. After making a close inspection of the fortifications of Carthage from the sea Scipio had no inclination to undertake a siege of the city. Then, too, he had never wished to destroy Carthage.

Hannibal seems to have read Scipio's mind. There will always be a question as to how much the two of them talked over at their meeting before Zama. We only know what Scipio himself chose to make public years afterward. Certainly both gained an unusual understanding of the other's character.

For Hannibal at Hadrumetum put his faith in Scipio's word. Scipio's terms would at least spare the city and leave its inhabitants free to adjust themselves to another mode of life that would still be Carthaginian.

In the event, Scipio's terms of peace revealed slight changes from his stipulations of the previous year. Those additions were demanded, in most cases, by the Senate. They were:

Surrender of all war vessels except 10, and of all elephants.

Agreement to enter upon no war in future in Africa without the consent of the Roman government.

Payment of 10,000 talents of silver over 50 years.

Carthage to become the friend and ally of the Roman Republic.

So at long last the city of Carthage was compelled to accept the condition that the Barcas had vowed they would never accept, of being a friend of the Romans.

Yet by Scipio's insistence the great city retained her autonomy; the Carthaginians themselves were not to be harmed and they kept their government, farms, and city-owned territory as before the war. Thus, by Scipio's terms, there was no interference with their civilian life. There was no demand for the surrender of Hannibal.

Roman insistence brought further details into the capitulation: the vessels stranded and stripped near Carthage were to be paid for in full. And Masinissa was to be rewarded by full kingship over all Numidian lands. As for the deserters, the annals relate that according to Roman

228

custom all Roman citizens surrendered were crucified, and the Italians put to death.

The annalists say that when Publius Cornelius Scipio returned in triumph to Rome in the following year (201) he brought to the treasury 123,000 pounds of silver. Crowds gathered from the farms to hail him along his route. Yet his triumph seems to have been more a popular than an official one. The throngs in the Forum may have felt that their eccentric commander had failed to bring the Carthaginians properly to their knees after the ordeal of the war. In the Senate the Claudian faction envied Scipio's unprecedented success. Few of his friends remained alive. (Of the wartime leaders only Varro, the forgotten man of Cannae, survived.) Newcomers resented the way he had imposed his own terms on their discussion of peace. Many feared that popular adulation might raise him to the throne of kingship. In the end the Senate contented itself with voting him the honorary titles of *princeps senatus* (roughly, First Citizen) and *Africanus*.

"What is certain," Livy remarks, "is that he was the first general to be distinguished by the name of a nation conquered by him."

He would not by any means be the last.

VI. Pursuit to the East

"You Must Teach Me the Way of This House."

When Hannibal rode into the land gate of Carthage in 202 he entered a city almost entirely strange to him. He had left it as a boy of nine years, following his father about. Probably he remembered the street and the garden of the Barca mansion, and the corridor to the curtained prayer niche inside the terrace that faced east. Only in that secluded part of his dwelling could he be alone now. Elsewhere a multitude of people pressed around him, earger to look into his face, to pull at his sleeve with whispered questioning, to gain some knowledge from the man who had been for so long the destiny of the city.

Hannibal had left the last armament behind him at the barracks of Hadrumetum, where the garrison troops remained with stragglers from Zama and the transport ships. From there the Council had recalled him almost at once, and he had come to the strangeness of the great city untouched by conflict. Whether his wife survived to greet him is not known, but his son could not have been alive. Unfamiliar faces of cousins intent on trade and of politicians who had backed the Barca cause—these filled his anterooms, and sometimes he found their clipped talk

231

harder to understand than the Greek of the lost Magna Graecia. When he left the crowds to go up to his terrace, the gaily colored brick walls around him seemed less real than the remembered roofs around Tifata or the sun-mellowed columns of the Lacinian temple.

Hannibal was forced to play a dual role again. He became more silent, testing his thoughts before he spoke. One conviction possessed him: the war lay behind him and his city; it was imperative to look ahead toward what might be accomplished without arms. Yet—although the western Numidians had been broken and driven to the mountains—the people of the city still looked upon him as their commander, able to conjure up some hidden resource to gain a victory that would preserve them from the terms of the peace.

Once in the Council he lost control of himself and strode up to the speaker's stand where a young noble of the Hanno faction cried out for his fellow citizens to arm themselves to defend their walls and hold fast to their battle elephants and triremes. Hannibal caught the arm of the speaker, wrenching him down from the dais. Shouts of protest assailed him, and the Shofet motioned him back.

Hannibal took the stand. "I ask your forgiveness. When I left Carthage I was a boy of nine; I am more than forty-five years old now." He fought back his temper and tried to jest. "You see I know something about war encampments but I am not familiar with your rules. You must teach me the way of this house."

When he had their attention, he challenged them. "Rome also has suffered. What terms would you have granted her, if the gods had willed it so. Not many days have gone by since most of you were in fear of great disaster. What assurance did you have then that the city would be preserved to us without a Roman proconsul seated here in authority over you? What we have in store for us will bring us no ease of body. But your minds! You know all the terms. Be glad of that and accept them. They can not now be changed, except for the worse."

His plea led the Council to accept the terms of peace. But it added to his enemies among the dominant oligarchs. The difference of viewpoint between the soldier without an army and the civilian lords of the city came to a head very quickly.

After five months—that is, early in 201—all captives were mutually exchanged, the expenses and damages of Scipio's army paid, and the treaty signed, and sanctified by Roman ritual. The last Roman troops put to sea from Castra Cornelia and Tunis. Scipio, now *Africanus,* had laid down harsh conditions yet had carried out his own part in them to the letter. He left to Carthage "the boundaries possessed by the Republic at the time of my landing in Africa." Hannibal respected this forbearance of his great antagonist. It must have seemed little less than a miracle to him when the familiar standards of the Roman maniples were carried to the Sicily-bound transports. (Already the army was required for a punitive expedition against Philip of Macedon.)

Nevertheless, the first payment of the indemnity was due—some 16,000 pounds of bar silver. Little coined money remained in the treasury, and the administrative Committee of the Hundred faced the necessity of raising this large amount of bullion when silver had ceased to come in from the mountains of Spain and overseas trade was still in chaos. The Hundred (who appear sometimes as the Thirty) decreed a tax on personal wealth to raise the silver. And this, in turn, brought angry protest and loud grieving from many in the assembled Council.

The indemnity tax violated tradition. During peace in the past the government of Carthage had paid its way usually by customs dues and levies on trade monopolies. The chief magistrates drew only token salaries. (No less a judge than Aristotle had described this government as good, without a tyrant in its history.) In the crisis of the war, Carthage had exerted herself too late in the day to increase her armed forces, to strengthen Spain and Hannibal in Italy. A tax on profits had been paid then. Now the Hundred demanded a levy on capital, which would fall inevitably on the most wealthy citizens.

One of them appealed against it as a hardship not to be endured. Hannibal laughed.

"It amuses the Lord Hannibal son of Hamilcar," cried the orator, "to see our tears as we suffer under the hardships he had brought upon us."

Hannibal rose from his seat. "I am not amused. I laugh to see you weeping at the least of your hardships. You, who have watched the end of your army and fleet and the passing of the power of Carthage, now shed tears at the loss of a part of your private wealth."

Then, or later, he tried to make his viewpoint clear to the Council. His speech is known only by fragments written down at second hand. Apparently the man who had always been a soldier voiced a warning. Carthage, he believed, had relied upon trade with other nations in ancient times. In so doing, she had held herself apart from politics at first; but it proved to be impossible to trade with nations without association with their governments. Carthage could not remain a carrier of trade and nothing else. She sought peace as a protection, while being unwilling to act to preserve it. "No great state can remain long at peace, both outward and inward."

Hannibal warned his hearers that Carthage faced the task of existence among the other warlike peoples of Africa; in her new destiny there could be no immunity for private wealth.

And now the cleavage between the commander and the merchants became wider. During too many years the feeding of his followers and the unending watch over their security had been a preoccupation of Hannibal, and toward the end it had become an obsession. Fabius had been close to the truth when he said that Hannibal needed to contrive each day to find food for the morrow. Now he felt the impact of his surroundings within secure walls among nobles who possessed villas to pleasure them, filled with the gleam of alabaster and the scent of myrrh. Their elder women donned purple wigs and strings of pearls to watch the song and dance of mimes. They smelled of costly unguents.

Hannibal had been too long in the camps. Moreover he was in the anomalous position of being the first citizen of the city—as was Scipio in Rome—without civil authority. He resigned as commander after the departure of the Roman troops. He was still the favorite of the volatile Assembly of the People—who did not suffer overmuch from a levy on wealth. And presently he departed on a personal inspection of the suburbs and outer lands from the

Syrtes to Cirta. After this journey he made a startling proposal to the Council. He would undertake to raise the yearly indemnity payments without the aid of any levy. The expenses of the government and the payments to Rome as well could be met from routine revenues.

How Hannibal accomplished this has not been related in detail. The man who had brought order into tribal Spain and had engineered an army over the Alps did not find it a difficult task to renovate the tax collection in Carthage. He tore apart the tax system to do away with the hierarchy of officials who passed on coins with sticky hands. Burned areas were reforested, dry lands had water channeled from the rivers; ex-soldiers were turned into the farms.

The year arrived when the new Hannibalic economy met routine costs and paid the silver talents to Rome. When one angry official refused to obey Hannibal's order, the soldier haled him into the Council under guard to exhibit him as one of the reasons why the old order failed.

Then Hannibal proceeded to renovate the government by removing the lifetime privilege of the Hundred, of whom he was one. He argued that members of the supreme body must not enter it through family influence to remain until death. The members should be elected yearly, and their re-election should depend on their record during the year. With the enthusiastic support of the popular assembly he won this battle. As Shofet and virtual dictator, he led the city toward its reconstruction.

It is hinted and often said that in doing so Hannibal worked to restore the military power that had been stripped from Carthage. That, however, may be no more than the endemic suspicion in Roman minds of a Carthage secretly arming. No evidence during the brief years of Hannibal's influence supports it. Armed detachments went with the southbound caravans into the interior; at sea the ten triremes served as guards against pirates. No interference in troubled Spain—his former dominion—can be traced to him; no build-up of war material seems to have taken place under his austere economy. Whether he negotiated with Philip of Macedon, then engaged in a futile resistance to expeditions from Italy, remains a controversial point. The indications are that Hannibal and his renovated Hundred attempted to channel the reviving trade of the city toward the east. Their hegemony of the western Mediterranean was lost. But in the east they could renew commerce with the great markets of Alexandria, Rhodes, and ancestral Tyre as well as mighty Antioch, terminal of the trans-Asia trade.

In his ruthless reconstruction, Hannibal had made enemies among the aristocracy of Carthage. It was no longer a case of opposition to the Barcid faction but of antagonism to a dictator with the unsteady support of the populace. His new enemies sent their spokesmen to the Senate on the Tiber with the plausible story that while they themselves sought to maintain true friendship with Rome, Hannibal was contriving in his usual manner to resume his lifelong conflict with the city that had humbled him. It was a good story, and by that time it found ready listeners.

In 195 a commission went from the Senate to investigate the African affairs and to bring charges against Hannibal.

Hannibal Puts to Sea

Ironically the peace of 201 found Rome, the victor, deeply inmeshed in conflict while Carthage, the vanquished, became free to go about her affairs. In great measure this paradox was the consequence of the peculiar war Hannibal had waged. In the west of Rome's new imperium the Spanish peoples remained unsubdued and restless under martial law; in the north the unpredictable Gauls still struggled to hold their old frontier, while the savage Ligurians roved free as bandits. Then, too, a ghost of Hannibal had appeared along the troubled Po. A wounded Carthaginian officer named Hamilcar had been left behind by Mago. Now this Hamilcar took command of the resistance forces. The Senate demanded that the Council recall its rebellious officer, and the Council replied with truth that it had no means of doing so.

This episode increased the dissatisfaction of the Fathers

236

at Rome. There was a vague feeling that—as so often happens—in winning the war they had managed to lose the peace. (Even at the last negotiation, the bearded Carthaginian statesmen *still* protested that Carthage had not been responsible for the war. This argument about an ideological war guilt was foreign to Roman thought, and it exasperated them. By their laws those who had taken arms against the *Civitas Romana* were the guilty, the war criminals, so to say. So it befell that at the signing of the peace the statesmen of the Senate found themselves in agreement only with the Carthaginians of the Hanno faction, who now said that Hannibal had begun the conflict.) It had needed all Scipio's persuasion and popularity to have the Senate approve the peace terms.

Moreover as the war prisoners came back from Carthage—many being of senatorial rank—they brought tales of the luxuries they had beheld in the African city, the curtains of spun glass, the incense burners of wrought silver, and the scented steam of the bath chambers. That year (200) the Senate ordered the building of the first public bath. Furthermore the Senate had to deal with social as well as economic dislocation within its own frontiers. Since freedmen and ships' crews had been enlisted in the armed forces, few laborers remained to harvest the grain of Sardinia or Sicily. Italian farm lands lacked cultivators. An import of slave labor could fill this need, and patrician landowners now had money enough from war contracts to purchase slave labor—but where were able-bodied workers to be bought except in the Greek markets, or gathered in by new campaigns?

Quite illogically but quite characteristically, the first act of the Senate was to embark on a campaign of retribution against Philip V, who had become the ally of Hannibal after Cannae. The doors of the temple of Janus remained open.

The project of the Macedonian war was violently opposed by all popular assemblies. In their exhaustion they wanted only one thing, the return home of the armed forces. Scipio Africanus must have advised against the new campaign, because he was the popular idol of those years and the plebeians would not have voted against him. In spectacular triumph the war elephants of Africa—sent from Carthage in fulfillment of the peace terms—had paraded through the Circus. (They were not yet used in the gladiatorial games.) Now the prized elephants were sent off to aid the campaign against the Macedonians.

Scipio's seeming inaction during these critical years has never been satisfactorily explained. His popularity could have won him the title of king, but he never wished that. Perhaps he was too weary after ten years of campaigning to feel any interest in the machinations of politics. He seemed to accept the leadership of the Claudian faction and to withdraw to the Greek books and talk that had pleased him so well at Syracuse. Someone said that the lion of Africa became a caged animal, brought out to go through its tricks.

He was still *princeps senatus* and still idling when 197 brought news of the military victory of Cynoscephalae in Greece over the army of Philip, and of the great uprising in Spain—which he had dreamed of making a Roman Hispania. The unaccountable Spanish pride caused the most varied peoples to rebel against Roman officers as rulers. The unwarlike Turdetani soon rebelled with the combative Celtiberians. When the Consul commanding north of the Ebro ordered the surrender of all weapons—Scipio had adapted the Spanish sword and spear for use in his legions—some of the barbaric northerners killed themselves with the weapons that they would not give up. Manlius, the Consul, warned them that rebellion injured them more than the Roman occupation troops. "There is only one way to prevent this, and that is to arrange matters so that you will no longer be able to rebel."

The shadow of Hannibal still lay over Spain, as over the troubled Po. It seemed unaccountable now to the leaders of the Senate that Hannibal had been left to his own devices by the terms of peace; unmistakably he was restoring the strength of Carthage. To what end? Scipio, it seemed, had counted on Masinissa to act as a counterbalance to the enemy city, but the King of the Numidians was still occupied in regaining territory and building palaces. It had to be taken into account that the persuasive Hannibal might win back the confidence of Masinissa, to put himself again at the head of the formidable Numidian horsemen and invade strife-torn Spain.

Then, early in 195 arrived the Carthaginian nobles who complained that their autocrat, Hannibal, had corresponded with the defeated Macedonians, to create a new alliance against Rome. Hannibal, they said, was using public revenues to fortify Carthage secretly.

Accordingly the commission of the Senate was named to journey to Carthage to bring charges of conspiracy against Hannibal. This drew a protest from Scipio Africanus.

"It is unworthy," he declared, "for Rome to concern herself with the internal affairs of Carthage, or to take the side of those who accuse Hannibal."

In due course the investigators sailed. They did not find Hannibal in Carthage.

He was still in the city the day the commissioners landed, to be escorted with all ceremony to their quarters on the Byrsa. He showed himself in the streets elsewhere as usual, and in the evening he went out of his mansion to stroll toward a postern gate in the city wall. There he left his two servants and mounted the horse awaiting him outside. He was last seen cantering off without belongings or attendants, as if for a ride in the cool of the evening.

That night and the next day Hannibal rode 140 miles to one of his villas on the east coast below Hadrumetum. By the villa in a tiny harbor a fast sailing vessel waited for him, with garments and a few personal treasures and a stock of gold and silver aboard. At once he put to sea into the quiet sand-barred waters of the Little Syrtes, wherein the legendary isle of the Lotus Eaters lay. It was not a traveled waterway. When the shore vanished behind him, Hannibal headed east.

His flight astonished Carthage, and the populace thronged up to the Byrsa to demand tidings of their idol. The Roman commissioners could do nothing, except to state that his flight from them proved that he must have had treasonable correspondence with Philip.

Apparently Hannibal never explained why he left Carthage. He would have been wiser not to antagonize the magnates of the city. Obviously he had learned of the decision in Rome to bring charges against him. A generation before, other Roman envoys had demanded the surrender of all the Barca brothers, and the Council had refused to recall him from New Carthage. Whenever the Roman authorities sought Hannibal, he managed to be far from Carthage.

This time a mischance almost prevented his escape. When his vessel put in to shore for the first night, at the small port of Cercina, Hannibal found the place filled with traders' ships. They were Phoenicians from Tyre, who recognized him and gave him joyful greeting. Hannibal responded in the same spirit that he was departing on an embassy to Tyre. Then, to honor the occasion, he invited the ship captains and merchants to dine with him on the shore. Midsummer heat held the low sandy coast, and Hannibal suggested that the Phoenician guests bring their own awnings from their vessels drawn up on the beach. Sails made the best awnings, he pointed out, if erected on spars. At the same time he brought cool and inviting jars of wine from his own vessel, anchored offshore. The jars bore the seals of fine Greek vintners.

The feast so well arranged by Hannibal lasted through the cool of the evening, and the good mariners of Tyre drank on through the hours of refreshing starlight.

They did not wake until the sun was well up. The vessel of their host was gone from its anchorage. It took quite a while for the captains to rerig their ships, and much more time for them to round the cape of the Sacred Mountain to gain the harbor of Carthage. By then Hannibal was far away to the east.

He landed at Tyre.

The Three Thrones of the East

As soon as his ship passed the hills of Crete Hannibal found himself under a milder sun on a sea studded with drowsy islands. The deep blue of tranquil water reflected the clear sky. Storm-bound Sicily and wind-swept Spain seemed to belong to a different sea. The human habitations differed as well; here in the east the cities were ancient as Chronos himself who emerged from the beginning of time. Tyre rose in tenements smelling of freshly dyed cloth on its tiny island; its people had become merchandisers, no longer interested in politics except in the details of money exchange.

They greeted Hannibal with surprised reverence. His name had become a legend on this eastern coast. After a very brief stay he crossed to the shore. Here he stood on the home of the Phoenicians, the land of Canaan and the god El. Beyond to the east lay the Red Lands of folk memory. In an odd sense, as exile Hannibal was coming home, and welcome awaited him everywhere. Declining a showy chariot, he mounted a horse to ride beneath the dark heights of the Lebanon to the headwaters of the Orontes and on to the gate of Antioch.

There the people thronged into the streets at his coming, to welcome him as a gift from the gods. A king's son touched earth before him and lute players escorted him to a palace prepared for him.

This was the court of Antiochus the Great, most powerful of the monarchs of the eastern Hellenistic world.

It is apparent now that that world was in decline, yet lighted by an afterglow so strong that it still appears as one of the greatest of ages.

Alexander of Macedon had been its architect in joining Greek culture to the older wisdom of nearer Asia. In the century and a quarter after his death his half-formed empire had broken apart politically yet had endured in its society, and progressed vastly in the sciences and amenities of life. Archimedes was gone. Over in the Musaeum of Alexandria Eratosthenes, blind, was ending his long life by refusing to take any more food. Eratosthenes, that giant of the Five-Minds, had measured the earth to within 50 miles of its true circumference, and had written his appreciation of the comedies of Aristophanes. Others would read Aristophanes after him, but no one would calculate the true size of the earth as accurately for eighteen centuries. Apollonius, who succeeded him as librarian of Alexandria, would excel as critic and imitator, to begin an era of little books for little minds. And this era of afterglow would be known from its great library of remembered wisdom as the Alexandrian Age.

Politically the empire of Alexander the Great survived in three kingdoms, one centered in Egypt, one in Syria-Persia and the farther east, one in Macedonia itself with a fragile hegemony over the illustrious Greek cities. They were still alike in many respects—in their maritime economy, urban centralization, and increasing wealth. All shared the Greek language, thrived on expanding overseas trade—except perhaps for Macedonia—and lifted the standard of living of the upper classes very high indeed. They waged limited warfare over their fluid frontiers, chiefly in the connecting link of Palestine, and across the strait of the Dardanelles and among the rival cities of Greece. This warfare usually resulted in sieges, marches, and countermarches—maneuvering for some objective. It bore no resemblance to the total conflict between Rome and Carthage. And Hannibal sensed this difference at once. In addition to the three great kingdoms islands like Rhodes maintained independent fleets, city centers like Pergamum exerted power, while mountain folk like the Celts, called Galatians, or the Bithynians in Asia Minor, preserved their isolation.

Of the three Hellenistic kingdoms, Egypt on the African coast seemed to be the natural ally of Carthage, and Hannibal might have gone to Alexandria except for one circumstance. Egypt, under Ptolemy V, was then receding from the sea and from the Palestine frontier. In doing so it withdrew far from the advance of the Romans. His former ally, Philip, had retired perforce from Greece after the defeat at Cynoscephalae. Philip had always undertaken more in imagination than he had accomplished in reality.

There remained Antiochus III of Syria-Persia. Less than ten years before, this youthful lord of Antioch had returned from a great sweep through Asia as far as the mountain barrier of India in the very footsteps of the great Alexander, whom he hoped to rival. Antiochus had brought back with him a veritable armament of battle elephants, swift Parthian horses, and innumerable riders. With treasures past counting, Antiochus had the resources that Hannibal had always lacked. Moreover, his sweep across the trade routes had channeled the silk and precious goods of Asia into his terminal port of Seleucia, near Antioch, and away from Alexandria. Holding, as it were, the gorgeous east in fee, Antiochus now looked toward the Dardanelles beyond Asia Minor and to Greece beyond the Dardanelles. He looked on them as irredenta, since they had formed part of Alexander's domain, while he himself was Alexander's true successor. And precisely there the Roman legions had intruded.

At this juncture of affairs Hannibal appeared in readiness to serve Antiochus against the Romans. They had been in touch with each other by letter. (And distrust of their correspondence had impelled the Roman Senate to hurry its commissioners to Carthage.) The great general and the impulsive monarch met that summer in the sunlit gardens of Ephesus, on Antiochus' northern frontier, where the masts of war galleys choked the harbor. The meeting must have affected Hannibal as a dream fulfillment. Yet it was urgent for him to discover what reality might lie behind this dream of power.

It was the last place on earth his enemies could have wished him to appear.

Late in the Hannibalic War a Roman delegation had brought back a very odd prophecy from the revered shrine at Delphi. The Delphic oracle predicted that Rome would gain the victory in the end through a king of Asia, or of the east. That might have applied to a certain Attalus, king of Pergamum and friend of the Republic. But there is a possibility that the well-informed priests of Delphi had anticipated the expansion of Roman power into the east.

That came to pass almost immediately after Zama. True, the city on the Tiber faced west, and had no visible concern with the Hellenistic states. But there was the demand for cheap slave labor, the demand of new shipping interests for a share of the carrying trade hitherto a monopoly of *Punics,* the craving of tired people for the luxuries of the east, for silk and pearls and the scents of Araby—and the general conception that the Roman state was losing the advantages of its late war in the ensuing peace. So the truce of 201 opened a floodgate to movement toward Greece. Philip had served as a convenient *casus belli,* and now Antiochus stood squarely on the horizon.

Just what quarrel the Senate had with the monarch of nearer Asia remains obscure. Rhodes as well as Pergamum complained that his presence in Asia Minor meant that he would use Greece as a base for invasion of Italy. But the two small cities had made the same complaint against Philip. It was a far-fetched warning, yet most convenient.

That the Senate could take advantage of it was probably due to the astuteness of its commander in Greece, the victor at Cynoscephalae. Quinctius Flamininus imitated the policy of Scipio Africanus without Scipio's sincerity of purpose. Once he had broken Philip's military force, he refused to humble Macedonia by invasion. Then, in a famous and very clever speech at the Isthmian games, Flamininus made declaration of the full freedom of all Greek cities. This oral declaration might not have impressed his Hellenic hearers, but Flamininus proceeded to do the unexpected by withdrawing all Roman garrisons from Greek soil. (They were needed that year to take the field against the Insubres on the Po.) And the overjoyed Hellenes rewarded him by releasing all the Greek slaves who had been Roman soldiers taken captive by Hannibal. In withdrawing Flamininus left the remnant of the Macedonians as a counterpoise against the volatile Greeks, while he left Greek soil a vacuum to be filled by the first comer with power. By all indications that would be Antiochus the Great.

It was a diplomatic trick, neatly turned, and it deceived the Greeks most of all. They were intoxicated by their autonomy, under the protection of Rome, the one supreme military power. Oddly enough the first to invite Antiochus in were the Aetolians, who had been the earliest ally of the distant Republic, only to be abandoned by the Romans. They desired a "Hellenic liberty" of their own.

The nicety of the trap laid by Flamininus and the Senate (during their preoccupation on the Po front) lay in its invisibility. No veritable frontier of Greece existed; the ports of the ancient Ionian coast on the Asiatic side were as Hellenic as Athens; Ephesus, where Antiochus gathered his forces, housed the shrine of the Greek goddess Artemis. Quite openly all Roman armed forces had been withdrawn. If Antiochus now entered this benevolently liberated zone, from what could he claim that he wished to free the Greeks, the openly declared friends of Rome?

Hannibal did not need his one good eye to perceive the trap. He had seen it work in Spain when the legions had marched in to aid the Saguntians as the declared allies of Rome. The legions were still there.

And as in Spain he conceived all three means of defense against the advance of the Romans; an alliance, this time of the Hellenic states; a fleet to hold the sea routes; an expedition against Italy itself. This plan would have succeeded twenty-four years before, and Rome would have fallen if it had not been for the failure of the Carthaginian fleet. And now, at the other end of the Mediterranean it needed to be set in motion quickly or not at all. Antiochus, that is, had to strike with all his wit and power while the Gauls were still in arms on the Po and the Spaniards still unsubdued beyond the Ebro—and Carthage still intact.

Hannibal offered to lead the overseas expedition; he asked for a force of 100 decked ships, 10,000 armed men, and 1,000 horse. He would take this fleet to Carthage and from there make the diversion against Italy while Antiochus completed his Hellenic alliance in the east.

Hannibal Listens to a Philosopher

Antiochus was about ten years younger than his great general. Very intelligent and quick to make a decision, he had been surprisingly successful—too successful for his own good. The satraps of his eastern lands had bowed to his will as if to a divine being. Just then, moreover, he was thoroughly exasperated by Roman tenacity. His envoys at the nebulous frontier of the Dardanelles had met with

245

only tiresome negation on the part of the envoys of the western Republic who needed—it seemed—to journey back to report every word to their Senate—and Falmininus. By degrees it became clear that Rome would not recognize his claim to any portion of the Macedonian empire beyond the straits. Rome, on the contrary, claimed to be the protector of the existing (Philip's) Macedonia. And Rome questioned Antiochus' presence in the Greek cities of Asia Minor, especially his encirclement of Pergamum, an ally of the Senate and the Roman People. Finally the Roman envoys very calmly delivered an ultimatum: Antiochus must not set foot on the soil of Europe. Exasperated, the Syrian King proceeded to do that at once. Was he not the successor to Alexander who had emerged from those same hills of Europe?

Antiochus understood the merits of Hannibal's plan, and perceived just as clearly its consequence: a major war with Rome which he did not desire and had not prepared for.

"Have you ever thought," the Carthaginian asked, "what it means to be declared an enemy of Rome?"

The Syrian monarch could smile at that. Millions of people served him from the waters of the Indus to the ruins of ancient Troy. He did not fear an invasion by barbarians across the western sea. They could not, in any case, get at his domain in Asia. He merely wanted what he could rightfully claim, overlordship of the eastern shores of Greece. Being a Greek, Antiochus could grasp all the intellectual aspects of the matter; he could not decide so clearly how to act.

He approved of Hannibal's expedition but delayed in preparing for it. As to his fleet, that was efficient enough, under a capable admiral, Polyxenidas; while the Roman navy had been pretty well disbanded after the peace with Carthage. Although Rhodes possessed a strong battle fleet and remained hostile, there seemed to be no danger upon the sea. Only in the third undertaking, the formation of an alliance, did the master of Antioch act promptly. A daughter, Cleopatra, was given in marriage to Ptolemy of Egypt; in Asia Minor the rude Galatians, the Cappadocians of the mountains, and the Bithynians of the eastern

Mount Olympus were won as allies. Over in Greece the hardy Aetolians waited to join him.

Hannibal perceived a certain familiarity in this shadowy alignment. The more primitive folk rallied to them, while the nobles of the cities, cultivated by Roman envoys, remained antagonistic. As months went by in mingled feasting and preparation at Ephesus, Hannibal failed to hide his anger at the delay.

He had one incurable weakness. It was necessary for him to work alone, concentrated on his task, sharing his thoughts only with those who understood him. Hasdrubal and Mago had sat with him for unending hours, considering the innumerable facets of a plan. Only Carthalo and Hanno had shared his thoughts in Italy. As for the men of the army, they respected his isolation because of the actions that came out of it. Hannibal had held his men as only Alexander had been capable of doing before that time. But he could not play the part of a jovial leader of magnates. He had failed to do it in Capua, and in Carthage itself.

In Ephesus it was not merely that he was a Semite among Greeks. He kept to his chamber, drinking no more than one bowl of wine, usually alone, while courtiers thronged to the table of Menippus, chief adviser of Antiochus. Menippus insisted that the strongest peoples in Greece, led by the Spartans, would hasten to join Antiochus the Great if he showed himself on their shores.

Too often Hannibal lost his temper. Once, at a parade past of horsemen from the Ionian cities, Antiochus, who enjoyed parades, asked if these were not enough for the Romans.

"Enough for a mouthful—yes," Hannibal made answer.

Among the many philosophers at the court a certain Phormio prided himself on his reading of ancient texts relating to the art of war. Phormio could quote the *Anabasis* of Xenophon or even Homer at will. After he had made one full oration on the secrets and science of warfare, the listeners turned to Hannibal, who had kept silence through the talk, to ask his opinion.

"I have heard many old fools speak out," the Carthaginian said, "but never such a fool as this."

He would have been wiser to flatter Antiochus and to humor the prating Phormio. He could not do it. With difficulty he concealed his anger at each month's delay. Yet the powerful Seleucid monarch was no sluggard; it took many months to bring in new levies of horsemen from the caravan routes, to build battleships of the Roman type in Tarsus and Tyre, to fortify his ferry over the Hellespont at Abydos, and to bring the highly discordant eastern Mediterranean states into some kind of mutual security league. Meanwhile favorable news came in: his very able admiral Polyxenidas inflicted punishment on the hostile fleet of Rhodes, while the Roman armies and fleets appeared to be doing nothing at all.

On his part Hannibal distrusted this appearance of Roman inaction profoundly. Tyrian traders bringing olive oil from Sicily told him that new galleys were arriving from Tarentum and Croton—now naval allies of Rome—to strengthen the fleets guarding Sicily (where Hannibal had hoped to make his diversion) and new legions manned the coasts around Messina. Already the seemingly quiescent enemy had countered any move by Hannibal toward his former battleground of Magna Graecia. The Tyrian merchant sent to Carthage to sound out the possibility of support for Hannibal there had been captured and turned over to Roman commissioners who failed to draw his secret from him yet held him for further questioning.

Behind this curtain of inaction, the enemy forces were gathering. With every passing month they took more weapons from the hands of the Spaniards, and reduced the numbers of Gauls able to bear arms. Hannibal abandoned all thought of his own expedition to Italy. Yet there was still time to seize command of the eastern sea, the Aegean waters off the vital Ionian coast.

At Delos in the Aegean Scipio Africanus appeared, seemingly on a pleasure cruise. Hannibal warned Antiochus from his own bitter experience that it would be useless to lead an army into Greece unless his fleet held mastery over the Greek waters.

"No more than two Roman galleys have been seen there," Antiochus objected. "How can I drive away a fleet that does not exist?"

He was a little wearied by Hannibal's urging to make haste. Moreover Roman envoys landed at Ephesus to negotiate even in this last minute. One of them, in Antiochus' absence, called frequently at Hannibal's quarters. Publius Villius seemed to have no animosity against the Carthaginian. He made a point of saying so to Hannibal. But a rumor ran through the streets that Hannibal, who avoided the courtiers of the palace, talked amiably enough with the Roman envoy. (Villius' exchange of messages with Eumenes, lord of Pergamum, was not observed.) While he waited for his audience with Antiochus this same envoy of Rome gave expression to the benevolent desire of his government for the full independence of the great cities of the Ionian coast, especially of historic Rhodes, progressive Pergamum, and Ephesus itself. In diplomatic terms he expressed his surprise that the Ephesians should be laboring in shipyards and arsenals to increase their armaments. Against whom? Even Hannibal, Villius admitted to the Ephesians, thought it was all rather ridiculous.

To Antiochus himself, however, Villus offered no more than the ultimatum of Rome, not to enter Greek territory with his armed forces. After dismissing the Roman envoys in exasperation, Antiochus called in his councilors. Hannibal, however, was not summoned to this conference of decision. The rumor of his talks with Villius had reached the ears of the Syrian king, Menippus, the minister, argued that the Carthaginian could hardly be entrusted with the command of an army—that Antiochus himself should lead them to victory.

In fact the council was quite unanimous—sensing the mood of its master—as to what Antiochus should do. Antiochus should go as the gods willed upon a ship and spread his banners to the wind, to "fill all Greece with armed men and horses, and line the coasts with his ships."

The king agreed that this should be done, after he had offered sacrifice at the altar of ruined Troy. When he left the council chamber he found Hannibal waiting for him alone in the corridor. No one else at the moment cared to be seen in his company.

249

Hannibal asked what decision the council had reached, and when he heard, he said, "Then you will give the Romans a cause for their war."

When Antiochus merely agreed, Hannibal looked at him for a moment of silence. "Why do you distrust me?" he asked abruptly.

Antiochus told him that he had been too much in talk with the Romans.

"You have heard a rumor," the Carthaginian said. "But there is a story that even Antiochus had not heard. When I was a boy nine years of age my father Hamilcar took me with him to offer sacrifice at the altar of Melcart. He took my by one hand, led me up to the altar, and put my other hand on the sacrificial lamb. He asked me to swear that I would never be a friend to the Romans, and I did so. Now I am an exile from my home in your court. I came because there is strength here with weapons to withstand the Romans. If your couriers deny this, let them tell me so. I tell you, by the memory of my father, that I am among the first of your friends."

Antiochus believed him and kept him as adviser on the expedition to Greece. The convoy from Asia crossed the Aegean to the friendly port of Demetrias just before the autumn storms of 192. The fleet was strong enough but the expedition numbered no more than 10,000 with 500 horsemen and 6 elephants. And in Greece Flamininus, as envoy of the Roman Senate, had already bound Philip of Macedon to inaction; the Spartans who had rebelled at the tidings of Antiochus' coming had been suppressed. Only the Aetolians joined his encampment with some 4,000 armed men. His force, therefore, was large enough to provoke a war, too small to wage one.

Over in Italy the Roman commands had burned the last towns of the Ligurians and had taken the surrender of the Boii. In Spain they had crushed the revolt as far west as the middle Tagus. When the winter storms ended they were able to bring back one army to land unopposed on the western coast of Greece.

Hannibal selected a narrow pass to defend against the stronger Roman columns. The pass lay between marshes stretching to the coast and a cliff in low hills. It was called Thermopylae. The Syrian Greeks built defenses across the bed of the pass, while the Aetolians mustered to guard the tracks over the hills above.

The veteran Roman army made only a brief inspection of the pass after its approach march. Some of the legions made a show of attack, while other columns climbed the hills to force the line of defense. In a few hours it was all over, with Roman cavalry pursuing the broken Syrians to keep them from forming again. The redheaded Cato, serving as a legate in the campaign, coined one of his ironies after the affair. "King Antiochus could not even hold Thermopylae."

Antiochus rode headlong to his ships with some 500 followers, and sailed at once for Ephesus.

The affair at Thermopylae caused little excitement in Rome, where a Consul, Nasica, was celebrating his triumph over the Boii with herds of captives and their horses and chariots in the parade and a sworn statement that more than half the 50,000 Boii had been killed, and trophies of 1,471 necklaces of chieftains, 247 pounds of pure gold, 2,340 pounds of silver, wrought and unwrought, and 234,000 coins without a copper piece among them.

Actually on the heels of this triumphal parade, M. Fulvius Nobilior, the praetor in Spain, received an ovation from the city. In his procession the carts were loaded with 130,000 silver coins, 12,000 pounds of silver, and 127 pounds of gold.

After this the main armies and the fleet were ready to move against Antiochus in the east. Scipio Africanus joined the new expedition as director of operations. Oddly enough he owed his recall to service to Hannibal. Rome feared Hannibal anew, now that he was with Antiochus, and summoned the victor of Zama to the front.

In Ephesus Antiochus wanted to forget the unfortunate winter in Greece and the fate that had befallen the Aetolians who had joined him there. In his familiar gardens, he

251

felt the security of his great domain. Then, too, his councilors reassured him that the sea barred the way of his enemies. It would be surprising, they said, if the Romans ever managed to transport a great army across the sea.

Hannibal was with him during this talk, because Antiochus had found the silent Carthaginian to be right after Thermopylae. And Hannibal failed to agree with the Greek councilors. "I am only surprised," he said, "that the Romans are not already in Asia."

He dismissed the sea as a barrier. "It is a shorter crossing from the Greek shore to Asia than from Italy to Greece."

As to the motive of the Romans in coming—"Antiochus possesses more than the Aetolians had."

Hannibal had information from sources of his own. "Their fleet has been assembling at Malea for a long time. New vessels and a new commander have come out to it."

When Antiochus, disturbed by his warning, asked if he should not open negotiations for peace, Hannibal said it would be useless now. There was only one way to safeguard the kingdom of Antiochus and that was to defeat the Romans at sea. This time the Syrian king took the advice of the man who understood better than anyone else how the Romans waged war. Commanding all his shipyards to begin the construction of heavier and loftier galleys, he journeyed north to fortify the Asiatic shore of the Hellespont. Hannibal went south to raise a fleet at Tyre.

Within a few months the hope of success at sea became dim. For the Roman battle fleets arrived off the coast, to be joined by those of Rhodes and Pergamum, to beat back the lighter triremes of the hard-fighting Polyxenidas—himself an exile from Rhodes—and to blockade him with the main Syrian fleet in the roads of Ephesus. More ominously, Scipio Africanus was marching the legions overland from Greece toward the Dardanelles. There the water barrier would be narrow indeed, yet still requiring transports and a guardian fleet to get the army of invasion across to Asia.

At Tyre Hannibal decided that he could wait no longer. One last chance remained—to gather the ships at Tyre and Tarsus and lead them north to Ephesus to join the surviving vessels of Polyxenidas against the Roman block-aders. If the Roman battle fleet could be destroyed, the Syrians might reach the straits before Africanus. If no more than two score Syrian galleys survived to reach the straits, the legions could not cross. The chance that all this could be accomplished was slight, and Hannibal must have realized as much.

Ironically, the greatest of soldiers went out to his last battle on shipboard.

Encounter at Sea

Heading north in fair weather, Hannibal hugged the coast in all its confusing pattern of islands and headlands. He had skilled seamen of Tyre to direct him, but the force of his fleet was in the new, orversize galleys with lofty decks and heavy oar banks. The flotilla of open craft following behind like minnows could do little but pick up survivors. Passing the bare hills of Rhodes the fleet entered hostile waters and prepared for action by lowering masts, stowing the great sails. The galleys crawled forward under the slow swing of the oars—not to tire the rowers. In this sluggish fashion they formed a battle line abreast. Thus the right end of the line of giant galleys brushed the shallows of the shore, the left end with the handier vessels held the open sea. Here Hannibal took command, while Apollonius, a Syrian courtier, led the ships of the right wing.

They were wise to move in readiness. When they rounded a long headland they sighted the fleet that had come to meet them. With sails set and oars in motion, slim triremes of Rhodes came on in line ahead in the wake of their admiral's ship. A fair sight on the smooth sea rippled by a wandering breeze.

On the high aft deck between the brown bodies of the men gripping the steering sweeps Hannibal watched the spectacle of the meeting fleets, unable to judge what would happen. Bronzed nobles of Tyre told him that the dangerous Rhodians had been caught unaware, under sail. The advantage lay with him. A hammer struck the shining copper plate beside him. Its clanging strokes quickened, and the Tyrians shouted. While armed men took up their shields and moved to the railings, the thresh of the great oars quickened beneath Hannibal. The galley moved more swiftly through white water. The shouting spread from vessel to vessel into a roaring.

The strangeness of it tensed Hannibal's body with anticipation. Between him and the shore nearly a hundred great ships were straining toward each other. His eye told him that his line, moving more swiftly with each moment, would overlap the Rhodians.

The enemy admiral-ship had streamers flying as it turned seaward to gain room. Its mast came down and its oar beat quickened. Others followed it seaward. The Rhodians were skilled seamen. Their triremes seemed to fly across the prows of the heavy Tyrian craft. With all their swiftness, they could not come up into battle line before their admiral crashed into the oar bank of the Syrian galley. Their rearmost vessels were still crowded together against the shore. Hannibal had won the opening move of the strange sea battle. And very soon the Rhodian admiral flew a black streamer, a distress signal, from the stern.

Two hours later Hannibal's great ship was still whole and moving through the combat with slow oar beat. But the aspect of the fleets had changed. By deft handling the Rhodian galleys at the shore end had driven between the heavier Syrian penteconters, stripping the oar banks from their sides, and then wheeling to ram the drifting giants. Those giants had been designed to meet the clumsy Roman craft filled with legionaries in readiness to board and fight hand to hand. But there was not a Roman ship in this battle off Cape Side. The triremes of Rhodes fought as the Carthaginian fleets had fought generations before. Their beaks slashed and crippled Hannibal's vessels.

Near the shore Apollonius was giving way, turning to escape with his injured ships. A Rhodian squadron was coming up from the shore end to sweep around Hannibal's line. Beside him the Tyrian shipmasters lowered their heads and opened their hands. "Withdraw," they told him. "Lord Hannibal, we can do nothing more."

When he gave his consent, two of the steermen ran to the signal hoist. They flung out a long red streamer and pulled at the cord that raised it to catch the wind.

The Tyrians on the swift open boats came in with sails set to take the crippled galleys in tow. They edged in to the shore where the Rhodians could not maneuver after them. At sunset the enemy turned away.

Hannibal had saved all except one of his ships, but had failed to reach the blockaders at Ephesus.

Months later Polyxenidas made a last attempt to break out of Ephesus and was defeated. At Abydos Antiochus learned of the loss of his fleet and abandoned the defenses of the Dardanelles. It was useless to wait there in the forts to withstand Scipio Africanus when the victorious Roman fleets could ferry him across to any point on the Asian shore. So it happened that Africanus made quite a festive crossing, to regale his leg-weary legionaries upon the supplies abandoned by the Syrians.

For the first time a Roman army entered Asia. Leisurely it moved south past the ruins of Troy. There was something odd about Scipio's behavior at this point.

Triumph and Fall of Scipio Africanus

Although an adversary, Scipio's life toward the end bore a close relationship to Hannibal's. Both masters of warfare seemed to have no feeling for its pageantry and no craving for personal gain by means of it. Whatever ambition had actuated Publius Scipio in his younger days had left him now. There remained his pursuit of an ideal which he never ventured to define.

He seemed to believe that in entering the east the Romans must use their arms only to protect Greek culture—that they must control rather then pillage.

In crossing the Hellespont he had been careful to win the rather barbaric king Prusias of Bithynia to neutrality. Perhaps the journey through ancient Ionia had its effect on the soldier devoted to Hellenic literature. It is certain that here, as in Africa, the eccentric Scipio thought through the meaning of events around him to a conclusion. And the conclusion he arrived at was that the destiny of Rome called for the great city to be the protector of these weaker Hellenistic states, not their conqueror.

His behavior now may have been influenced by a generous—and politic—gesture of Antiochus in returning his son, captive in a naval engagement, without ransom. Yet such a personal favor would hardly have weighed against carrying out Scipio's mission as leader in the war for Rome. True, he was there officially merely as the adviser of his brother Lucius, the Consul. While still marching at ease he sent Antiochus his conditions for peace: surrender of all of Asia Minor to the Taurus Mountains, and payment of the cost of the war. At Ephesus Hannibal advised Antiochus to accept the conditions.

The proud monarch of the near east, however, would do no such thing. As he retreated south he gathered in the levies from Asia and prepared to make a stand. Then Scipio sent the remarkable message that caused so much debate thereafter: he urged Antiochus on no account to give battle unless he, Scipio, should be present. What Scipio meant by that has never been made clear. What actually happened was that, falling sick, he remained behind the army.

His legate took command at the battle that followed at Magnesia near to Ephesus and the winding Meander River. There the veteran legions broke the host of Antiochus into fragments of fugitives. Hannibal, like Scipio, had been far from the scene.

From beyond the barrier of the Taurus Antiochus sent envoys to ask what terms the Roman general would grant. Curtly Scipio answered that his terms were the same as before the battle of Magnesia.

That ended the war but not the participation of the Roman Senate. The leaders in the Forum considered the wealth of Antiochus to be too great, the terms granted by Scipio too mild. The Senate debated, listened to Cato, and added conditions of its own. A huge indemnity of 15,000 talents must be paid, the fleet and elephants of Antiochus surrendered, with a pledge that he would undertake no future war on his western frontier without the consent of the Senate. And Hannibal must be surrendered.

In due time (188) Antiochus agreed to the treaty, thereby withdrawing from the Mediterranean shore. The stubborn Aetolians, who had been granted a six months' truce by Scipio (to enable him to proceed with the Syrian campaign), were confronted with a demand for unconditional surrender. Even the stalwart Rhodians, who had gained victory at sea for the inept Roman fleets, were treated rather as inhabitants of a subject city than as men of an independent republic. Pergamum, the weaker of the two cities, was given the lion's share of the spoils. Although the Macedonians were still to be subdued, the outline appeared of a changed Hellenistic world, of client kings and cities dependent on the will of the distant Senate. While this maintained the fiction of Flamininus, of autonomous Greek states, the fiction became more apparent. Very soon Roman magnates established business centers in Athens; slave markets moved into Delos, which Roman interests supported against Rhodes, the wartime ally. That historic city was forced to yield to Delos as the center of the eastern Mediterranean trade.

Eventually Pergamum, the remaining ally of Rome in Asia, was stripped of its new possessions. The reason: Pergamum exercised too great a power.

It was really the inflexible Cato who pressed the charges against Scipio. Cato had a hard hatred for the enervated Hellenistic world with its soft manners and devotion to Greek letters. Cato would wear only cheap garments and drink only the wine of the slaves; he made telling gibes at Aemilia, the wife of Scipio, who adorned herself with Asiatic pearls. His devotion was given to an abstract thing, the Roman of ancient tradition, steel-hard, merciless, and uncomplaining. He became increasingly envious of the handsome Scipio, conqueror of Africa and now victor in Asia. They headed rival factions in the Senate, but Cato's animosity was a personal matter. Specifically Cato charged—through other spokesmen—that Scipio had kept for himself a sum of 500 talents of silver paid by Antiochus after Magnesia for the support of the Roman troops. And he complained of the lax discipline and appearance of eastern luxuries in Scipio's encampments.

Scipio met the charge in his own eccentric way. Bringing his account books into the Senate chamber, he tore them up and asked his accusers to look for proof in the fragments. Then he asked the Senators why they did not choose to investigate through whom 15,000 talents of silver had come into their treasury, and by whose means they had been made masters of Spain and Asia and Africa.

It was the last public speech of Scipio Africanus. After that, in reality a poor man, he went into voluntary exile.

In his fall he kept his strange relationship with Hannibal. Scipio had fought ineffectively for an ideal, the liberation of the Hellenic states; Hannibal had attempted to aid them in an alliance against Rome.

When the Roman commissioners sought Hannibal after the peace, he was not to be found in Ephesus or Tyre. For a while he disappeared. He turned up in an island ruled by pirates. So the Roman commissioners called them.

The House in Bithynia

The craggy island of Crete should have been a safe asylum. It lay quite far from the traveled sea routes but not too far to prevent its highly independent mariners from raiding the traffic lanes. Otherwise events passed it by, and forgetfulness shrouded it as well as the waters of its river Lethe. Hannibal went inland to a plain dark with olive groves, where some houses clustered around a temple, at Gortyna. He made no attempt to hide his identity; perhaps he could not have done so. Obviously he sought an out-of-the-way spot to consider what he was to do next.

The Gortynians remembered him well because of the jest he played on them. He still had some bullion with him, and he made quite a point of depositing heavy jars in the treasury of the temple, where the priests could guard them. Silver and gold coins glinted in the openings of the jars, and only Hannibal knew that weighty lead lay beneath the salted coins. He took a receipt from the well-pleased guards of the temple. His real treasure had been stored in some hollow bronze statues of Phoenician gods, which he left standing by the path to his house. The statues attracted no attention at all.

Crete sheltered many strange gods and varied peoples as well. Among these were several thousand former Roman prisoners of war, now slaves of the sea captains of Knossos and Kydonia. It must have amused Hannibal to discover them working in the fields—these aging men who had marched to the Trebia and Cannae thirty years before. He was more than sixty years old, and at times he felt the weariness of those years.

What befell at Crete is revealed only in an obscure chapter of Roman naval annals. After the peace with Antiochus the galleys of the Republic continued to explore and transport troops along the newly opened coasts of Asia. In due time a certain Fabius Labeo brought a squadron to the harbors of Crete. Apparently this particular Fabius ordered the Cretans to cease fighting among themselves and also to cease annoying the new Roman merchant marine. In so doing he discovered the presence of the Roman prisoners of war. Now Fabius obviously knew nothing of Hannibal's presence at Gortyna. But it is a curious circumstance that Gortyna was the only town to give up its prisoner-slaves. Either the temple priests— mindful of the weight of those treasure jars—kept Hannibal's secret, or something passed between them and the officious commander of the fleet.

In any event, Hannibal disappeared from his house, taking with him the bronze statues of his pathway. There is no record of the scene at the temple when the Roman officers or the Cretans eventually opened the jars in the temple. Instead, we know that Fabius claimed an official triumph for his Cretan campaign, and although the Senate did not award it—because the release of a scant 4,000 captives was hardly the equivalent of the killing of 5,000 enemies—the head of Fabius was struck upon a minting of gold coins in consolation.

This time Hannibal went far east through the straits to Bithynia. There, on the shore of the quiet inland sea of Marmora (the Propontis) he should have been beyond the reach of Roman legions or galleys. Apparently Scipio Africanus learned that Hannibal was there, but Scipio kept his counsel, being then beyond the Roman frontiers.

And now obscurity deepens about Hannibal. He has a small dwelling at Libyssa, a fishing village on the lovely inlet that ends in Nicomedia. On his daily rides he never loses sight of one landmark, the snow-sprinkled peak of a mountain named Olympus in forgotten times by some homesick Greeks. At times he rides to the rude court of King Prusias, who had been an ally of Antiochus in the lost war. Thus he is the guest-friend of Prusias, whom he advises in matters of statecraft—Prusias being illiterate and not very bright in mind. He still has his books, and perhaps here he writes the brief study of history for the people of Rhodes.

The sea of Marmora is really a backwater of the troubled Mediterranean, a sanctuary of dark hills above tranquil water, between the strife-torn Dardanelles and the citadel of Byzantium. Venturing inland, Hannibal might have heard the chanting of the Galatians, the Celtish mountain folk still carrying their long shields and broadswords and singing their bravery like the Boii and Insubres of a former day. Already the Romans are considering the subjection of the Galatians. Then, too, their client king of Pergamum across the mountains has his quarrels with Prusias.

As usual, Hannibal prepares a hidden way out of his house. It is a large house although lacking all comforts, with six doors opening out of it. By turning aside into a cypress garden Hannibal can leave by a small opening in the stone wall around the garden. It is a lonely place, unlikely to attract attention. For the first time Hannibal appears to make no attempt to keep in touch with outer affairs. Except for the servants of Prusias he seems to have no visitors.

The Bithynian king kept his secret. The time came, however, when envoys of the small kingdom were summoned to Rome to explain their differences with Pergamum, now the friend of Rome. And in a conference at the Forum one of the envoys mentioned Hannibal's name.

Flamininus happened to hear it. The name, of all others, haunted the memory of the men who now ruled the

Mediterranean. From their first entrance into the hidden land beyond the Pyrenees to their last campaigns into Asia Hannibal had confronted them.

The quick-witted Flamininus took his information to the Senate, to have it debated. What was Hannibal concocting in Bithynia? By the terms of the peace with Antiochus he should have been surrendered.

After due debate the Senate authorized Flamininus to demand that Hannibal be given up to him.

When the Bithynian envoys returned home, Flamininus accompanied them, with an escort. Landing at Nicomedia they went straightway to the presence of Prusias, who had summoned his servants and guards hurriedly to honor his visitor from Rome. But Prusias refused to give up Hannibal. He was a barbarian, and the great Carthaginian was under the protection of his hospitality. All Flamininus' arguments could not convince Prusias otherwise. "If you will take Hannibal," he said, "you must do it yourselves."

As soon as Flamininus left, Prusias sent armed guards of his own to take post at all entrances to the house in Libyssa.

There a servant observed them and reported to Hannibal that unknown armed men stood outside the gates. Hannibal went to the main entrance and recognized the Bithynian guards. Turning back he went through the rooms to the cypress garden. Outside the escape door another pair of armed men waited.

After a moment he returned to the dining chamber and asked the servants who gathered there for a bowl of wine. "It is time now," he said, "to end the great anxiety of the Romans who have grown weary of waiting for the death of a hated old man."

With the wine he drank the poison he had kept by him in these last years. "Flamininus is hardly a worthy descendant," he said then, "of the men who warned Pyrrhus against the poison prepared for him."

So died Hannibal in the year 183.

Across the sea Scipio Africanus also died in that year, after giving order that he be buried outside Roman territory. "Thus he exiled himself," Livy wrote, "not only in his life but in his funeral as well."

261

Note on Hannibal

Hannibal son of Hamilcar left the world as quietly as if he had walked out of the hidden gate in his garden. Few of us know that his grave may be near there in a crypt above the modern Turkish village of Gebze, overlooking the waters of the Gulf of Nicomedia. He left no explanation behind him.

What kind of a man was he, in the eyes of his contemporaries? Clearly he avoided attracting attention to himself. The story that he went about at times disguised may be no more than a rationalization of this peculiarity. His only intimates were his two brothers, and Mago spoke for him in the Council at Carthage until after the war. No coin has been found bearing his portrait head, although many yield the likenesses of the Greek monarchs and Roman generals of his day.

His private life, in striking contrast to that of Alexander of Macedonia, remained simple and withdrawn. He did not care for wine, and only one woman is connected with his life. Apparently he possessed a residence in Carthage and an estate near Hadrumetum, but he never seemed to be concerned about them. His enemies said he was avaricious; yet, in contrast to the Romans, he levied no contributions on wealthy cities like Capua and Tarentum and made almost no demand on the treasury of Carthage. His rigid renovation of the revenues of Carthage at the end must have penalized his own wealth as well as that of others. As for his temper, the few occasions on which he lost it have become anecdotes, so we can be sure that he kept it, with his emotions, under habitual control. After a triumph he appears to have been too preoccupied with what to do next to show any elation, although he sometimes decreed a festival for his followers.

Polybius says that the Carthaginians called him avaricious and the Romans called him cruel. So they did, at a later date. The Hannibalic War was unrelenting on both sides; Hannibal almost depopulated Latium. But he did not show the merciless rigor of Hamilcar in the war with the mercenaries. Perhaps because of that bloody severity, which he witnessed as a young boy, Hannibal reveals a dislike of killing; no massacre of prisoners can be laid to him, and no killing off of the inhabitants of a captured town—a detail that became almost customary with Roman troops. His care in giving fitting burial to the slain Roman commanders contrasts with the savagery of the living Romans in throwing Hasdrubal's head to the Carthaginian sentries. It was hardly a moral question in that age. Men like Gracchus and Marcellus simply cut down a hostile people wherever found; Hannibal, a man of higher culture, preserved human life where possible.

Was Hannibal superstitious? It is not easy to say in the case of a Carthaginian of his day. Certainly he never claimed attributes of divinity like Alexander or the "divine" Caesars of the later empire. Nor did he claim aid from the unseen gods as did Scipio, whether from conviction or policy. Apparently Hannibal depended on his own efforts, and his remarks of record to his army urged only realistic effort for tangible rewards.

Here we touch upon Hannibal's genius. He was among the greatest of the leaders of men; he broke through the older pattern of government by a council or elders to prove that the most ordinary human beings could accomplish things undreamed of in the world's philosophy. In this respect he may be compared with Alexander alone, with one decisive difference. The volatile Alexander managed to get under the skin of all the peoples he led; he created the embryo of a new state, the Eurasian, which failed to endure as a whole yet survived in its parts to form the Hellenistic governments. Hannibal never ceased to be a Carthaginian, apart from the Europeans, even the Greeks. Moreover Alexander proved to be an irresistible attraction to the storytellers, who enlarged his deeds into a mythical epic. He became, as it were, the hero of a world cycle. In Hannibal's case his enemies wrote the record of his life, turning it by degrees into a fable of their own. ("His cruelty was inhuman, his perfidy worse than Punic": Livy.)

Yet Livy and his fellows could not manage to obscure Hannibal's unique leadership. For thirty-six years his personality was the touchstone of the entire Mediterranean and because of him events thereafter took a different course. Some ideas that we assume to be modern derive from him, more than from Alexander. This may explain the paradox that while Hannibal was pretty much a stranger to his own time, he is familiar to our thought. We understand his way of doing things: how he financed his army from the silver of the Spanish mines, and got Alpine clothing from the tribes of the Island, and an entire new issue of weapons and armor from the Romans after Trasimeno. His heterogeneous army of the small nations has been duplicated at various times, but Hannibal made the concept work. Something very like it is materializing along the southern Mediterranean today from Egypt to Morocco, but without a Hannibal to lead it. His method of waging war against the *minds* of the Romans we call "psychological warfare." His intelligence service could be used as a model today.

We would be quite at home with Hannibal, too, in estimating the natural resources—"strategic materials"—on the enemy's side, and how we might deny them to the enemy. He never seemed to lose sight of the esparto grass and the horse herds of his cherished Spain; or of the copper and tin deposits as well as the invaluable silver, or the grain of Sicily, the hides and iron ore of Sardinia, and above all of the timber and harvests wherever they might be. It is fascinating to follow his countermarches across Italy to gather in the Roman harvests. Perhaps the critical point in this struggle for resources came when the Romans in desperation bought a shipment of grain from Egypt—only to lose the grain convoy to a Carthaginian fleet, forewarned by Hannibal's intelligence. And when Scipio Africanus at last became master of the Spanish mines, in time to ship silver to the relief of Rome.

The economic factors—so familiar to the conflicts of the modern world—in the Hannibalic War have never been given a qualified analysis. The masterly studies of Tarn and Griffith have been confined to the Hellenistic states, that is, to the eastern Mediterranean. One writer (Rose) goes so far as to attribute the decline in Carthaginian naval supremacy to the loss of shipbuilding materials after the Roman seizure of Sicily, Sardinia, and Corsica. But it was more probably due to lack of manpower toward the end of the great conflict for the Mediterranean. Contrariwise, the old historical falsification that Carthage was a citadel of vast wealth opposed to a poverty-ridden Rome has gone unchallenged until today. Modern scholars speak as a matter of course of the "Mammon" of Carthage confronting a Rome that had nothing "but its virtue and its poverty." In reality Carthage, being a commericial and cultured metropolis, possessed more coined money than her antagonist in 219. The Carthaginian shekel was standard as far east as Rhodes. The closing of the sea lanes, however, injured her export trade, and the coined reserve of the Byrsa was exhausted at least twice in the conflict. Rome always possessed greater natural resources, and her confiscation of precious metals gave her vastly more wealth toward the end. (In 157 B.C. the Roman treasury held 16,810 pounds of gold, and 22,070 pounds of silver, with 61 million pieces of coined silver. Very little of all this had been produced by the mines of Italy.) Hannibal, far from being Mammon's commander in chief, never possessed adequate means for his great undertakings, and he took pains not to draw upon the limited resources of his city. Few modern writers have given clear thought to this or to the great Roman predominance in manpower. According to Strabo—almost the only authority—the population of Carthaginian territory in Africa was under 700,000, while that of the peoples under the Roman imperium amounted to some 6,000,000.

So Hannibal was forced to improvise means as he went along, from the doctoring of his horses to the sale of his prisoners of war. He was constantly finding unexpected ways out of his difficulties. He invented, as it were, a course of action that no one could predict. Sempronius, Flaminius, Marcellus, and a long roster of Romans tried to outguess him, and guessed wrong. Hannibal had a way of changing his plan almost in mid-stride. While moving up the coast of Spain in 218, he shifted overnight to the incredible plan of the march through the Alps to Rome; then instead of marching on Rome after Cannae, he changed his strategy to the formation of the Mediterranean alliance and the economic squeeze of the enemy capital. At Zama he came into the field with a formation entirely unexpected by the astute Scipio. From first to last his actions filled the Romans with astonishment. No one else ever managed to hide an entire army above a mist through which the enemy marched unsuspecting, or to transform an open plain like Cannae into a death trap. No one except Alexander managed to maintain an army on a hostile continent for nearly a generation.

Hannibal was the greatest of soldiers. It is not easy to make comparisons between him and the other noted military leaders of history. His achievement was unique. Among the Asiatics the Mongol Subotai led horse archers to victory over open plains. In Europe both Frederick of Prussia and Napoleon possessed a certain superiority in weapons; they operated from homeland bases against hostile alliances. When the Napoleonic armies ventured farther afield as in Spain, Egypt, and Russia, they fared badly. We cannot picture Hannibal leading a great army toward Moscow in June of 1812 in the hope of winning a war by one decisive battle. Nor can we imagine him ordering that army into the frontal attack against the lines of Borodino. Again it is necessary to turn to Alexander for a true comparison. Both the Carthaginian and the Macedonian pressed unrelenting attack against the enemy's capital and army; both sought to destroy the enemy's power to resist by any available means. But, again, would Hannibal have driven his followers on across the Indian rivers to seek the nebulous end of a continent, until they mutinied against him? Of Hannibal the annalists relate: "His army had endured hardships that no one believed an army could endure ... Yet, holding them together, he kept so large an army from sedition against himself or within its own ranks."

Modern military critics often allege that Hannibal was unable to undertake a siege. In the words of Major General J. F. C. Fuller: "He could adapt himself to every circumstance except one—siege warfare." But it is very doubtful if he ever sought to turn his solitary field army into a besieging force, operating from trenches with engines. He had captured engines enough from the Romans; yet that particular form of battle was the one in which his Latin enemies excelled. That was proved by Marcellus at Nola. In the event, Hannibal did become master of most of the cities of southern Italy by other means, and without wasting lives of his men against stone walls. Modern critics fail to understand that the Carthaginian always had the stronger battalions against him. ("His army was not so numerous as highly efficient": Polybius.) He sought at every point to draw his enemies into open plains, where his matchless cavalry could maneuver. Until he turned to the defensive, after 207, in the highlands of Bruttium. His great adversary, Africanus, avoided being pinned in siege lines at Utica, and refused to approach the walls of Carthage. Stalingrad is only one of many instances where a powerful army of invasion wasted itself against a city.

As for Scipio Africanus, equal to Napoleon as a tactician, he nevertheless learned strategy from Hannibal. In fact to defeat Hannibal the Roman state had to evolve the total mobilization and the methods of the empire that it soon became. Scipio was the forerunner of Sulla and Gaius Julius Caesar. In this evolution the Romans followed the Carthaginian rather then the Macedonian methods, but they followed them to a different end than Hannibal. To him warfare was not an end in itself. He fought for the preservation of Carthage.

"The Carthaginians fought for their own preservation and the sovereignty of Africa, the Romans for supremacy and world dominion": Polybius.

We can do no more than imagine the consequences if

the Romans had accepted a peace after Cannae, or the Carthaginian fleets had been able to master the sea lanes. The only clue to such a Hannibalic peace lies in his brief administration of the Spanish peoples, and we have only fragmentary data on that. Apparently he had given increased governmental powers to the Iberian princes of the south and east. Spain might have enjoyed local autonomy under the Carthaginian commercial imperium. Exploration of the Atlantic shores would have been pushed, with control retained over the western Mediterranean islands—Port Mahon in Minorca still bears the name of Mago—while the independence of the Ligurians and Cisalpine Gauls would have been established. Capua would have become the capital of a Greek-dominated southern Italy. And possibly Etruria and Samnium would have been freed as a counterpoise against Roman Latium. How long such a state of affairs would have lasted is another question. Very probably it could not have endured beyond Hannibal's life span. He warned the Carthaginians that their empire could no longer be sustained by commerce alone.

There is a warning to the modern world, as well, in Hannibal's life. It is that warfare need not be a vast conflict of technological skills and accumulation of weapons of destruction. Regardless of its mechanisms, war remains an equation of human beings, and their minds. It has never ceased to be an art, in which a supreme artist may appear out of a pass of the Alps to prevail over money- and man- and weapon-power. No amount of stock-piling of things can offset a superiority in minds. In 219 the Roman state was prepared for war in the usual manner; the Carthaginian was not. "Of all that befell both the Romans and the Carthaginians the cause was one man and one mind—Hannibal's."

Delenda Est Carthago

Hannibal had postponed the destruction of Carthage for fifty years.

The manner of that destruction should be told here as the epilogue of his story. Because from the terms first offered by Regulus in Africa to the final decision of Cato and his party in Rome more than a century later there is a continuity of purpose, and it is idle to suppose that the son of Hamilcar was not aware of that purpose to make an end of his city. It is given here only in a brief continuity of dates, with the steps taken by the Romans.

The peace treaty of 201 imposed by Scipio and accepted by Hannibal pledged the city of Carthage freedom from harm "as friend and ally of the Republic of the Roman People" with her boundaries to be preserved as in 218, but with the condition that Carthage must not make war in Africa without the consent of the Senate. Carthage had offered to pay off the indemnity before the payments of the last years fell due. This offer was refused. Accordingly, the last payment was made to Rome in 152 B.C.

In 167 in Macedonia the last effectual resistance to Roman rule ceased; in 155 in Dalmatia also. In 154 the lagging conquest of the Ligurians was completed, with the removal from their lands of 40,000 survivors. Resistance in Spain, flaring up in 154, virtually ceased after the killing of all male Lusitanians (on the Atlantic coast—Portugal today) by the praetors Lucullus and Galba after the inhabitants had surrendered on terms that merely exiled them from their land.

At this point, when Rome had received the last indemnity from Carthage, the situation of the peoples in the western Mediterranean resembles very much (except for Spain) that faced by Hannibal at New Carthage in the year 219.

Polybius comments: "A people who surrendered at discretion to the Romans first gave up their land and the towns in which they lived; then they yielded up themselves, males and females, their waterways, ports and temples and tombs. So that the Romans became absolute masters of everything they owned and they themselves possessed nothing more."

Carthage had kept the terms of the treaty of 201 faithfully, even giving some ships and money to aid their Roman "friends and allies" against Antiochus while Hannibal lived. Now they violated one clause of the treaty in assembling an army to resist the aged Masinissa, who had been encroaching on the boundaries of Carthaginian territory. Seven times before then they had appealed to the Senate to mediate between them and the oncoming Numidians. Roman commissions sent to Africa usually favored their client king, whose territory now dwarfed that of the city of Carthage (regardless of the agreement of the peace of 201 that the Carthaginian boundaries were to be kept unchanged). The Carthaginians were defeated in their attempt to resist the Numidians by arms.

Thereupon a fresh commission went from the Senate to Africa, and it included Cato. The former Censor and ascetic had won some military glory, had shared in the crushing of Spanish resistance (oblivious of the assurances given by Scipio Africanus of the benefits to be received from Roman rule), and had increased his wealth by shipping ventures and participation in the new slave trade in Delos. Now he brought back his evaluation of the city of Carthage: that it prospered again, with expanding overseas trade in rivalry to the Roman. He quoted a saying in the city: "Carthaginians will always be safe when one of their admirals can dip his hand into the sea." He showed the senators a fresh fig, brought in two days from Carthage to Rome, and he declared the city to be dangerous. He repeated his *Delenda est Carthago.*

There were others who did not agree. Publius Cornelius Scipio Nasica declared: "And I say that Carthage must not be destroyed."

There were still others who foresaw danger if the warlike Numidians became masters of the great city. The question was debated in secret session, and history has much to say of the reasons given for or against the elimination of Carthage from the Mediterranean that had now become the Mare Nostrum. The final decision: to destroy the city with as little expense as possible.

A Carthaginian embassy, arriving in Rome to express contrition for the act of war against Numidia and to inquire what compensation must be given, received the unintelligible demand: "Give satisfaction to the Roman People." No more than that.

A second embassy seeking to learn the particulars of this demand, learned only that: "The Carthaginians know well enough." With that they were dismissed.

Thereupon, in 150, war was declared against Carthage. With the mobilized army and fleet the two Consuls crossed to Sicily to prepare to invade Africa. A third embassy went from Africa to Rome with full powers to effect a treaty; it announced that Carthage surrendered herself to the discretion of the Roman Senate, in readiness to provide satisfaction. Again the Carthaginians asked: what satisfaction must be given? The Senate, however, made only one demand, for 300 children of the Hundred or leading families to be delivered as hostages within 30 days. Delivery was to be made to the Consuls in Sicily since a state of war existed. This was done. But the Consuls refused to discuss further conditions of peace; that, they said, could only be done in Africa.

Then the Roman army of invasion sailed to Utica without opposition. Utica had already accepted friendship and alliance with the Romans. There the Carthaginian envoys were received with full military parade; they stood within the lines of armed soldiers beneath the balustrade of the dais on which sat the two Consuls who were now arbiters of their fate. The Consuls then demanded "without deception or fraud" the surrender of all weapons, engines, and munitions of war of the city of Carthage. This was done.

Then, after the giving up of the young sons of the leading families and all weapons, 50 Carthaginian councilors, priests, and magistrates took their places in the parade of the legions and standards, to hear the terms of surrender, which had not been revealed until then.

The Consul who made the announcement said that it could be put in a few words. The Carthaginian people, he explained, would not be harmed; they could go where they wished in Africa to build a new city, but this must be 80 stadia (about 9 miles) from the seacoast. Because the city of Carthage must be destroyed.

The frantic outcry of the Carthaginian envoys ended in one plea; they could not leave their temples and their ancestral graves. The Consul replied that they would have liberty to visit the sites of their temples and graves.

The Carthaginian spokesmen then begged that their

lives be taken instead; their people had no livelihood other than traffic upon the sea. The Consul told them they could make a living from tilling the soil inland instead. He himself could not alter the conditions because he had orders which must be carried out as given.

When the Carthaginians started to leave the ranks of the legionaries they stopped to say one thing more. "You will not see any of us alive again."

That proved to be true. A few of the fifty fled into the country from Utica; most of them were killed within the gates of Carthage by the infuriated populace. The city, tricked to its destruction, rose to defend itself with the courage of desperation.

It is one of the ironies of history that without leadership, weapons, engines or munitions, the people of Carthage fought well. Warcraft appeared from the inner harbor, and the last army of Carthage was made up of all its families, armed anew by its artisans.

For three years they beat back the Roman legions from their suburbs and defeated them in the field. Victory in the Third Punic War—as the Roman annalists called it—was not gained as cheaply as the Senate had anticipated. It might not have been won at all if a very able man—"a sage among shades," Cato termed him—had not taken command in Africa in the third year. He was Scipio Aemilianus, adopted as son by the eldest son of Scipio Africanus. Very much as Africanus had done, he restored the confidence of the harassed legions, and began the siege of the great city with professional acumen, cutting off food supplies and inching his forces within the walls by the blasting force of engines.

Still the Carthaginians fought in their streets and held each lofty building until it was burned or demolished beneath them. The fighting penetrated day by day through smoke and demolition to the vicinity of the Byrsa height.

Polybius, a soldier himself, although a Greek held as hostage at the time, watched the holocaust of the last days from the side of Scipio Aemilianus. He said that Hasdrubal, leader of the resistance on the Byrsa, came out to ask for truce from Scipio when the fighting had become hopeless. There was a silence then, except for the conflagration around the temple enclosures. The surviving

273

Carthaginians no longer looked like human beings. One of them, a woman, appeared on the terrace of the temple of Melcart. She wore her finest garments and had her children with her. Around her the grimy skeletons of men threw timber and oil down into the flames beneath the terrace. This woman called out, and after a little her voice could be heard where the Roman commander stood with the hopeless Hasdrubal. She pointed at him when she cried: "That is not my husband at the feet of the Roman officer. That is a coward, a vagabond who will suffer more torment than I will."

They watched the robed woman seize her young children and throw them down into the furnace of flames and leap down after them. It is odd that the history of the city of Carthage, which began with the legend of one woman, should end with the anecdote of another in the year 146 B. C.

It puzzled Polybius to hear Scipio Aemilianus quote the lines from Homer that told of the towers of Troy going down in flames. Scipio was thinking that Rome might go the way of Carthage in time.

When a commission arrived from the Senate to inspect the ruins, Cato ordered the demolition of temples and buildings that had escaped the flames. The massive structures of brick and limestone, however, could not be entirely razed. Vast heaps of ruins remained along the peninsula among the ancient graveyards.

What was entirely destroyed by the action of the Romans was the life of Carthage. Some 50,000 inhabitants who survived were sold off as slaves, or escaped into the depths of Libya and Numidia (now made Roman provinces, with Spain and Sicily). No group of refugees seemed to be large enough to settle a town of their own, and Carthaginian ships disappeared from the seas. Libraries that had not burned up were distributed to the Numidian princes who could read Punic. Apparently they had contined works of history, of the new sciences, and the lives of philosophers and kings. There must have been accounts of great voyages and textbooks on agriculture because the Romans translated one of those and made use of it for a long time. The conquerors settled eventually upon the name of "Africa" for the province that had been

Carthaginian territory (and that of Asia" for the coast where Hannibal had died across the sea). Curiously enough the Carthaginian speech survived for centuries after all the life-customs and traditions of Hannibal's city had been lost to memory. It must have been an eloquent language because traces of it were preserved as late as the fifth Christian century, when Saint Augustine was bishop in Hippo Regius, on the eve of the downfall of the Roman state.

But in 146 other rival communities vanished from the shores of the Mediterranean. Corinth lost its freedom. Corinth had been the last center of Greek resistance. Macedonia became a province ruled by martial law. That—with Spain, now Iberia—completed the roster of the peoples who had stood against Rome under Hannibal. They were all subjected.

Acknowledgment, and Appeal, to Scholars

The writer is indebted above all to the lifetime works of Stephen Gsell on the Carthaginians and of G. de Sanctis on the Roman annals. In the all-important matter of Spain he has relied on the massive *Historia de España* (*Tomo* I, *Volumen* III, Madrid, 1954) by Ramón Menéndez Pidal, and on the able elucidation and analysis thereof by Philip Lemont Barbour.

He acknowledges the great aid given by many translators of the Loeb Classical Library texts of Diodorus Siculus, Silius Italicus, Polybius, and Titus Livius. And by those painstaking scholars who have correlated the existing works of Cornelius Nepos, Fabius Pictor, Justin, Appian, and Zonaras with the above texts. For geography, the Loeb edition of Strabo, edited by Horace Leonard Jones, had been of value at every stage. The work of the master W. W. Tarn on Hellenistic civilization and military affairs is exceptional in that it draws upon every facet of that confused and brilliant age.

Among viewpoints of today, Delbrück, Kahrstedt, and Veith give closely reasoned interpretation of the military aspect of the conflict between Rome and Carthage, although they seldom agree among themselves or with the unacademic Maj. Gen. J. F. C. Fuller. (All of them persist in calling Hannibal's forces mercenaries, which they were not, opposed to an army of patriotic Roman citizens—an army which was in reality composed 60 per cent of other Italian conscripts.) The Hannibalic War at sea has been carefully, not to say arduously, examined by J. H. Thiel (*Studies on the History of Roman Sea-Power in Republican Times,* Amsterdam, 1946). Among the legion of books on Hannibal's probable route over the Alps, the deft and delightful *Alps and Elephants* (London, 1955) of Sir Gavin de Beer is the newest and most enjoyable, even if it may not be the final word on that controversial topic.

In the internal politics of Rome and the relation of Scipio Africanus thereto the two studies of Howard H. Scullard served as guide (*Roman Politics 220–150 B.C.,* Oxford, 1951; and *Scipio Africanus in the Second Punic War,* Cambridge, 1930). Among the French writers— who all have special interest in the African coast—Father Lapeyre and A. Pellegrin in their *Carthage Punique* (Paris, 1942) summarize the evidence of the ancient life of Carthage. And Gérard Walter in *La Destruction de Carthage, 264–146 av. J.C.* (Paris, 1947) rebels with good reason against the Roman interpretation of the history of those years.

That interpretation is still found in modern works dealing with Hannibal's time. Our few naval experts are concerned only with the steps by which Roman sea power gained mastery over the Mediterranean; the many military experts confine themselves to the battlefields as described by Latin annalists, without wondering overmuch how those battles came to be fought. (Fortunately Livy and his fellows faithfully relate the details of Hannibal's mastery; it was creditable to Roman prestige to have first resisted and then defeated such a master of warfare.) Because the Roman annals survive, to a great extent, in our time, and because the Carthaginian accounts have perished, scholars have tended to concentrate on Livy and Polybius and the material used by them, regardless of the certainty that a great deal happened that left no evidence to us. Silence cannot speak for itself.

So our histories still reflect what was written for the Roman youth to read in the Augustan age.

That, at least, was the time when the curious guilt complex appeared in the Roman recording of events. In Hannibal's day the Romans were hardly troubled by a guilt complex. A victory then by any means was evidence of the good will of the war-gods, and accordingly reassuring. Even Stoic morality had barely entered Roman thought. Vergil could write in glorification that it was Rome's mission *"parcere subjectis et debellare superbos"* without reflecting that there was no great glory in sparing those who submitted and in crushing those who were too proud to submit.

It is not clear why the annalists felt the need to apologize more than a century after Carthage was destroyed. Perhaps that destruction had come to seem uncalled-for; perhaps the Hannibalic War had grown, in memory, to be the great epic of the advent of the Roman Empire. But Livy and his contemporaries did feel the need to apologize, more than the Greek Polybius who witnessed the war's end.

So they began to draw the likeness of a *perfida Carthago,* wealth-ridden, treacherous—"pleading with uplifted arms for a treaty they mean to break." Rome had been the one to break the treaties of 241—in the seizure of Sardinia and Corsica, and in beginning the war of 218 (Livy falsifying that fact by making Hannibal carry out the actions of 218 in the previous year)—and of 201, in the invasion planned by Cato's faction but carefully concealed from the Carthaginians. Since there is no mistaking Roman cruelty, Livy pictures Hannibal as cruel and "his perfidy worse than Punic."

Since Hannibal, in the minds of the propagandists, was at once the great antagonist of the proto-Roman Empire and the archleader of the discredited Carthaginians, his likeness was drawn in a very odd fashion. This likeness will not stand analysis, or what Scullard calls the test of "probability and common sense," but it has endured in the pages of history until now.

It is that of a boy of a race scheming to achieve the downfall of Rome, a boy sworn in childhood never to relax his enmity; growing to manhood in a Spain prepared as a base for attack on the Latin race; drawing his city of Carthage into war, half unwillingly; beginning the war by starting on the journey by land, as his father had planned, to the gates of Rome, and there losing his one chance for victory after Cannae, eventually to be recalled by a Carthage that had failed to support him in Italy; then cursing his city and fate as he sails back to Africa—in a way not specified—there to be finally overcome by a Roman Consul. Yet he still conspires for the victory that escaped him, egging on Antiochus III to combat, and when finally cornered by Flamininus in Bithynia (no mention being made of the order of the Senate to bring Hannibal back captive) he kills himself praying that the anger of the (Roman) gods of hospitality will avenge him after his death.

I appeal to the scholars of a new generation to re-examine the evidence of history in this case, to restore the reality of Hannibal, his people, and his city.

Index

Index

A

Abydos (Hellespont), 248, 255

Adriatic Sea, 40, 41, 99, 104, 106, 111, 115, 121, 125, 130, 138, 145, 153, 167, 182, 183, 187

Aegates Islands, 153

Aegean Sea, 248, 250

Aemilian family, 101, 190

Aemilian-Scipionic party, 110, 113, 142, 193

Aeneas, 203

Aetolians, 172, 187, 244, 247, 250, 251, 257

Africa, 10, 16, 30, 32, 33, 35, 38, 41, 45, 48, 54, 60, 82, 84, 169, 178, 187, 189–203 211–16, 222, 223, 234, 238, 255, 257, 266–73

Alexander the Great, 10, 27, 28, 242, 243, 246, 247, 263, 264, 265, 267–73

Alexandria, 28, 29, 100, 134, 161, 236, 241, 242

Allobroges, 64, 66, 108

Alps, 29, 47, 48–49, 53, 57, 59, 60, 61–68, 70, 71, 84, 85, 90, 103, 131, 137, 145,
154, 174, 181, 182, 189, 211, 214, 267, 269, 278

Anabasis, by Xenophon, 247

Antioch, 236, 241, 243

Antiochus III the Great, 13, 241–57, 259, 261, 271, 280

Apennines, 85, 86, 92, 99, 107, 124, 130, 154, 160, 182

Apollonius (critic), 241

Apollonius (admiral), 253, 254

Appian Way, 164, 165, 168

Apulia, 105, 130, 167, 170

Archimedes, 28, 134, 149, 150, 151, 160, 241

Aristophanes, 241

Aristotle, 233

Arno River, 87

Asia, 89, 242, 243, 246, 250, 252, 255, 256, 257, 258, 259

Asia Minor, 33, 242, 244, 246, 256

Astapa, 188, 192

astrology, 66

astronomy, 4

Athens, 10, 244, 257

Atlantic Ocean, 15, 16, 17, 18, 33, 48, 158, 205, 269

Attalus, 243

Aufidus River, 105, 114, 121, 125, 183, 185

Augurs, 81, 90, 123, 142, 174

Augustine, Saint, 275

Azores, 17

Bruttium, 137, 170, 172, 186, 194, 200, 205, 224, 268

Buteo, 127

Byblos, 3

Byrsa, 9, 12, 13, 15, 31, 35, 43, 203, 210, 211, 239, 266, 273

Byzantium, 260

B

Baecula, 180

Bagradas River, 10, 203, 204, 210, 215, 219, 227

Balearians, 51–52, 67, 80, 162, 205, 214, 219

Balearic Islands, 15, 41, 181

Barca family and faction, 5–8, 22, 23, 25, 29, 31, 40, 49, 54, 56, 130, 131, 152, 179, 189, 205, 210, 228, 231, 236, 240

Basques, 25, 52, 55, 57, 181

Bellona, 101, 193

Berbers, 19, 51, 72, 86, 120, 178, 224

Betis (Guadalquivir) River, Valley, 18, 19, 26, 59, 135, 192

Bithynia, 255, 259, 260, 280

Bithynians, 242, 246, 259

Bizerta (Hippo Diarrytus), 215

Boii, 55, 56, 59, 60, 65, 69, 70, 75, 83, 125, 128, 130, 250, 251, 260

Bomilcar, 54, 57, 137, 152, 172, 211

Brennus, 42, 83

Brindisi (Brundisium), 153

Bruttians, 135–37, 144, 145, 154, 173, 187, 213, 219, 226

C

Cádiz. See Gades

Caesar, Gaius Julius, 24, 26, 157

Campania, 107, 108, 131, 134, 135

Campanians, 141, 166, 169

Canaan, 3, 5, 241

Canary Islands, 17

Cannae, 98, 105, 110, 113–19, 121, 124, 125, 126, 127, 129, 130, 132, 137, 139, 141, 145, 148, 151, 153, 154, 155, 156, 161, 164, 167, 176, 179, 194, 196, 207, 259, 267

Cappadocians, 246

Capua, 34, 130, 132, 133–35, 136, 138, 141, 144, 161–63, 164, 165, 168, 169, 170, 195, 212, 247, 264, 269

Capuans, 154, 162–63, 166, 168

Carpetanians, 24, 26, 27, 56

Cartagena. See New Carthage

Carthage, passim. See also Byrsa; Carthage, Council of; and Carthaginians

Carthage, Council of, 6, 25, 31, 35, 38, 43, 46, 50, 54, 56, 113, 129, 130, 211, 216, 218, 219, 231, 232, 233, 235, 236, 263

Druids, 25, 68, 83

Pinnacle Books proudly presents

A BICENTENNIAL CLASSICS SERIES

Starting with four great American historical novels by Bruce Lancaster, one of America's most distinguished historians.

_____TRUMPET TO ARMS An exceptionally crafted romance spun beautifully amidst the fury of the American Revolution. (PB-887, 1.75)
"Explosive in style . . . *Trumpet to Arms* is always easy to read and strikes a note as stirring as a call to battle."
—*The Boston Globe*

_____THE SECRET ROAD A fascinating, yet little known account of the exploits of Washington's Secret Service. A gripping story of America's first espionage unit. (PB-889, 1.75)
"A veteran craftsman at the top of his form."
—*The New York Times*

_____PHANTOM FORTRESS A masterful treatment of the career of General Francis Marion, known to history as "The Swamp Fox." (PB-905, 1.75)
"History that is good and galloping, for competent scholarship underlies the romantic story."
—*New York Herald Tribune*

_____BLIND JOURNEY An absorbing tale of romance and adventure that moves from 18th-century France and its grandeur to the carnage of revolutionary America. A story no one should miss. (PB-915, 1.75)
"Romance, adventure . . . full pulsing life. Bruce Lancaster's best."
—*The Boston Herald*

Check which books you want. If you can't find any of these books at your local bookstore, simply send the cover price plus 25¢ per book for postage and handling to us and we'll mail you your book(s).

PINNACLE BOOKS
275 Madison Avenue, New York, New York 10016

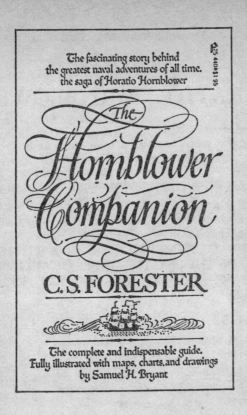

The fascinating story behind
the greatest naval adventures of all time.
the saga of Horatio Hornblower

P25 440A $1.95

The Hornblower Companion

C. S. FORESTER

The complete and indispensable guide.
Fully illustrated with maps, charts, and drawings
by Samuel H. Bryant

P440   THE HORNBLOWER COMPANION $1.95

TO ORDER

Please check the space next to the book/s you want, send this order
form together with your check or money order, include the price of
the book/s and 25¢ for handling and mailing to:

PINNACLE BOOKS, INC. / P.O. Box 4347
Grand Central Station / New York, N.Y. 10017

☐ CHECK HERE IF YOU WANT A FREE CATALOG

I have enclosed $_____check_____or money order_____
as payment in full. No C.O.D.'s

Name_____

Address_____

City_____ State_____ Zip_____
(Please allow time for delivery)

ATTENTION: SHERLOCK HOLMES FANS

DO YOU KNOW HOW TO?

(Pinnacle does and can help you!)